A HISTORY OF IRISH MUSIC

W. H. GRATTAN FLOOD

A HISTORY OF IRISH MUSIC

Introduction by
SEÓIRSE BODLEY

PRAEGER PUBLISHERS
New York . Washington

BOOKS THAT MATTER

Published in the United States of America in 1970
by Praeger Publishers, Inc., 111 Fourth Avenue,
New York, N.Y. 10003

First edition Dublin 1905
Second edition Dublin 1906
Third edition Dublin 1913

This Praeger reprint is a photolithographic facsimile
of the third edition and is unabridged even to the
extent of retaining the original printer's imprint.

© 1970 in Shannon, Ireland, by Irish University Press

Microforms

Microfilm, microfiche and other forms of micro-publishing
© Irish University Microforms, Shannon, Ireland

Library of Congress Catalog Card Number : 74–112029

Printed in the Republic of Ireland

INTRODUCTION

Perhaps the importance of Grattan Flood's 'History of Irish Music' lies elsewhere than in its value as a work of reference. It has been for long the object of both praise and blame, and by the exacting standards of modern scholarship it leaves a great deal to be desired. Among its more obvious defects is its mixture of patriotism and scholarship. Certainly it would be hard to imagine that its author examined the motivation of some of his assertions. However much one might sympathise with his desire to claim for Ireland some famous figures of musical history, one finds it difficult to accept claims made without indication of sources. The frequent lack of references is disturbing. On the credit side it must be said that here is an attempt to cover the entire history of Irish music. The range of the work is wide indeed, and the author's knowledge is extensive if not always reliable. The value of this work lies mainly in its importance as a possible starting-point for further research. Anyone contemplating such work, or merely cultivating an interest in the history of Irish music, must find it valuable as an indication of the main lines to be followed.

Grattan Flood laboured under a difficulty that must hamper all researches into the earlier periods of Irish music—namely the absence of even a fair-sized body of extant secular music. Contemporary descriptions of early Irish music, and other clues as to its style, are important and relevant. But how frequently one longs for some actual *music*. One can of course understand why the Celtic bards on the Continent avoided writing down their compositions to prevent the dissemination of their craft among the common people, and insisted that their students rely on memory. If the attitude of the bards in Ireland was similar, one can only regret its consequences for us to-day.

One important and tantalising new piece of evidence with regard to music in Ireland came to light as recently as 1959. In that year some slate fragments bearing musical notation were discovered in the ruins of an ancient church near Smarmore, Co. Louth. Professor Thurston Dart has placed these as dating from the second quarter of the fifteenth century. The notation is that used for 'measured' music. Even though the slates give only single melodic lines, the notation indicates that they belong to a polyphonic style. The Smarmore slates are at present in the National Museum of Ireland.

Other items, a study of which might help to fill some of the gaps in Grattan Flood's history, are the Late Bronze Age Horns, the crotals from the Dowris hoard (from a musical point of view more properly called simply bronze rattles), and such depictions as the Last Judgement scene on Muireadach's Cross, Monasterboice (c.900) with its three musicians.

Grattan Flood's remarks on the scales of Irish music are of interest, if incomplete. While the pentatonic scale undoubtedly influenced Irish music, one wishes

that he had elaborated on the evidence for the conclusion that 'the old Irish scale was pentatonic'.
Likewise the hexatonic scales are not examined. His
discussion of the flat *v.* the major 7th in the scales is
also incomplete, insofar as both are often freely inter-
changed in the performance of some Irish songs. The
practice of instrumentalists in altering certain notes of
the scale, is perhaps also relevant here. His remarks on
phrase-length are useful. The reference to five-bar
phrases, in particular, is easily validated. On the other
hand the attempt to claim for Ireland the invention of
musical form puts rather a strain on the facts, to say
the least!

In many ways the most problematic period of Irish
music is that stretching from the middle ages to the
sixteenth century. Though Grattan Flood has collected together many interesting accounts of Irish
musical activity in this period, it must be admitted
that they do not add up to a very coherent picture.
For all that, this section of the book is of value for
some useful, if disjointed, information. With the
chapters on the seventeenth century, information is
more extensive and an over-all view of musical
activity begins to emerge.

Some aspects of the later periods have been re-
searched since this history was originally written, and
the reader would be advised to study some of the more
recent works in conjunction with the relevant chapters
of Grattan Flood. In particular Donal O'Sullivan's
study of Carolan, Charlotte Milligan Fox's *Annals of
the Irish Harpers* and Ita Hogan's book on Anglo-Irish
music, 1780–1830, come readily to mind.

The period 1701–41 is one that could usefully bear further research. Apart from questions of fact regarding possible inaccuracies in this history, some aspects of the work could be expanded without undue difficulty. A short list of the music-publishers in Dublin is given on page 269 of this work. A more complete list might include the following:

Robert Thornton, Bookseller, Leather Bottle, Skinner Row.

Edward Sandy's, Custom Printing House in Essex Street.

Thos. Benson, Shakespeare's Head, Castle Street.

Pamphlets Shop, Skinner Row, opposite the Tholsel.

Neale of Christ Church Yard.

R Norris, Bookseller at the corner of Crane Lane, Essex Street.

G Risk, G Ewing, W Smith, Booksellers, Dame Street.

Joseph Leathly, Abraham Bradley, Thos. Moore, Booksellers, Dame Street.

Sarah Hyde, Bookseller, Dame Street.

J Moy, Skinner Row.

G Risk, Shakespeare's Head, Dame Street.

Mr Manwaring, Musick Shop, College Green.

G Ewing, Angel & Bible, Dame Street.

C Wynne, Parrot, Caple Street.

Oli Nelson, Milton's Head, Skinner Row.

In quite a number of instances Grattan Flood seems inaccurate, or at least incomplete, regarding matters of fact. He refers, for instance to Geminiani as arriving in Dublin in 1738. On December 4th, 1733, the Dublin Evening Post announced his arrival in the city. His first concert was held on December 17th, 1733. The author also mentions that Cousser was appointed master of the choristers in Christ Church Cathedral in 1710. The Chapter Acts of this cathedral do not refer to this appointment, nor do they mention Cousser's name.

In a short introduction it is not possible to give an account of all the doubts which arise concerning matters of fact in this history. My purpose has been to warn the reader against approaching much of this work uncritically. Grattan Flood's claim to have spent twenty-six years amassing material speaks of a great dedication to the subject. Nonetheless this history should be read with the greatest of care and caution.

The following books and articles are among those which might be consulted with reference to Irish music:

Rimmer, Joan, *The Irish Harp* (Cultural Relations Committee of Ireland, 1969).

Fox, Charlotte Milligan, *Annals of the Irish Harpers* (London, 1911).

Hogan, Ita Margaret, *Anglo-Irish Music 1780–1830* (Cork, 1966).

O'Sullivan, Donal, *Carolan* (London, 1958).

Armstrong, Robert Bruce, *The Irish and Highland Harps* (Edinburgh, 1904; reprinted IUP 1970).

Fleischmann, Aloys & Gleeson, Ryta, 'Music in Ancient Munster and Monastic Cork' (*Journal of* the *Cork Historical and Archaeological Society*, Vol. LXX, 1965).

Bliss, A J, 'The Inscribed Slates at Smarmore' (*Proceedings of the Royal Irish Academy*, 64, C2).

Finally, I should like to express my gratitude to Michael Herity, MA, PhD, FSA and Bernadette O'Rahilly, BMus, both of University College, Dublin, for their advice concerning particular aspects of Grattan Flood's *History of Irish Music*.

Seóirse Bodley

October 1969

A HISTORY OF IRISH MUSIC

A HISTORY
OF IRISH MUSIC

BY

WM. H. GRATTAN FLOOD

Mus.D., National University of Ireland;
Vice-President of the Irish Folk-Song Society;
Member of the Royal Society of Antiquaries of Ireland, etc., etc.

THIRD EDITION

DUBLIN
BROWNE · AND · NOLAN · LIMITED
AND AT BELFAST, CORK AND WATERFORD
1913

BROWNE AND NOLAN, LIMITED, PRINTERS, DUBLIN

DEDICATED

TO

EDWARD MARTYN, Esq.,

THE FOUNDER OF THE PALESTRINA CHOIR

AND

THE MUNIFICENT PATRON OF

TRUE CHURCH MUSIC IN IRELAND.

PREFACE

ALTHOUGH Erin is symbolical of Minstrelsy there has never yet appeared anything like a trustworthy History of Music in Ireland—that is to say, of genuine Celtic-Irish and Anglo-Irish Music. We have absolutely no compact record of the " divine art," wherein the Celts of Ireland pre-eminently excelled, or of its professors and exponents during sixteen hundred years of authentic history.

Innumerable magazine articles, and references to the " land of song " have been published during the past century, but to the serious student of Irish music no standard work was at all available. True it is, no doubt, that the sources of information may almost be regarded as an *embarras des richesses*, yet these are so scattered, and in some cases so difficult of access, that the task of wading through such voluminous material would be no light one.

Hitherto the principal authorities on the subject have been Walker, Bunting, Hardiman, Petrie, Beauford, Drummond, Renehan, Pilkington, O'Curry, and Conran ; whilst some little information is to be met with *passim* in Rimbault, Chappell, Burney, Hawkins, Crotch, Busby, Rockstro, Davey, Moore, Hudson, O'Daly, Joyce,

Moffat, Sparling, Graves, and O'Donoghue. The *Dictionary of National Biography* and Grove's *Dictionary of Music and Musicians* are somewhat deficient in their treatment of Irish musicians ; and it is no exaggeration to add that the information vouchsafed of the thirty natives of Ireland who are included in the former colossal work of reference is unreliable, whilst the number of omissions is simply appalling.

O'Curry says : " Much has been confidently written on the ancient Irish music and musical instruments, particularly by Mr. Joseph Cooper Walker and Mr. Edward Bunting ; the former chiefly from imagination, and the latter from induction, aided by a high musical education. Walker seems to have been the sport of every pretender to antiquarian knowledge, but more especially the dupe of an unscrupulous person of the name of Beauford—not the learned author of the *Memoir of a Map of Ireland*, but another clergyman of the name— who unblushingly pawned his pretended knowledge of facts on the well-intentioned but credulous Walker."

All Irish students must be for ever grateful to O'Curry for having gathered together what has well been described as " a mine of information " in his *Lectures on the Manners and Customs of the Ancient Irish*, edited by Dr. W. K. Sullivan. The section dealing with " Music and Musical Instruments in Ancient Erin " cannot be ignored, especially in connection with Dr. Sullivan's learned Introduction and Notes ; yet, I must rather unwillingly acknowledge that many of his theories and conclusions are at variance with the result of recent scholarship. During the past thirty years our knowledge of matters relating to Ireland has been wonderfully added to ; and the investigations of erudite writers have cleared away the almost impenetrable haze which had so long obscured the state of civilization as regards literature, art, and music in pre-Norman and mediæval days.

No further apology is therefore needed for offering the present work to the reading public. Twenty-six years of unwearied research have resulted in a colossal amount of material, but I have endeavoured to condense my matter so as to produce a concise history. Moreover, I have avoided as far as possible all technicalities, and thus hope to make these pages more popular, and within the scope of the average reader.

It would be ungrateful not to mention the valuable assistance received from numerous kind friends, and from the Librarians of the home and continental libraries. As far as possible, all references have been verified at first hand; whilst, from the sixteenth century onwards, the State Papers and contemporary documents have been laid under tribute. Files of newspapers, commencing with the year 1728, have proved of much service, and rare magazines and chapbooks have been consulted. Dr. Henry Watson and Dr. Culwick lent me some unique music books, and Mr. T. L. Southgate allowed me to use his exceedingly scarce edition of Playford's *Dancing Master* (1652). The Lord Abbot of Mount Melleray, Mr. F. J. Bigger, Mr. Andrew Gibson, Mr. Barclay Squire, Mr. David Comyn, Dr. Douglas Hyde, Mr. H. F. Berry, Dr. W. H. Cummings, Dr. Cox, The O'Neill, The Lady Abbess of Stanbrook, Mr. Dix, Father G. O'Neill, S.J., and others helped me in many ways.

I must especially thank Father Maurus, Prior of Mount Melleray, for his kindness in reading through the proofs, and supplying many valuable suggestions. His unrivalled knowledge of Irish was ever at my service in the case of archaic Irish names of songs, dance-tunes, etc., some of which proved a stumbling-block to O'Curry and Hardiman.

Above all, I must thank my subscribers—whose names will be found at the end of this volume—for their material support in the expense of publication.

In conclusion, it is my earnest wish that the result of my labours will prove, in the words of O'Heerin, "an addition of knowledge on holy Ireland."

WM. H. GRATTAN FLOOD.

ENNISCORTHY,

November 1*st*, 1904.

PREFACE TO THE SECOND EDITION

I GLADLY take the opportunity of a second edition to make numerous corrigenda, and also to utilise some musical data (furnished by Dr. Watson, Mr. W. J. Lawrence, and other kind friends) which only came to hand since the publication of the work. The almost universal chorus of approval from home and foreign journals, and the numerous congratulatory letters received from competent critics, fully justify the appearance of a long looked-for volume. It is satisfactory to learn that the first edition was exhausted within three months, and this is all the more remarkable, as I had been warned that books relating to Ireland do not sell. Apart from the wider circulation which a second edition will ensure, I feel flattered that my labours in the cause of Irish music have elicited such friendly recognition on all sides.

W. H. G. F.

February, 1906.

CONTENTS

HISTORY OF IRISH MUSIC.

CHAPTER I.

ANCIENT IRISH MUSIC.

MUSIC is a universal language, appealing to the very soul of man, and is the outpouring of the heart, whether to express joy or sorrow, to rouse to battle or soothe to sleep, to give expression of jubilation for the living or of wailing for the dead, to manifest sympathy with society or devotion to the Deity. It is, as Thomas Davis writes, "the first faculty of the Irish." He goes on as follows :—

"No enemy speaks slightingly of Irish Music, and no friend need fear to boast of it. It is without a rival. Its antique war-tunes, such as those of O'Byrne, O'Donnell, MacAlistrum and Brian Boru, stream and crash upon the ear like the warriors of a hundred glens meeting ; and you are borne with them to battle, and they and you charge and struggle amid cries and battle-axes and stinging arrows. Did ever a wail make man's marrow quiver and fill his nostrils with the breath of the grave, like the *ululu* of the North or the *wirrasthrue* [ᴀ ᴍᴜɪᴘᴇ ɪᴦ ᴄᴦᴜᴀᵹ] of Munster ? "

In ancient Ireland the systems of law, medicine, poetry, and music, according to Keating, "were set to music, being poetical compositions." Vallancey tells us that the bards, specially selected from amongst noble youths of conspicuous stature and beauty, "had a dis-

tinctive dress of five colours, and wore a white mantle
and a blue cap ornamented with a gold crescent." The
curriculum for an *ollamh* (bard) extended to twelve
years and more, at the expiration of which he was given
the doctor's cap, that is, the *barréd*, and the title of
ollamh.

Keating assures us that Cormac Mac Art, *Ard Righ*
[Head King] of Ireland (A.D. 254-277), had in his court
ten persons in constant attendance :—1, A Prince for
companion; 2, a Brehon; 3, a Druid; 4, a Chief Physi-
cian; 5, an *Ollamh*; 6, an *Ard File* [head poet]; 7, an
Ollamh re ceoil "with a band of music [*oirfideadh*] to
soften his pillow and solace him in times of relaxation :"
8, three stewards of the household. The *ollamh*, or
ollav, be it understood, was the Chief Bard, whilst the
oirfideacha were the instrumental musicians. Cormac
himself was styled " Ceolach," or the Musical.

Dr. Douglas Hyde, in his monumental *Literary History
of Ireland*, gives by far the clearest and most succinct
account of the bardic classifications. The real poet was
the *file* (of which profession there were seven grades),
to whom the bard was the merest second fiddle. The
Bards were divided into the *Saor* or patrician class, and
Daor or plebeians—with eight grades in each class.
They were poets, not musicians—a fact which has not
unfrequently been overlooked by writers on this subject.

It is now absolutely certain that the Irish were a
literary people long before the coming of St. Patrick
and we have Ogham stones yet preserved which date
from the third century. The codices of St. Gall and
Bobbio—valuable as they are—must yield supremacy to
the oghams, which undoubtedly furnish us with speci-

mens of Gaelic grammar earlier than any known writings. The Irish alphabetic inscriptions in ogham which have survived the hurly-burly of seventeen centuries are mostly on stone, though they were also written on rings, wooden tablets, ivory, bone, gold, silver, lead, crystals, twigs, etc. So far, that is up to the present year (1904), about 340 oghams have been discovered ; and whilst some of them are decidedly Christian, the greater number are pagan. Moreover, the deciphering of these quasi-cryptic oghams has been a veritable triumph for the authenticity of ancient Irish history and tradition.

Sixty years ago the savants sneeringly asserted that our ogham inscriptions were "mere tricks of the middle ages, and founded on the Roman alphabet." Now, however, owing to the researches of Brash, Ferguson, Graves, Rhys, Barry, Power, Macalister and others, the reading of the mystic strokes is almost an exact science. The very word *ogham* suggests at once a musical signification, and, therefore, it is of the very highest importance to claim for Ireland the earliest form of musical tablature.

In MacFirbis's MS. Book of Genealogies, there is mention of the three great Tuatha de Danann musicians, viz., *Music, Sweet,* and *Sweet-String, i.e.,* CEOL, BIND, and TETBIND, whilst the chief harper was named Uathne, or Harmony. Our most ancient writers agree that the Milesians, in their first expedition to Ireland, were accompanied by a harper. The *Dinn Seanchus*, compiled by Amergin MacAmalgaid (MacAwley), *circ.* A.D. 544, relates that "in the time of Geide, monarch of Ireland, A.M. 3143, the people deemed each other's voices

sweeter than the warblings of a melodious harp ; such
peace and concord reigned among them that no music
could delight them more than the sound of each other's
voice." In the same ancient tract there is mention
made of music, in the *Vision of Cahir Mor*, King of
Ireland. However, passing over the ages that may be
regarded as quasi-fabulous, we come to the close of
the third century, when we are on fairly solid historical
ground. At this early period the number of Irish
minstrels was very great; and there is a record of *nine*
different musical instruments in use.

Heccataeus, the great geographer quoted by Diodorus,
is the first who mentions the name *Celt*, and he describes
the Celts of Ireland, five hundred years before Christ,
as singing songs in praise of Apollo, and playing melo-
diously on the harp. The Galatians, who spoke Celtic
in the time of St. Jerome, sang sweetly.

There is scarcely any room for doubt that the pre-
Christian inhabitants of Ireland had the use of letters,
the ogham scale, and the ogham music tablature. The
Bressay inscription furnishes an early example of music
scoring; and it is quite apparent that the inscriber
regarded the ogham and the quaint tablature employed
as one and the same—in fact, three of the mystic strokes
are identical with three musical signs.*

Inasmuch, therefore, as there are genuine ogham
inscriptions dating from the third century, we are forced
to believe that the music tablature also co-existed at the
same early period. Not a little remarkable is it that
the very name of ogham writing, namely, *Bethluisnin*,
or Birch Alder tree, is derivable from a tree or branch ;

* See " Ogham Readings," *Journal R.S.A.*, 1857, p. 328.

and the Irish letters—sixteen in number—are perfectly unique of their kind. Moreover, the trees were called after the letters, and not, as some have alleged, the letters after the trees.

The music pupils in pre-Christian Irish schools had their *music staves ;* and O'Curry describes for us the Headless Staves of the Poets, *i.e.*, *squared* staves, used for walking (or purposes of defence), when closed, and for writing on, when open, in the shape of fans. And, regarding the advanced state of our ancient bardic poetry, Constantine Nigra writes :—" The first certain examples of rhyme are found on Celtic soil and amongst Celtic nations, in songs made by poets, who are either of Celtic origin themselves or had long resided among the Celtic races. . . . Final assonance, or rhyme, can have been derived solely from the laws of Celtic philology."

Archbishop Healy tells us that St. Patrick " taught the sons of the bards how to chant the Psalms of David, and sing together the sweet music of the Church's hymns." He adds : " They might keep their harps and sing the songs of Erin's heroic youth, as in the days of old. But the great saint taught them how to tune their harps to loftier strains than those of the banquet hall or the battle-march."*

Apropos of the Psalms of David, Biblical commentators agree that the music of the Apostolic age was derived

---

* As regards the absurd theory that St. Patrick introduced letters into Ireland, it is only necessary to quote Colgan, the venerable hagiologist, who tells us that Dubhthach MacLugair, Arch-Poet of Ireland, had taught St. Fiacc of Sletty, and " had sent him a little before into Connaught *to present some of his poems to the princes of that country*." St. Patrick may possibly have introduced the *Roman* letters, but it must be borne in mind that the pre-Patrician Irish had their *Irish* alphabet centuries previously.

from the Jewish psalmody. The Apostles themselves
"adapted" the psalm tunes of the Temple, but, as the
Hebrews had no musical notation, the Synagogal chants
and melodies, which must have been simple, were handed
down traditionally. Very little is actually known of
even the shape of the Jewish instruments, as not a
single *bas relief* exists by which we can accurately
judge. However, in regard to the vocal department,
we can assume that a *monotonous recitative* gradually
developed into occasional modulations, and, in process
of time, worked up to an ambitious form of *roulade*.
An irregular form of chant, designated *cantillation*, was
the primitive system of psalm-singing; and it is worthy
of note that the modern Arabs recite the Koran in this
manner.

Many elaborate essays have been written on Hebrew
accents, but, unfortunately, it seems that these accents
expressed both the *interval*, or movement of the voice,
and also the *melodic succession* of notes, with an array of
embellishment. Moreover, as Sir John Stainer says,
"some of the vowel accents of Hebrew became tonal
accents if placed in a particular place with regard to the
letters forming the words," which, of course, increases
our difficulty in attempting any translation. As is well
known, the Hebrews utilized poetry and music as a sort
of medium for religious worship, whereas the Greeks
cultivated music and the kindred arts solely for art's
sake—and thereby evolved an ideal mythological world.

Most musicians are now agreed that the early Christian musical system was not altogether founded on the
Greek *modes*, as, apart from other arguments, the ecclesiastical modes could in no wise be accommodated to

Pythagorean tonality. Moreover, for over three hundred years, the early Christians, that is, the Christians of the Catacombs, could not possibly have any ornate form of service ; and the music of that period must needs have been of a primitive nature.

Dr. W. H. Cummings, one of the most eminent living English musicians, thus writes : "I believe the Irish had the diatonic scale as we have it to-day. It was the advent of the Church scales which supplanted that beautiful scale." More recently, Father Bewerunge, Professor of Ecclesiastical Chant in Maynooth College, expresses his conviction as follows :—

"It is thought that the old Irish melodies contain within them the germ that may be developed into a fresh luxuriant growth of Irish music. Now, *the Irish melodies belong to a stage of musical development very much anterior to that of Gregorian chant. Being based fundamentally on a pentatonic scale, they reach back to a period altogether previous to the dawn of musical history.*"*

On Easter Sunday, 433, Duththach (Duffy) MacLugair, chief bard of Ireland, gave his adhesion to the tenets of Christianity, as propounded by St. Patrick; and soon after, the Irish minstrels, almost to a man, imitated his noble example. However, so far from the ecclesiastical chant introduced by St. Patrick in aught affecting the music of ancient Erin, it was exactly *vice versa.* O'Curry, Dr. Sullivan, Archbishop Healy, and others are in error when they assert that Gregorian chant coloured much of the music in Ireland from the fifth to the eighth century. As a matter of fact, "Gregorian" music only dates from the year 593; and it was the

* *New Ireland Review*, March, 1900.

Gallic (some say *Ambrosian*) chant which St. Patrick taught.* Even assuming that the *plain song* of St. Gregory reached Ireland about the year 620, which is improbable, Irish psalmody and hymnody were distinctly *Celtic* in the first half of the seventh century, and were mainly " adaptations " of the old Irish pre-Christian melodies.

* The learned Usher informs us that " St. Jerome affirmed that Mark the Evangelist *chanted as the Scots do*," etc.

CHAPTER II.

IRISH MUSIC FROM THE 6TH TO THE 9TH CENTURY.

THE *Carmen Paschale* of our Irish Sedulius (Shiel), written in the fifth century, was, according to Dr. Sigerson, " the first great Christian epic worthy of the name," the Latin metre of which is decidedly Irish in its characteristics. But, from a musical point of view, the beautiful *Introit* of the Mass of the Blessed Virgin—" Salve Sancta Parens enixa puerpera Regem," which is still sung throughout the Western Church, is the most glowing tribute to the estimation in which this worthy Irishman's compositions were held by the compilers of the Roman Missal and Gradual. Again, in the Roman Liturgy we find our Irish composer's abecedarian hymn commencing " A Solis ortus cardine " ; and, as Dr. Healy writes, "several other expressions in the Divine Office are borrowed from the *Carmen Paschale* of Sedulius."

Some critics have, as might be supposed, questioned the *nationality* of Sedulius (for there is no contrary opinion as to the *authenticity* of. his writings), but this point is set at rest by another Irish scholar of European fame, Dicuil the Geographer. This Dicuil, who flourished about the year 795, wrote a celebrated treatise *De Mensura Orbis Terrarum*, and, in the second section of his fifth chapter, he quotes twelve poetical lines from Theodosius, regarding which he observes that the faulty prosody had the authority of Virgil, " *whom in similar cases our own Sedulius imitated*." Needless to add that the mention of "*noster Sedulius*" by Dicuil, fellow-countryman of the Christian Virgin, should be held as conclusive.

In 544, Amergin MacAmalgaid mentions the Irish Harp; and, at one *Feis* there were over a thousand bards present—each *ollamh* having thirty bards in his train. It is interesting to notice that the last *Feis* at Tara was held by Dermot MacFergus, in 560. As a result of the Synod of Drumceat, near Limavady, in 590, the chief minstrels were prohibited from pursuing the nomadic life they had previously been leading, and were assigned apartments in the mansion houses of the princes and chiefs.* The *Annals of Ulster* chronicle the death of Ailill the Harper, son of Aedh Slaine, who was killed in the year 634.

Another early reference to the Irish Harp is in a distich on the death of St. Columba (*d*, 596), wherein we read of a " song of the *Cruit* without a *ceis*," that is, " a harp-melody without a harp-fastener [*ceis*]," or an air played on an untuned harp. Regarding our Irish *cruit* Sir Frederick Gore Ouseley, Bart., Mus.Doc., says :— " *From its very construction we must assume that Harmony was known to the ancient Irish.*" Moreover, the Irish Harmony was distinctly in advance of Hucbald's (840-930), which only allowed fourths, and fifths, and octaves, with occasional elevenths and twelfths, whereas the Celts admitted major and minor thirds as consonant intervals.

Not only were our ancestors acquainted with Harmony in the sixth century, but they had an acquaintance with discant or primitive counterpoint From a

* At this Synod, according to Dallan Forgail, were: " Twenty Bishops, two score priests, fifty deacons, and thirty students; " and he adds that the Bishops and priests were " of excellence and worth," and were famed for " singing psalms—a commendable practice."

passage in Adamnan's *Life of St. Columba* we gather
that the Irish monks sang canticles in counterpoint.
St. Adamnan uses the phrase "*modulabiliter decantare*,"
which clearly indicates discant ; and, in the ancient Irish
glosses of the eighth century "modulantibus " is glossed
by *donaibhi bindigeddar*, that is, "to those who make
melody." Hucbald, in the ninth century, describes
organising as "modulatio." Furthermore, John Scotus
Erigena, the world-famed Irish philosopher, who died
circ. 875, is the first authority to allude to discant or
organum, which subsequently developed into counterpoint. This he does in his tract *De Divisione Naturæ*
(864), as will be seen in Chapter VII.

In connection with the subject of ecclesiastical chant
it is as well to emphasise the fact that whilst the Irish
at the close of the sixth century had a form of music
tablature, a knowledge of the diatonic scale, harmony,
counterpoint, and musical form, the plain-song of Rome
was in a very elementary stage, and was only known
traditionally until collected and arranged in an
Antiphonarium by Pope St. Gregory the Great, in 593.
Dr. Haberl adds :—" Whether Pope Gregory made use
of the letters of the alphabet or of symbols (points,
accents, etc.) to designate the sounds is uncertain ; but
it is certain that whatever signs he adopted they were
not adequate to determine the intervals with exactness."
In fact, not a single authentic liturgical chant-book in
existence goes back farther than the eighth century, or
early in the ninth, as some assert.*

* From the *Book of Lecan* it would appear that St. Gregory the
Great was of Irish origin, his descent being traced from Cairbre
Musc, son of Conaire II., Ard Righ (Head King) of Ireland,
A.D. 212-220.

All musical persons have read of the world-renowned monastery of St. Gall, in Switzerland, but the fact is too often ignored that its foundation, in the year 612, was the work of the Irish saint Cellach, whose name has been latinized *Gallus* or Gall.   This great Irishman, a student of Bangor, Co. Down, the friend and disciple of St. Columbanus, died October 16th, 645, aged 96, and, at his demise, the fame of his music-school became known far and near.

About the year 653, St. Gertrude, of Brabant (daughter of Pepin, Mayor of the Palace), abbess of Nivelle, in Brabant, sent for St. Foillan and St. Ultan, brothers of our celebrated St. Fursey (Patron of Perrone), *to teach psalmody to her nuns.*   These two Irish monks complied with her request, and built an adjoining monastery at Fosse, in the diocese of Liege.

St. Mailduff, the Irish founder of Mailduffsburgh, or Malmesbury, in England, flourished in 670, and composed many beautiful hymns.   He is best known as the tutor of St. Aldhelm, who tells us that the English students of his time flocked daily in great numbers to the schools of Ireland " of unspeakable excellence," and that Erin, " synonymous with learning, literally blazed like the stars of the firmament with the glory of her scholars."

Davey, in his *History of English Music,* mentions, with pardonable pride, the fact that St. Aldhelm (*d.* 709) is the first English writer who alludes to *neums,* or musical notation signs, but he conveniently ignores the equally well-known fact that the illustrious Saxon saint owed his knowledge of neumatic music tablature and liturgical chant to our countryman, St. Mailduff.

In regard to the so-called Gregorian *Sacramentarium* which Pope Adrian sent to the Emperor Charlemagne by John, Abbot of Ravenna, between the years 788 and 790, Dr. Haberl, one of the greatest living authorities on Church Music, says that "it was altered in the copying, and Gallican elements were introduced." Moreover, it contained only the Roman Station-festivals, *with additions made by Popes that came after Gregory*," so that Duchesne justly observes that "it should rather be called the *Sacramentarium Hadrianum*." The Pope also sent two famous Roman singers, Peter and Romanus (author of the Romanian notation) to the Irish monastery at St. Gall's, who brought with them a faithful copy of the Gregorian *Antiphonarium*, but Duchesne considers that this great musical work was also altered by the monks of St. Gall. In any case, owing to the very imperfect method of notation by *neums* (which really were only aids to memory, or a form of mnemonics to indicate the rendition of the liturgical chant as taught orally), it is only within the past twenty years that a scientific attempt to solve the puzzles of neum-accents has been made by the learned Benedictine monks of Solesmes. Certain it is, however, that the Celtic monks, from the time of Sedulius, unquestionably introduced and composed many original melodies for the early plain-chant books, and these musical arrangements were afterwards retained in the service of the Church. As a matter of fact, the name *Cantus Gregorianus*, or Gregorian Chant, is first mentioned in the ninth century, by Pope St. Leo (847-855), in a letter to the Abbot Honoratus, *e.g., dulcedinem Gregoriani carminis.*

Dungal, an Irish monk, who founded a great school

at Pavia, was a particular friend of the Emperor Charlemagne, and at his death, at Bobbio, in 834, he bequeathed
to that Irish monastery his library, including *three fine
Antiphonaries*, which are now in the Ambrosian Library
of Milan.

In reference to St. Gall's, Ekkhard, the historian of
the monastery of St. Gall's, who wrote in the earlier part
of the eleventh century (1036), says :—" Moengal came
from Rome to the Abbey of St. Gall in company with his
uncle Mark, *to visit their countryman Grimoald*, who was
elected Abbot of that monastery about the year 840."
This testimony of a distinguished German historian is
convincing as to the nationality of Grimoald, Abbot of
St. Gall's, and also of Mark and Moengal. Were it
not for such an authority, some persons would be very
sceptical as to the fact of any Irishman rejoicing in the
seemingly German name of Grimoald. It is as well to
explain—even to the Irish reader—that many of our
countrymen who went abroad were " re-christened,"
inasmuch as the Irish Christian names—to say nothing
of surnames—were not sufficiently intelligible or
euphonious for Continental taste. Therefore, do we find
Moengal figuring as Marcellus, just as *Maelmuire* appears
as Marianus and Mylerus; *Maelmaedhog* as Malachy;
Gillaisu and *Cellach* as Gelasius ; *Gilla in Coimded* as
Germanus ; *Tuathal* as Tutilo ; *Donal* as Donatus; *Aedh*
as Aidan and Hugh, etc.

In the year 870, the above-mentioned Moengal (Marcellus) was appointed head master of the Music School
of St. Gall's, under whose rule it became "the wonder
and delight of Europe." " The copying of music became such a feature of the work done at St. Gall's that

the scribes of this monastery," as Matthew writes in his *History of Music*, "provided all Germany with MS. books of Gregorian Chant, all beautifully illuminated." Moengal died September 30th, 890, and had as his successor his favourite Irish disciple Tuathal, whose name is Latinized Tutilo.

Tuathal, or Tutilo, was even more famous than his master Moengal, and was not only a wonderful musician, but was also famed as a poet, orator, painter, goldsmith, builder, and sculptor. We are told that he was a skilled performer on the *Cruit* and the *Psaltery*. Père Schubiger published many of the *Tropes* composed by Tutilo, two of which, "Hodie cantandus," and "Omnipotens Genitor," betray all the well-known characteristics of Irish music. This marvellous Irish monk died at an advanced age, on the 27th of April, 915.

Although music was the great feature of St. Gall's, literature was by no means neglected—in fact, to the Irish scribes of St. Gall's we owe the preservation of priceless manuscripts of the seventh, eighth, and ninth centuries. It was mainly from the glosses of the Irish MSS. at St. Gall's, dating from 650-900, that Zeuss deduced the rules which formed the basis of his *Grammatica Celtica*, in 1853. *Inter alia*, these glosses incontestably proved that part-singing was known to the Irish of the seventh century. Dr. Sigerson in his *Bards of the Gael and Gall*, gives us a charming translation of " The Blackbird's Song," written in Irish by an Irish monk of St. Gall's about the year 855, and published by Nigra in 1872.

O'Curry says that we have Irish lyrics of the ninth

century which will sing to some of our old tunes ; and,
he quotes a boat-song by Cormac MacCullenan, Prince-
Bishop of Cashel, who died in 908, which would seem
to have been written for the melody of " For Ireland I
would not tell her name "— " Ⰰⱁ Éⰺⱕⰻⰻ 'ní ⱀⰵóⱃⰰⰻⱀ
cé ⱄⰻ." Let me add that the first Ode of Horace sings
admirably to the Irish melody " Ⱅⰰⰻⰿⱃⰵ ⰰⰿ ⰽⱁⰽⰽⰰ 'ⱃ ⱀⰰ
ⱁⰻⱃⰻⰽ me," as pointed out by a writer in the London
Sun, of October 18th, 1844.

The *Liber Ymnorum Notkeri,* one of the most ancient
MSS. belonging to St. Gall's, is fully " noted," and was
illuminated by an Irish scribe.   Dr. W. K. Sullivan
says that "the initial letter of the Easter Sequence,
commencing ' Laudes Salvatori voce modulemur sup-
plici,' is an excellent example of the interlaced Irish
style of ornament, with the interesting peculiarity that
the trefoil or shamrock is used as a prominent feature
of it."

St. Notker Balbulus, the author of this valuable book
of hymns, about the year 870, shed undying lustre on
the music school of St. Gall's, but he is best known to
students of liturgy as the inventor of *Sequences.* This
honour must be shared by Moengal, who gave Notker
the first pattern *Alleluia,* and revised his pupil's work
Although the original meaning of Sequence was a pro-
longation of the last syllable of *Alleluia* by a series of
neumes, jubili, or wordless chant, yet the name was
more generally given to a melody *following the Epistle,*
before the Gospel. We need only refer to an ancient
Irish authority quoted in the *Book of Lismore* for an
explanation of the term *Sequence ;* and it is added
that " Notker, Abbot of St. Gall's, made [invented]

sequences, and Alleluia after them in the form in which they are." In process of time a special Sequence was introduced for every Sunday and feast-day, but Pope Pius V. eliminated all but five.

Among the numerous Sequences composed by St. Notker is the famous one on the Bridge, the "*Antiphona de morte*," commencing *Media vita in morte sumus*—."In the midst of life we are in death "—which was almost immediately adopted throughout Europe as a funeral anthem. Not unfrequently are the words " In the midst of life we are in death," quoted as Scriptural, but the text is only one of the many contributions to the Sacred Liturgy due to Irish writers and composers.

RESPONSORIUM: MEDIA VITA.

[Composed by Blessed Notker Balbulus, 870. Modernised from the St. Gall copy by Wm. H. Grattan Flood.]

Sancte - - - - - - - De - us

Sancte - - - - - - - for - tis   Sancte

- - - mi - ser-i -cors Salva - - tor   a -

marae morti   ne tra - - das - - - nos.

V. In   te   spe-ra - ve - - - - runt pa -

tres   no - stri: spe - - ra - ve - runt et

li - be-ra - - sti   e - os.
                        Sancte Deus, etc.
                        al fine.

NOTE.—This exquisite *Responsorium*, also called *Antiphona de
Morte*, from the fact of having been the favourite "anthem" sung
at all "offices for the dead" during the Middle Ages, was suggested
to Blessed Notker *balbulus* (the stammerer) by his Irish master,
Moengal, or Marcellus, about the year 870. Not only was it super-
stitiously supposed to be a preservative against death, but the singing
of it was believed by many to cause death ; and hence, the Council
of Cologne, in the twelfth century, forbade the chanting of "Media
Vita" without the express permission of the Ordinary of the diocese.
The neum-accents merely served as a mnemonic guide for the precentor or choirmaster, showing the number of notes to be sung and
the manner of grouping them, but leaving the interpretation as to
exact intervals and phrasing to the Cantor, who was required to
know all the liturgical chants "in theca cordis." St. Notker also

But why dwell longer on St. Gall's.   All Europe must acknowledge its indebtedness to Ireland more or less. The learned Kessel, writing of our Irish monks, says:—

" Every province in Germany proclaims this race as its benefactor.   Austria celebrates St. Colman, St. Virgilius, St. Modestus, and others.   To whom but to the ancient Scots [Irish] was due the famous ' Schottenkloster' of Vienna ?   Salsburg, Ratisbon, and all Bavaria honour St. Virgilius as their apostle. . . . Burgundy, Alsace, Helvetia, Suevia, with one voice proclaim the glory of Columbanus, Gall, Fridolin, Arbogast, Florentius, Trudpert, who first preached the true religion amongst them.   Who were the founders of the monasteries of St. Thomas at Strasburg, and of St. Nicholas at Memmingen, but these same Scots ? . . . The Saxons and the tribes of Northern Germany are indebted to them to an extent which may be judged by the fact that the first ten Bishops who occupied the See of Verden belonged to that race."

I have now reached the limit of the present section, namely, the close of the ninth century.   The reader has seen that the ancient Irish were acquainted with the ogham music tablature in pre-Christian ages ; they had their battle-marches, dance tunes, folk songs, chants, and hymns in the fifth century ; they were the earliest to adopt the *neums* or neumatic notation, for the plainchant of the Western Church ; they modified, and introduced Irish melodies into, the Gregorian Chant ; they had an intimate acquaintance with the diatonic scale long before it was perfected by Guido of Arezzo ; they

elucidated the " Romanian " signs as taught by Romanus, in 795, as we learn from a letter of his, in a manuscript of the thirteenth century, preserved at St. Thomas's, Leipzig.   The earliest known theoretical treatise on church music was by a priest, Aurelian of Réomé, in his *Musica Disciplina* (850), who described the system as devised for the Western Church by Pope St. Agatho (678-682).   St. Notker died a centenarian on April 6th, 912.

were the first to employ harmony and counterpoint; they had quite an army of bards and poets ; they employed blank verse, elegaic rhymes, consonant, assonant, inverse, burthen, dissyllabic, trisyllabic, and quadrisyllabic rhymes, not to say anything of *caoines*, laments, elegies, metrical romances, etc. ; they invented the musical arrangement which developed into the sonata form , they had a world-famed school of harpers; and, finally, they generously diffused musical knowledge all over Europe.

CHAPTER III.

ANCIENT IRISH MUSICAL INSTRUMENTS.

THE subject of ancient Irish musical instruments is involved in much obscurity, which has been intensified by the absurd theories of archæologists about a century ago. Walker, whose book on the Irish bards was published in 1786, was, unfortunately, misled by Beauford and others; and no writer tackled the question properly till O'Curry's *Lectures* made Irishmen feel that a knowledge of the Gaelic language was absolutely essential for the elucidation of this and kindred knotty points.

Zeuss's *Grammatica Celtica* (1853) was the first book to give a real clue to the nature of many old Irish instruments; and the musical references were taken from the glosses written by the Irish monks of St. Gall's, which commentaries make the basis of this epoch-making work. These glosses, as mentioned in the first chapter, date from 650 to 900, and are without any doubt the earliest MSS. we possess which throw light on various musical allusions. However, it remained for O'Curry to present the clearest and most succinct account of references to music, scattered as they had previously been in a very fragmentary way throughout the hundreds of ancient Irish manuscripts critically examined by that much-lamented Gaelic scholar.

To the reader who wishes for an exhaustive account of ancient Irish musical instruments, I can unhesitatingly recommend O'Curry's admirable *Lectures*,

though I do not acquiesce in some of his opinions.
Were that eminent Celticist now alive, he himself would
have altered not a few of the conclusions arrived at;
but, all the same, his list of the instruments played on
in pre-Norman days, as recorded in the oldest Irish
MSS., is very interesting. Recent Celtic scholarship,
especially by German, French, and Irish writers, has
been freely availed of in collating the various passages
quoted by O'Curry, and I have summarised his list, with
some necessary modifications, as follows :—

1. *Cruit* and *Clairseach* [harp] ; 2. *Psalterium, Nabla,
Timpan, Kinnor, Trigonon*, and *Ocht-tedach* [stringed
instruments] ; 3. *Buinne* [oboe or flute] ; 4. *Bennbuabhal*
and *Corn* [horns] ; 5. *Cuislenna* [bag-pipes] ; 6. *Feadan*
[flute or fife] ; 7. *Guthbuinne* [horn] ; 8. *Stoc* and *Sturgan*
[trumpets] ; 9. *Pipai* [pipes] ; 10. *Craebh ciuil* and *Crann
ciuil* [musical branch or cymbalum] ; 11. *Cnamha* [casta-
nets] ; 12. *Fidil*.

Omitting the 10th and 11th, which, after all, were
not musical instruments in the restricted sense, we
thus find nine instruments in general use among the
ancient Irish. The professional names of the various
performers were :—

1. *Cruitire* [harper] ; 2. *Timpanach* [timpanist] ; 3.
Buinnire [flute player] ; 4. *Cornaire* [horn player] ; 5.
Cuisleannach [player on the bag-pipes] ; 6. *Fedanach*
[fife player] ; 7. *Graice* [horn player] ; 8. *Stocaire* and
Sturganaidhe [trumpeter] ; 9. *Pipaire* [piper].

The CRUIT is called *crwth* by the Welsh, and *crowde*
by the English. Originally a small harp or lyre, plucked
with the fingers (as in the case of the Roman fidicula),
it was subsequently played with a bow, and is mentioned

by an Irish poet who flourished about four hundred years before Christ. It is justly regarded as the progenitor of the *Crotta*, the German *Rotte*, and the Italian *Rota*. St. Venantius Fortunatus (the great Christian poet, A.D. 530-609) calls the *Cruit* a CROTTA; and we learn from Gerbert that it was an oblong-shaped instrument, with a neck and finger-board, having six strings, of which four were placed on the fingerboard and two outside it—the two *open* strings representing treble *G*, with its lower octave. In fact, it was a small harp, and was generally played resting on the knee, or sometimes placed on a table before the performer, after the manner of the zither.

The CLAIRSEACH was the large harp, "the festive or heroic harp of the chiefs and ladies, as also of the bards," having from 29 to 58 strings, and even 60, but as a rule 30 strings. Its normal compass was from *CC* (the lowest string on the violoncello) to *D*, in all 30 notes, that is, about four octaves. It was generally tuned in the scale of *G*, but, by alteration of one string a semitone (effected by means of the *ceis* or harp fastener), the key might be changed to *C* or *D*. "In those keys the diatonic scale was perfect and complete, similar to ours now in use." It may also be added that the ancient Irish played the treble with the left hand, and the bass with the right.

Among early representations of the Irish harp we find one in a MS. of St. Blaise, quoted by Gerbert, dating from the close of the ninth century. Another one is on the panel of a sculptured cross at Ullard, Co. Kilkenny, dating from the tenth century, and which, as Dr. Petrie points out, is "the first specimen of the harp without a fore-pillar that has hitherto been found outside of Egypt."* There is a good representation of an 8-stringed harp on the metal shrine of St. Maedhoc, dating from the 9th century. Cambrensis alludes to the harp of St. Kevin (*d.* June 3, 618) as held in great reverence by the natives, and to this day considered a valuable relic. An 11th-century harp is drawn on the cover of an Irish manuscript in the Stowe Library, and another drawing of a harp of 23 strings is found on a relic case (dated 1350) containing the *Fiacail Phadraic* (tooth of St. Patrick), formerly belonging to Sir Valentine Blake. This shrine case was ornamented by Thomas, 8th Baron of Athenry.

The so-called "Brian Boru's Harp," though not dating from the time when the hero of Clontarf flourished, has a venerable antiquity, and was almost certainly a harp of the O'Briens. It really dates from about the year 1220, having been made for the famous Donnchadh Cairbre O'Brien, King of Thomond, whose death is recorded on the 8th March, 1242-43. A detailed account of its workmanship is given by Petrie and other writers ; and it is here sufficient to mention that it is furnished with 30 metallic strings, having a compass from *C* below the bass stave to *D* above the treble stave.

One of the most veracious of Irish chroniclers, Tighernach, who died in 1088, has preserved for us a poem, dating from 620, wherein the Irish harp is extolled. Walker says that " the *cionnar cruit*, or *Kinnor*, had ten strings, and was played on with a bow or

---

* There are still preserved Egyptian harps dating from B.C. 2000, but it was during the rule of Rameses II., *cir.* B.C. 1284, that the harp, from being triangular shaped, assumed its present form. The Egyptians had various other instruments, such as the lyre, single and double flutes, trumpets, timbrels, sistra, etc. Harps are sculptured on the High Crosses of Monasterboice and Castledermot—not later than the 10th century.

plectrum." He describes it as "similar to the *canora cythara* of the Latins of the Middle Ages, and the origin of the modern guitar." Another form of *cruit* was the *creamthine cruit*, which the same author tells us was "the *crwth* of the Welsh," and is said to be the parent of

BRIAN BORU'S HARP.

the violin, "but having only six strings." We also have a record of the *Fiddle* being used in Ireland as early as the seventh century, as is quoted by O'Curry from the poem on the Fair of Carman. In regard to the very favourite and oft-quoted instrument known as a *timpan*, it has been variously explained as a drum, or a sort of tambourine, whilst an Anglo-Saxon MS. makes it equivalent to a bagpipe! Dr. W. K. Sullivan cautiously tells us (relying on the authority of Dr. Charles O'Connor) that it " was a bowed instrument," whilst the credulous Walker gravely assures us that " a Timpanist |player on the timpan] was simply a musical conductor."

The *timpan* was, in reality, a small stringed instrument, having from three to eight strings. and was played with a bow or plectrum, being also called a *benn crot*, or peaked harp, by an ancient Irish writer. Recent research has almost conclusively proved that the *Kinnor* and the *Trigonon*, or three-stringed *timpan*, are identical, whilst the *Nabla*, or *Psalterium*—a favourite Celtic instrument from the seventh to the eleventh century—was generally of eight strings, and hence called the *Ochtedach*, or the eight-stringed.* We meet with constant allusions in the old annalists to *timpans* and *timpanists* ; and a skilful performer on the *timpan* was held in the highest esteem.

Let me here mention a comparatively unknown item of musical history in regard to Irish surnames. The CURTIN (MacCurtin) family is so named from a hereditary skill on the *cruit*; whilst the family names TUMPANE and TUMPANY are derived from a musical ancestry—famous *timpanists,* or performers on the *timpan.* The music of this latter instrument was generally known as a *dump* ; and various dumps are to be

---

* Euclid, a name dear to the heart of most schoolboys, tells us that Terpander (who founded the celebrated Lesbian School where Sappho was taught), about the year B.C. 670, invented a new system of musical notation, and extended the tetrachordal lyre to one of seven strings, known as the heptachordal lyre. The *Nabla* is described in an old Irish tract as " a ten-stringed *cruit* "; and St. Isidore says that " there are ten chords used in the Hebrew *Psalterium,* from the number of the Decalogue."

met with in MS. music books of the sixteenth century. A similar musical origin is traced for the surnames Harper, Piper, Fiddler, etc., whilst the family of MacCrossan (now Englished Crosbie) are so-called from the Irish word *Crossan*—a travelling musical comedian.   The Cronins or Cronans are in like manner designated from a family of street singers.*

The *Buinne* was a primitive oboe, or a flute, and it is glossed by Zeuss as equivalent to *tibia*.   O'Curry equates it with " trumpet in the shape of a horn," whilst Dr. O'Sullivan says that it is the Romance *Buisine*, or Bassoon, but I am more inclined to the view of the eighth-century Irish monks, which makes it a sort of pipe, or flute, or *cambucus* (crooked flute, as it is styled by Archbishop Kilwarby, in 1275).   Moreover, we read that the Irish were wont to sing to the accompaniment of the *cruit* or the *buinne*, which renders it most probable that this latter was a delicate instrument of the flute genus.   In a poem by William de Machault, a writer of the fourteenth century, there is a reference to our Irish *buinne* as " La flaute bretaigne," which, in English, was given the name of " Recorder," or " Flute a Bec."

In the twelfth-century manuscripts we meet with allusions to the *bennbuabhal,* a horn of a very resonant character, and *corn* (Chaucer's " corn pipe," and the Welsh " pibcorn,"†) which were horn-pipes.   From the Irish *corn-pipe* came the instrument (as also the dance) called hornpipe, which instrument survived till the

---

* Similarly, the family name *Mac an Bhaird*, or Ward, which really means "son of the bard," is derivable from a bardic origin, just as the *Brehons* (who in some cases changed their names to *Judge*) are the descendants of Irish Judges.

† The " Pibcorn " was played in Wales till near the close of the eighteenth century.

.seventeenth century. As we have the hornpipe dances called from the *horn-pipe*, so we have the jig dance from the *geige* or *fidil*. The term "lilt" is from *lilt-pipe*, a form of shepherd's pipe—in fact a simple reed—replaced in after days by the human voice singing the syllables *la la la* to the tune—and hence called "lilting" a tune. Chaucer writes thus in his *House of Fame* :—

> " Many a flower and *liltyng horne*,
>   And pipes made of greene corne."

The *Guthbuinne* was also a horn, but more of the bassoon character. (Compare the "gait-horn" and the "wayt" or oboe.) Of course there is no difficulty in identifying the *feadan* with the fife ; and O'Curry has given many references to it from ancient manuscripts. The *Stoc* and the *Sturgan* were forms of clarions or trumpets, though some authors assert that they were horns— whence the name "stock-horn." We learn from the Brehon Laws that cooks and *trumpeters* were to have a special supply of "cheering mead."

Although there is mention of the bagpipe in the Brehon Laws of the fifth century,[*] this instrument did not come into prominence until the eleventh century. Dr. W. K. Sullivan tells us that the old Irish bagpipe was inflated by the mouth, "and was in every respect the same as the Highland bagpipe of to-day." In the State Papers of the fourteenth century, the bagpipe is expressly termed "the music of the Irish Kernes."

---

[*] In one of the ancient Irish historic tales describing the palace of Da Derga at Bohernabreena (Bothar-na-Bruighne), it is stated that "nine pipers, who came from the fairy hills of Bregia," did honour to King Conaire, by their performances. Their names were Bind. Robind, Riarbind, Sihe, Dihe, Deichrind, Umal, Cumal, and Ciallglind, and they are styled "the best pipe-players in the whole world." In this tale the set of pipes is called *tinne*, whilst the band of pipers is named *cetharchoire*, indicating the four parts of the pipe.

One of the earliest drawings of this warlike instrument is in a MS. in the British Museum, dated 1300, describing the Irish who accompanied King Edward to Calais, in which manuscript there is an illuminated initial letter with the quaint device of "a pig, as gravely as possible, playing on the bagpipes." Lovers of mediæval art will be interested in knowing that there is a splendid painting still preserved at Vienna of an Irish piper, by the celebrated Albrecht Dürer, dated 1514 ; and in Ferguson's *Dissertation* (in Bunting) there is an illustration of "a piper heading an irruption of the native Irish into the English Pale in the sixteenth century."

We are given by Stanihurst, in 1584, a most graphic description of the Irish bagpipes of his time, as follows : "The Irish, likewise, instead of the trumpet, make use of a wooden pipe of the most ingenious structure, to which is joined a leather bag, very closely bound with bands. A pipe is inserted in the side of this skin, through which the piper, *with his swollen neck and puffed-up cheeks, blows in the same manner as we do through a tube.* The skin, being thus filled with air, begins to swell, and *the player presses against it with his arm* [fore-arm] ; thus a loud and shrill sound is produced through two wooden pipes of different lengths. In addition to these, *there is yet a fourth pipe, perforated in different places,* [having five or six holes], which the player so regulates by the dexterity of his fingers, in the shutting and opening of the holes, that he can cause the upper pipes to send forth either a loud or a low sound at pleasure."

Ullan Pipes and Cuisle Pipes are synonymous,

according to Vallancey, inasmuch as Ullan is derived
from *Uilleann*=elbow, and *cuisle* means a pipe, whilst
even in the last century pipers called their bellows *bolg
cuisleann*=fore-arm bellows. Walker adds : " In Ullan
Pipes we have, perhaps, the *woollen* Bagpipe of
Shakespeare, to which he attributes an extraordinary
effect" (*Merchant of Venice*, Act iv., scene 1).
The late Professor Morley, in his *English Literature*,
says : " The familiar presence of the bagpipe indicates a former Celtic occupation of the fens ;" and he
adds that " the drone of a Lincolnshire bagpipe is one of
Falstaff's similes for melancholy." Other Shakesperian
commentators assert that the " drone of a Lincolnshire
bagpipe " is not the music of that instrument, but is
intended to typify " the croaking of frogs in the fen
country." From the sixteenth century the Irish
Uilleann (" Union ") pipes were played as at present,
that is, the wind being supplied by a bellows (worked
by the fore-arm), just as were the *regal*, or *portative*,
organs of that date.

Regarding the introduction of the organ into Ireland,
Walker says that " there is no mention of an Organ in
our Ecclesiastical History till the year 1641, at the
Friary of Multifarnham," etc. This truly absurd statement will give the reader an idea of the value to be
attached to many of the facts (?) detailed by Walker,
and goes far to justify the strong language in which
O'Curry denounces such charlatans on the subject of
ancient musical history. Other writers have asserted
that the earliest notices of the organ in Ireland date
from about the middle of the fifteenth century ; but
recent research has shown that we can go back to the
first decade of the ninth century for the use of " the

king of instruments " in our lovely Hiberno-Romanesque
churches.*

About the year 140, according to Optatian, the organs
then in use had fifteen pipes, namely, fourteen notes for
the seven modes, and one additional for the *Proslam-
banomenos*, but, in A.D. 350, they were increased in size
to twenty-six pipes. In the year 660, Pope Vitalian
(657-672), as we learn from John the Deacon, introduced
organs into the service of the Church; and they were
soon adopted in the Irish Church, as also by the Anglo-
Saxons. Under date of the year 814, in the *Annals of
Ulster*, we read that the organ in the Church of Cluain-
crema (Cloncraff, Co. Roscommon) suffered destruction
by an accidental fire. It is almost unnecessary to add
that the Irish word *orgán* (oircin) is a loan-word from
the Latin *organum;* and *organum* in the Vulgate always
means a pipe. Before the death of Charlemagne (814)
the organs had fifty-two pipes, with two stops ; and subsequently, many improvements and additions were made.
During the Middle Ages it was the custom to designate
the king of instruments as " a payre of organs,"† a
designation which obtained as late as the year 1680.

The next chapter will be appropriately devoted to a
brief explanation of ancient Irish scales, and a summing-
up of the characteristics of our old melodies.

* Walker also informs us that "the Irish harp received considerable improvements from the ingenuity of Robert Nugent, a Jesuit,
in the 15th century [*sic*], who resided for some time in this Kingdom." Even assuming that 15*th* is a slip for 16*th*, Father Robert
Nugent did not flourish till the 17th century. As is well known, the
Jesuit Order was not founded till the year 1549 by St. Ignatius; and
it was only in 1561 that Father David Wolfe, S.J., founded the
Jesuit mission in Ireland.

† In the 14th century organ pipes were generally called "flutes,"
and hence the subsequent corruption of *flue* pipes for *flute* pipes. In
1667, Pepys, in his diary, under date of April 4th, alludes to "a fair
pair of organs."

CHAPTER IV.

ANCIENT IRISH SCALES.

THE construction of the old Irish scales has afforded a wide field for the most conflicting theories. Even Dr. Sullivan, in his critical introduction to O'Curry, says that the Irish scales were " manifold, and often apparently quite arbitrary, so that the principles upon which they proceed are sometimes incomprehensible to us." Dr. James C. Culwick would have us believe that the Irish scales numbered 15, and he compares our old " gapped" scales to those of the Chinese, Russians, and Zuni Indians. Father Bewerunge, the most recent authority on this subject, only admits four modes namely, Doh, Ray, Soh and Lah.*

From a long and careful study of some thousands of our ancient melodies, I have arrived at the conclusion that the old Irish scale was pentatonic, proceeding as follows: *C D EG AC*. By making each note in this first mode a *tonic*, or keynote, we naturally form four other modes—and thus we get five modes. These five are :—

1st. *C D EG AC*
2nd. *D EG AC D*
3rd. *EG AC D E*
4th. *G AC D EG*
5th. *AC D EG A*

The notes *F* and *B* are studiously omitted, and the arrangement is made throughout these five modes so as

* See *New Ireland Review*, for June, 1903.

not to include the fourth and seventh. This omission of *F* and *B* is largely the cause of the quaintness which characterises many of our oldest airs. Between the eighth and twelfth century, the missing, or absent notes of the above five scales were gradually supplied, and thus our ancient gapped scale became almost the self-same as five of the so-called Gregorian modes, namely :—

1. Intense Iastian.
2. Æolian.
3. Intense Hypolydian.
4. Iastian.
5. Relaxed Iastian.
6. Hypolydian.
7. Relaxed Hypolydian.
8. Dorian.

The third Irish mode (omitting *F* and *B*) is the same as the Phrygian mode in the *E* to *E* scale, with naturals only.* However, I would especially call attention to the beauty of airs constructed in the fourth Irish mode, at least, the variant of it which obtained in the early Anglo-Irish period, when the really characteristic note of this lovely mode had become definitely fixed by the inclusion of the missing seventh, that is *F natural.* This mode being subsequently played and sung in the modern key of *G major* (which, of course, has *F* as an *essential sharp*), had to *flatten* the seventh in order to meet the tonality of the Irish modes, and thus the airs written in this fourth mode were said to have been the *flat seventh.* One of the very best examples of the airs

---

* Mr. Fuller Maitland, in January, 1904, in an admirable lecture on Folk Music, quoted examples of the Dorian (D) mode, and also of the Ionian (C), Lydian (F) and Mixolydian modes, from the Petrie Collection.

written in this quaint mode is "An Maiopín Ruᴅò" which Moore sadly mutilated in his "adaptation" of "Let Erin Remember"—a mutilation which extended not only to the character of the mode, or scale, but to the very rhythm, or time-period, of the tune. In the light of this explanation it is amusing to read of the *flat seventh* as "one of the most certain indications of an ancient Irish air"! Indeed, for well nigh two centuries, we have invariably one writer copying another as to the "ravishing effect of the flat seventh," ignoring the real truth that it is the modern scale which must needs flatten the seventh in order to equate itself with the old Irish scale of the fourth mode.

Another very popular delusion, which has been quoted *ad nauseam* by English and Irish writers, is the apparent use of the *minor* mode by the ancient Irish. One constantly meets with allusions to the "grand old air in a plaintive minor scale," or to "a captivating ballad in a minor key, so characteristic of old Irish melodies," etc. As a matter of fact, some of our liveliest and most inspiriting dance tunes are in what one would call the modern minor key, whilst many *caoines* and dirges are in the major scale. Strange as it may seem, there is a vein of melancholy or tenderness throughout all our old tunes, which character is derivable from the peculiarity of scale construction. This is equally true of our hymns, folk-songs, battle-marches, jigs, cradle-songs, elegies, drinking-songs, etc.; and Moore has hit it off very aptly in his exquisite lyric, "Dear Harp of my Country," when he sings :—

> "But so oft hast thou echoed the deep sigh of sadness,
>   That ev'n in thy mirth it will steal from thee still."

According to Walker, the ancient Irish cultivated

three species of musical composition, answering to the three *modes* (the Dorian, Phrygian, and Lydian) which the Greeks borrowed from the Egyptians, namely, the *Goltraighe*, the *Geantraighe*, and the *Suantraighe*. Hardiman also writes :—"Among the ancient Irish the principal species of musical composition was termed *Avantrireach*. It consisted of three parts—*Geantraighe*, which excited to love ; *Goltraighe*, which stimulated to valour and feats of arms; and *Suantraighe*, which disposed to rest and sleep." I may add that the Irish affix, *draiocht*, or *traighe*, means a mode or measure. The ancient *Gol*, which dates from the remotest period, was a distinctive lamentation air ; and each province had its own *Gol*. Walker prints the four ancient Lamentation Cries for Connaught, Munster, Leinster, and Ulster. Petrie informs us that "the *Gol* answers exactly to the rhythm and cadence of those words which are recorded, in the *Book of Ballymote*, to have been sung over the grave of a king of Ossory, in the tenth century." Numerous *Suantraighes* are still preserved, better known as "Irish Lullabys," but the *Geantraighe* has more or less disappeared.*

Mr. Alfred Perceval Graves says :—"Ireland was the school of music for the Celts of Great Britain during the Middle Ages, and *her minstrelsy remained unrivalled* until the Irish Bard, famous for 'the three feats' of solemn [*goltraighe*], gay, [*geantraighe*], and sleep-compelling music [*suantraighe*], degenerated under the stress of the internecine conflict between Saxon and

---

* The commentator of the meeting at Dromceat by Dallan Forgall, preserved in the *Yellow Book of Lecan*, says that "it was a *cruit* without any one of three tunings (*Glesa*) which served to Craiftine the harper, namely, Suantraighe, Goltraighe, and Geantraighe, for the sleeping, he crying, and the laughing modes."

Gael in Ireland, into the strolling minstrel, and finally into the street ballad-singer."

Numerous dissertations have been written on the characteristics of Irish music, but as a nutshell summing up of the whole question, it may briefly be stated that nearly all our ancient tunes are of symmetrically short construction, having the emphatic major sixth, and the thrice-repeated final cadence (the thrice-struck tonic at the close)—and with an undercurrent of tenderness, even in the sprightliest tunes. Apart from an artistic construction peculiarly Celtic, there is an undefinable charm about our ancient melodies that cannot be mathematically expounded. Sir William Stokes, in his *Life of Petrie*, thus writes :—

"It was Petrie's opinion that the music of Ireland stands pre-eminent among that of the other Celtic nations in beauty and power of expression, especially in her *caoines*, her lamentations, and her love-songs ; the latter, by their strange fitfulness, and sudden transitions from gladness to pathos and longing, are marked with a character peculiarly her own. It may well be supposed that some of these delightful tunes are accompanied by songs of corresponding simplicity and pathos."

Petrie himself thus writes regarding our ancient folk-songs, and his description of their construction is applicable to numerous old melodies :—

"These melodies are all in triple or three-four time, and consist of two parts, or strains, of eight bars each, and the same number of phrases, divided into two sections. Of these sections, the second of the first part is, generally, a repetition—sometimes, however, slightly modified—of the section preceding ; and the second section of the second part is usually a repetition of the second section of the first part—sometimes also modified in the first, or even the first and second phrases—but as usual in all Irish melodies, always agreeing with it in its closing cadence."

Taken in general, from a technical point ot view, the ancient Irish can claim the credit of inventing musical "form"—in fact the germ which developed into the Sonata form. Dr. Pearce, no doubt, wishes us to believe that the latter development is due to the thirteenth century Wolfenbuttel melody of the Christmas hymn : *Corde natus ex Parentis*. However, there is not a shadow of doubt that we have Irish tunes long before this period—certainly before the Anglo-Norman invasion —which are characterised emphatically by an artistically constructed ternary or three-phrase arrangement, that is, a phrase of four bars, not unfrequently repeated, followed by an apparent modulation. Sometimes we meet with phrases of seven bars, namely, of four bars and three bars alternately ; whilst a rather unusual rhythm is also to be met with, consisting of four sections of five bars each, each section being barred according to modern ideas into equal or unequal phrases of two bars and three bars. A not unfrequent form of rhythm is nine-eight ; and we meet with numerous tunes constructed on the principle of four sections of two bars each in nine-eight time. The jigs in nine-eight time are known as Hop Jigs, Slip Jigs, or Slip Time, and, as Hudson remarks, are "the most ancient, as well as in general the most effective."

But here it may be objected that probably our ancient Irish music was not of a high order, according to the canons of modern criticism. To this I shall briefly answer by quoting five unquestionable authorities.

(1.) Sir Frederick Gore Ouseley, Mus. Doc., acknowledges that "long before Norman influence was brought

to bear on native art, there existed in Ireland traditional
melodies, the origin of which is lost in antiquity." (2.)
Sir Hubert Parry, after an exhaustive examination of
about three thousand tunes in various collections, gives
it as his opinion that " Irish folk music is probably *the
most human, most varied, most poetical in the world*, and
is particularly rich in tunes which imply considerable sympathetic sensitiveness." (3.) Sir Alexander
MacKenzie writes in an equally eulogistic strain. (4.)
Chappell, who was particularly biassed in favour of
English music, avows the "exquisite beauty " of our old
tunes ; and (5.) the late Brinley Richards was enraptured
with " their individuality and tenderness." It is unnecessary to quote the eulogies of Handel, Beethoven, Berlioz,
Pleyel, Haydn, and other great masters.

Our own Moore rather ignorantly alludes to the comparatively modern date of many of our "ancient"
melodies, the origin of which he is pleased to reckon as
" dating no farther back than the last [eighteenth]
disgraceful century." In his later years the " bard of
Ireland" grudgingly admitted to Dr. Petrie that he was
mistaken in his previous views, and he acknowledged
that "*the date of those airs is much more ancient* " than he
had stated. This admission, however, is not to be
found in the various editions of the *Melodies*. However, as Renehan points out, Moore, in his *History of
Ireland* (1840) admits " the superior excellence of the
music of Ireland *before the English invasion*." Recent
research has more than vindicated the undoubted claim
of ancient Erin to the possession of the loveliest airs in
the world.

CHAPTER V.

IRISH MUSIC BEFORE THE ANGLO-NORMAN INVASION.

ALTHOUGH in ancient Erin, from the ninth to the middle of the eleventh century, the Danish incursions, as well as internecine conflicts, were serious obstacles to the cultivation of music, yet this very period was one of the greatest lustre for Irish music on the Continent. Of course, there are not wanting a few zealots who would fain have us believe that the Norsemen actually contributed to the preservation of churches and monasteries and schools in Ireland. It is strange to find Dr. Sigerson, in his otherwise excellent book, *The Bards of the Gael and Gall*, enunciating and upholding these peculiar views in reference to the Norsemen as regards Irish literature and music.

All our ancient chronicles are at one in describing the terrible vandalism committed by the Danes in the island of saints and scholars. Keating distinctly assures us that the Norsemen sought to destroy all learning and art in Ireland. His words are most emphatic :—" No scholars, no clerics, no books, no holy relics, were left in church or monastery through dread of them. *Neither bard, nor philosopher, nor musician, pursued his wonted profession in the land.*"

To come to concrete examples, we are told that " Brian Boru's March" and " The Cruiskeen Lawn " are good specimens of " Scandinavian music." This statement is quite erroneous. Both of these airs are genuinely Irish in construction, though I gravely doubt whether either of them dates from the Norse period, or even from mediæval days.

Despite the troubled condition of Ireland during these two or three centuries, as Dr. Douglas Hyde writes, "she produced a large number of poets and scholars, the impulse given by the enthusiam of the sixth and seventh centuries being still strong upon her." Among the distinguished bards of the tenth century was Flann Mac Lonain. In one of his eight poems that have come down to our days he describes a harper called Ilbrechtach, of Slieve Aughty, near Kinalehin.

King Brian, ere his sad death at the glorious victory of Clontarf, in 1014, did a great deal towards repairing the ravages wrought during three centuries. According to the "Wars of the Gael with the Gall," a valuable manuscript that was written during the first quarter of the eleventh century, Brian "sent professors and masters to teach wisdom and knowledge," but he was compelled "*to buy books beyond the sea and the great ocean, because the writings and books of the churches and sanctuaries had been burned and drowned by the plunderers.*"

Whilst we must for ever lament the destruction of our ancient literary and musical manuscripts by the Norsemen, it is gratifying to know that some few musical treasures, written by Irish monks, still remain on the continent. Only to quote one instance, at Zurich, in the library of the Antiquarian Society, may yet be seen a fragment of an Irish *Sacramentarium* and *Antiphonarium*.

Our Irish St. Helias, a native of Monaghan, was elected Abbot of Cologne, in Germany, in 1015. He was the bosom friend of St. Heribert, and ruled the two monasteries of St. Martin's and St. Pantaleon's, from 1015 to 1040. Mabillon tells us that not only was St. Helias a most distinuished musician, but that he was "*the first to introduce the Roman chant to Cologne*,"* and he is, most probably, "the stranger and pilgrim" to whom Berno of Riechenau dedicated his well-known musical work, "The Laws of Symphony and Tone."† No greater tribute to the esteem in which the Irish monks were held at Reichenau can be cited than the fact that this monastery (founded in 724 by our Irish St. Pirminius) was placed under the patronage of St. Fintan, a Leinster saint, who flourished *circa* 830. Walafridus Strabo, Dean of St. Gall's, was Abbot of Reichenau from 824 to 849.

The famous Guido of Arezzo (born in 995, and died May 17th, 1050), Benedictine Prior of the monastery of Avellina, perfected the gamut of twenty sounds, and improved diaphony. He devised the hexachordal scale, *Ut, Re, Mi, Fa, Sol, La*, from the first syllables of the hymn to St. John the Baptist, commencing "Ut queant laxis." It is not a little remarkable that the melody to which this hymn was sung before Guido's time was not an original one, but had been, years before, composed for an Ode of Horace, commencing "Est mihi nonus," and which is to be met with in a Montpellier MS. of the tenth century. This interesting fact strengthens the view put forward in a previous chapter, that many Irish

---

* The *Annals of Ulster* tell us that Donnchad, Abbot of Dun-shaughlin, died on a pilgrimage at Cologne in 1027, as also did Eochagan, Archdeacon of Slane, in 1042; and, similarly, Brian, King of Leinster, died there in 1052. Of course, the great musical theorist, Franco of Cologne, must have imbibed some of the Irish traditions as to discant or organum.

† Mabillon, *Annales Benedictinorum*, tom. iv., p. 297.

melodies were similarly utilized, or "adapted," by Irish
scribes in various copies of the service-books between
the eighth and twelfth centuries. Let it not be forgotten
that the musical work of St. Ambrose was in great part
an adaptation ; and, later still, we find the great hymnist,
St. Venantius Fortunatus, setting some vintage songs
to religious words. Father Michael Moloney, of Ber-
mondsey, some years ago,* stated as his "firm belief,"
that "some day, not far distant, the fact that Gregorian
music was largely influenced by ancient Irish music
would be satisfactorily established."† From all the
proofs here quoted—cumulative evidence of the very
strongest kind—the reader must be convinced of the
deep debt which "plain chant" owes to the monks and
scribes of ancient Erin.

As amply and conclusively supporting my view I can
confidently quote the "organised" arrangement of *Ut
tuo propitiatus*, written by an Irish scribe about the year
1095, and interpolated in a tenth century Cornish manuscript now in the Bodleian Library (Bodley, 572). Professor Wooldridge says that it is one of the earliest
known examples of "irregular Organum" in contrary
movement, employing an independent use of dissonance,
and it is written in alphabetical notation. The hymn

* At the Irish Literary Society, London, on January 25th, 1900,
the present writer lectured on "A Hundred Years of Irish Music,"
when a vote of thanks was proposed by the Countess of Aberdeen,
and seconded by Father Moloney, the chair being occupied by Mr.
C. L. Graves, in the unavoidable absence of Professor Sir Charles
Villiers Stanford.

† Professor Dickinson, in his monumental book, *The Music of
the Western Church* (1902), unhesitatingly adopts the view of
Gevaert, that "actual adaptations of older tunes and a spontaneous
enunciating of more obvious melodic formulas " are the true sources
of the earlier liturgical chant.

itself is portion of the hymn to St. Stephen, and apparently was most popular in England, as well as on the continent, as we meet with a variant of it in the Sarum Antiphonal.   In 1897, Professor Wooldridge was of opinion that the hymn was of the same age as the whole of the Bodleian manuscript in which it is included, but, in 1901, as a result of closer examination, he agrees with the experts who assign its date as eleventh century, or certainly not later than the year 1100.

The score of the "organal" part, as stated in a learned article by Dr. Oscar Fleischer, in the *Viertel-jahrsschrift fur Musikwissenshaft*, 1890, is really an adaptation, or setting, of "a Gaelic folk song, afterwards worked upon by a learned composer of that period," the melody being "in a scale of the pentatonic character." I subjoin a translated modern version of this ancient Irish melody from the reconstruction as given by Dr. Fleischer :—

UT TUO PROPITIATUS.

11th cent. Bodl. MS.

In a rare vellum MS. in Trinity College, Dublin (H. 3, 18), compiled about the year 1490, there is an extract given from an *Irish* tract written at the commencement of the thirteenth century, which exhibits a full knowledge of the Guidonian system, and discusses at great length the etymology of the syllables *Ut, Re, Mi, Fa, Sol, La.* A translation of this extract is quoted in full by Dr. W. K. Sullivan, in his introduction to O'Curry's *Lectures.* A still more convincing proof that the Guidonian gamut was known in Ireland at the close of the eleventh century is the actual preservation of some Irish airs in Morris's Welsh collection, quoted by Dr. Burney, which are said to have been transcribed in the twelfth century.

The great monastery of St. Peter's, Ratisbon, was established by Muiredach (Marianus) Mac Robertaigh, in 1076; and St. James's, at Ratisbon, was founded in 1090, with Diuma, or Domnus, a monk from the South of Ireland, as Abbot—being built, according to the *Chronicon Ratisbonense,* "by funds supplied from Ireland to Denis, the Irish Abbot of St. Peter's, at Ratisbon." By a curious irony of fate, the music school of Ratisbon, originally founded by Irish monks, has been for some years past importing German organists to various Catholic churches in Ireland, whilst Ratisbon itself is the home of the great music publishing establishment of F. Pustet, the printer of various liturgical works used in the Western Church.

CHAPTER VI.

IRISH MUSIC BEFORE THE ANGLO-NORMAN INVASION
(continued).

DR. LEDWICH gave it as his opinion that "the incomparable skill of the Irish harpers, as attested by Giraldus Cambrensis, could never be predicated of unlearned, extemporaneous, bardic airs, but implies a knowledge of the diagram [*sic*], and an exact division of the harmonic intervals." On the other hand, Brompton, in the reign of Henry II., says that "the Irish harpers taught in secret, and committed their lessons to memory." The truth is that though the pre-Christian Irish had their ogham music-tablature, and the Irish of the seventh-eleventh century had the neumal accents, after which the Guidonian system was adopted, *very little use was made of written music*, inasmuch as the "divine art" was mostly taught orally, according to traditional rendering, just as the Gregorian Chant was taught on the continent. At the same time there were *written* copies of the musical services ; and Gerbert gives a "memoria technica," from the *Breviarium de Musica*, a manuscript of the eleventh century, in which the neumatic *names* and the *signs* corresponding thereto are given in hexameter verses. However, in a country so tenacious of its language, music, and customs as Ireland, it is not such a very great loss that no notated copies of our religious tunes or folk-songs exist prior to the eleventh century, as, even if such notated manuscripts survived, they would be absolutely unintelligible to latter-day musicians, and would only possess an antiquarian value. The self-same must be predicated of all written music until the year 1100. Dr. Haberl thus writes: " During the course of the twelfth century the various manuscript *codices* written in *neums* were transferred into the clearer and larger staff-notation. But, the character of these translations was very much determined by locality, as the possibility of multitudinous interpretations and renderings of the neumatic signs gave rise, in the eleventh century, to different ways of chanting one and the same text, *according to the teaching which the singer received in the several cathedrals and cloisters.*" And, in proof of the comparatively small number of written copies, he adds : " The old teachers relied for the method of singing the *neums* principally on oral traditions. They committed very little to writing, and that little was by no means clear or determined."*

To this opinion may be added the view of the late Mr. H. B. Briggs, in his *Structure of Plainsong*, who says that " Plainsong is recitative," and " no notation can exactly express the rendering that will be given to it by a good singer." It is as well to state that the one-line stave, suggested by the Irish ogham scale, was drawn horizontally across the parchment over the words which demanded a musical setting, and the letter F was placed at the beginning of it, meaning an F line, that is to say, indicating the nomenclature of all the neums on the line as F, thus affording a basis for musical pitch, from which was naturally evolved the present musical staff or stave.

* Haberl's *Magister Choralis* translated by the Most Rev. Dr. Donnelly, Bishop of Canea, and Dean of Dublin.

In the new organum of the eleventh century we find in use dissonances of the major and minor third, with the major sixth, and even the second and the seventh, as well as concords. At the close of this century and during the first half of the twelfth, many examples are preserved of hymns and songs containing "imitation" passages, which gave rise to Rondel. But, more particularly, the basis of the mensural system was laid when the *Virga* became the *Longa*, or long note, and the *Punctum* the *Brevis*, or short note.

I have mentioned above that there are old Irish airs preserved in Morris's Welsh collection, dating from the twelfth century, and which are quoted by Dr. Burney. This fact demands a brief reference to Wales, and to the debt which she owes to Ireland for her music.

In consequence of the constant intercourse between Ireland and Wales from the third to the eleventh century, Irish immigrants introduced Celtic minstrelsy, and taught the Welsh people the music of ancient Erin. This musical cult was most warmly taken up during the reign of Howell the Good (915-948). Numerous entries in the Irish Annals, from 950 to 1095, testify to the exodus of Irish harpers to Wales, culminating in the celebrated Eisteddfod of Caerwys, in 1100, which became the model on which the subsequent Welsh festivals were based.

About the year 1059, the King of North Wales was forced to seek an asylum in Ireland, and, whilst abiding with his Queen as an honoured guest in the "Sacred Isle," his son and heir, Griffith ap Conan, was born, who was carefully fostered and instructed in all the polite learning of that period. We are told that the young prince was particularly enamoured of Irish music, especially the martial tones of the bagpipe. Dermot Mac Maelnambo, King of Leinster, was at this time supreme monarch of Ireland, which position he maintained till his death, on February 6th, 1072. His rule is highly praised by Caradoc of Llancarvan (1156), who frankly asserts that "the Irish devised all the instruments, tunes, and measures in use among the Welsh."* When Prince Griffith came to man's estate, he returned to Wales in order to assert his undoubted right to his father's patrimony, then in the hands of a usurper called Traherne; and the decisive battle of Carno, in 1080, eventuated in his being placed on the throne of North Wales. No sooner was he securely established as king than, between the years 1085 and 1095, he invited over some Irish bards and minstrels, so as to put the music of Wales on the same lines as the Irish musical code.

At the Eisteddfod of Caerwys in 1100, King Griffith, in order to introduce the Irish bagpipes, gave particular prominence to pipe performances, and we read in the Welsh Annals that "*the prize was carried off by an Irishman, who received from the monarch a silver pipe as a reward for his skill.*" However, the crowning glory of this epoch-making Eisteddfod was the evening *Feis*, held under the presidency of the monarch himself, in which laws were enacted for the proper regulation of Welsh minstrelsy.

In order that the future Eisteddfodau should have a genuine Irish character, King Griffith sent to Murtogh

* Powell's *History of Cambria* (1584), p. 191. See also the Note to Michael Drayton's *Polyolbion* by Selden.

O'Brien, styled by St. Anselm "Muriardach, the glorious King of Ireland," for an eminent professor of music, to confer with three Welshmen in drawing up a musical code. King Murtogh (1089-1120) selected a distinguished minstrel called by the Welsh chroniclers "Matholwch the Gwyddilian," or *Malachy the Irishman*, who, in conjunction with the three Welsh bards, drew up rules, according to the Irish system, for orchestration, musical theory, and metre. We read that these doctors "laid down rules for the performance on stringed instruments, the harp and the cruit; and they also drew up twenty-four musical canons, and established twenty-four metres."[*]

The Welsh annalists tell us that these enactments of the four learned bards were confirmed at a *Feis* held at Glendalough, Co. Wicklow, by the said Murtogh O'Brien, King of Ireland, "who ratified them by his prerogative and influence, commanding all to maintain them ;" and thus was settled for ever the question of Welsh minstrelsy. It is interesting to add that a daughter of our Irish monarch was married to Arnuph de Montgomery, Earl of Pembroke ; and King Murtogh himself died as a monk in the famous monastery of Lismore, Co. Waterford, on the fourth of the Ides of March, 1120.

Under date of A.D. 1110, the veracious *Annals of Ulster* chronicle the death of Ferdomnach the Blind, Lector of Kildare, who is described as a Cᴘuıcıᴘeċᴅ, or "Master of Harping." Some years later, namely, in 1119, there is a record of the death of Diarmuid

---

[*] See the "Celtic Origin of the Welsh Eisteddfod" by the present writer in the *New Ireland Review* for March, 1898.

O'Boylan, "chief Music-master in Ireland," who was killed by some ruffians in his own house, as were also his wife and his two sons, "with 35 others, his guests and retainers."

In Dowling's *Annals of Ireland* in connection with the year 1137, there is chronicled the demise of Griffith ap Conan, King of North Wales, "born in Ireland of an Irish mother, who had led back with him from Ireland, harps, timpans, cruits, cytharae, and harpers." The intercourse between Wales and Ireland was very frequent at this epoch, and in 1142, Dowling has the following entry :—" Cadwallader, the son of Griffith ap Conan, was forced to fly into Ireland, and brought back with him, for 2,000 marks, the son of O'Carroll, captain of 1,000 fighting men, together with spoils and booty."

The Irish character of the verses written by Prince Howell, son of Owen, King of North Wales, about the year 1165, is most remarkable. This Howell (whose mother was the daugher of an Irish chieftain) assumed the government of his petty kingdom on the death of his father, in 1169, and ruled till 1171, when he came over to Ireland to claim the property of his grandfather, in right of his mother, the heiress. It is only pertinent to add that Welsh poetry and minstrelsy flourished exceedingly from 1140 to 1240, in which latter year Llewellyn the Great died.* With the decline of the Irish element, and the decay of the bards towards the close of the thirteenth century, came the conquest of Wales, and its annexation to the "predominant partner," in 1283.

Scotland, even in a greater degree than Wales, owes

* *Ibid.*

her music to Ireland, as a result of two colonizations from *Scotia Major*, or ancient Erin—the first under Cairbre Riada (*a quo Dal Riada*) in A.D. 130, and the second under Fergus, Lorne, and Angus, the sons of Erc, in A.D. 504.

Giraldus Cambrensis, in the twelfth century, writes as follows :—" Scotland and Wales, *the former by reason of her derivation*, the latter from intercourse and affinity, seek with emulous endeavours to imitate Ireland in music."   He adds :—" The Irish use and delight in but two instruments, the harp and the viol [ᴄᴘᴜɪᴄ] ; the Scotch in the harp, viol, and bagpipe ; the Welsh in the harp, pipes, and bagpipe.   The Irish also use *brass wires* for their harps in preference to those of gut."*

O'Donovan says that "the present language of the Highlands passed from Ireland into the Highlands about A.D. 504 ; and a regular intercourse has ever since been kept up between both countries, *the literature and music of the one having been ever since those of the other."*

Ruined churches and monasteries, shrines, wells, inscribed stones, and solidly founded tradition—all point to the very close kinship between the parent Scots of Ireland and their progeny in Caledonia, Alba, or Scotia Minor.   Somerled MacGillabride, Chief of Uriel (Louth, Armagh, and Monaghan), was recognised as King of Argyle, that is, Lord of the Isles, about the middle of the twelfth century.   In a naval battle which took place in 1156, this same Irish king (who died in 1164) captured Iona and the rest of the Southern Hebrides from Godred, Norse King of the Isles, and he induced Flaherty O'Brolcain (Brollaghan or Bradley), Abbot-Bishop of

* *Top. Dist.* iii. c. xi.

Derry, to take over the Abbacy of Iona *in commendam*, who accordingly did so, and retained his Presidency of the Columban monasteries till his death in 1175.

King Somerled's sons, Reginald, Dubhgall, and Angus, and their successors, held sway over the west of Scotland till the end of the fifteenth century, namely, 1493, when the Lordship of the Isles was surrendered to the Scottish Crown. " This will account for the old bonds between Scotia Major and Scotia Minor being drawn still closer, and for the number of Irish bards— O'Dalys and others—entertained at Dunstaffnage, Inverary, and other western strongholds, during this long period, and the vitality of the old stories and poems that originated in the native country of these minstrels."*

* *Dublin University Magazine* for January, 1864.

CHAPTER VII.

IRISH MUSIC BEFORE THE ANGLO-NORMAN INVASION
(continued).

IT would be merely slaying the slain to bring forward any of the silly arguments that formerly were availed of by Dempster and others to claim as natives of Scotland the ancient Irish Scots. It is now universally conceded that even at the close of the eleventh century the Irish were called Scots ; and John Major says that it is certain the present (fifteenth century Scots of Caledonia owe their origin to Ireland."

Even England must acknowledge its indebtedness for music to Ireland. "the lamp of learning in the West." from the fifth to the twelfth century. It was our Irish missionaries who introduced Irish music and inaugurated plain-chant at Lindisfarne, Durham, Ripon Lichfield, Malmesbury, Norfolk, Suffolk, Cornwall Glastonbury, etc. St. Bede and St. Aldhelm vie with each other in their eulogies on Irish scholars.

Old neumatic notation is to be found in a copy of the *Codex Amiatinus*, one of the three books which Ceolfrid, Abbot of Jarrow, took with him, in the year 716, to Rome, as a present to Pope St. Gregory II. These neums, which were written about the year 704, are set for the Lamentations of Jeremias ; and the saintly Abbot died on his way to the Eternal City, in 716. Ceolfrid was the tutor and predecessor of St. Bede ; and, as is well known, the monks of Jarrow and Wearmouth were taught by the Irish monks of

Northumbria, of which district our Irish St. Aidan was first Bishop.

The learned Alcuin studied at Clonmacnoise, in 755-760, under St. Colgu the Wise, whom he styles his "blessed Master and dear Father." In 803, as an old man, this great English scholar, when he had resigned his scholastic labours, querulously informs Charlemagne of "the daily increasing influence of the Irish at the school of the Palace."

Suidhne Mac Maelumai (O'Molloy), the thirty-fourth Abbot of Clonmacnoise, is justly styled by the old chroniclers as *doctor Scotorum peritissimus*, whose best known pupil was Dicuil the Geographer. In the year 890, he was one of the three Irish sages who were summoned to England by Alfred the Great, to devise a scheme of studies after the manner of the Irish Universities.

During the winter of the year 941, Muircheartach of the Leathern Cloaks (heir apparent to the throne of Tara) made a circuit of Ireland, and brought away with him the provincial princes or their sons to his palace at Royal Aileach, on the eastern shore of the Swilly, near Derry, where he detained them for five months, after which he sent them to the Ard Righ of Ireland, Donogh II. His secretary, Cormac an Eigeas, has left us an account of this circuit of Ireland, in which we read that the evenings were generally devoted to music :—

> " Music we had on the plain and in our tents—
> Listening to its strains we danced."

Towards the close of the eleventh century, Gilbert, Bishop of Limerick, made an effort to displace the existing Irish liturgical "uses" in favour of the Roman Rite, but was not successful. In his *De Usu Ecclesiastico* he tells us that there was a great diversity and variety in the Church offices in Ireland, so much so that even a learned cleric, accustomed to one particular form of liturgy, would be quite bewildered in a neighbouring diocese, where a different Use obtained. It is more than probable that the Ambrosian chant—introduced by St. Patrick—and the Irish modification of the Gregorian chant continued to be sung in most of the Irish churches till the year 1125.

St. Malachy, Legate of the Holy See, got the Roman chant adopted throughout the archdiocese of Armagh in 1148; and, a few years later, Donogh O'Carroll, Prince of Uriel, got a complete set of liturgical books—Antiphonaries as well as Missals—copied by an Irish scribe. This Donogh O'Carroll, the founder of the Abbey of SS. Peter and Paul, Knock, County Louth, and a munificent benefactor to Mellifont Abbey, died, according to the *Annals of Ulster*, on Thursday, the tenth of the moon, Kalends of January, 1170; and "he it was for whom were written the Book of Knock Abbey, and the chief office-books (books used for the singing of the Divine Office) for the ecclesiastical year, and the chief books of the Mass.*

John of Salisbury, about the year 1165, highly extols the music of Ireland; and his testimony is all the more valuable as he was not very favourable towards this country. He declares that in the Crusade of Godfrey of Bouillon, in 1099, *there would have been no music at all had it not been for the Irish Harp*, or, as Fuller says, "the consort of Christendom could have made no musick if the Irish Harp had been wanting."

* *Annals of Ulster*, vol. ii., pp. 160, 161.

The great St. Laurence O'Toole, Archbishop of Dublin, in 1165, dissatisfied with the Dano-Celtic system of liturgical chant in Christ Church Cathedral, introduced the Arroasian Canons of the Order of St. Victor—a reform of the Augustinians—who sang the Divine Office daily, presided over by the Archbishop himself.

Music was an especial feature in the school of the Culdees at Armagh, as has been amply demonstrated by the late Bishop Reeves. The *Annals of Ulster* give a lengthened obituary notice of Flann O'Gorman, "chief lector of Armagh and of all Ireland," in 1174, "on Wednesday before Easter, the 13th of the Kalends of April [March 20], in the 70th year of his age." He had been President-General of the Universities throughout Ireland, and was held in the highest esteem.*

Even after the formation of a Chapter in the Cathedral of Armagh, the Prior of the Culdees was invariably Precentor, or Chief Chanter, whilst the brethren of the *Colidei* acted as Vicars Choral.† These Culdees were the representatives of the old Columban order of monks ; and their school at Armagh lasted from the close of the ninth century to the time of Elizabeth. The diocese of Meath is still a silent witness of the ancient Celtic monastic form of church government, and has never had a cathedral body or Chapter, nor yet a Cathedral.

In 1168 died " the chief Ollamh of Ireland in harp playing," and in 1171, " the timpanist Ua Coinnecen, Ard-Ollamh of the North of Ireland, was

* *Ibid.*

† Among the treasures exhibited at the Gregorian Congress, in Rome, during Easter week, 1904, was a copy of St. Gregory's *Moralia*, in the last page of which was inserted the hymn, "O Christi Martyr "—of the Irish St. Kilian, *in musical notation of the twelfth century.*

killed by the Cinel-Conaill, with his wife and with his
people."

Irish bishops, priests, and clerics were accustomed,
in the twelfth century, to carry round with them small
harps, both for the purpose of accompanying the sacred
chant, as also for their own delectation. This fact is
expressly stated by Archdeacon Gerald Barry, from
personal observation at the close of the same century :—
" Hinc accidit, ut Episcopi et Abbates, et Sancti in
Hibernia viri cytharas circumferre et in eis modulando
pie delectari consueverint."*

The neums or accents of the Irish corresponding to
the Latin *Acutus, Modicus, Gravis*, and *Circumflexus*,
are : *Ardceol, Ceol, Basceoil*, and *Circeoil*, indicating
pitch ; whilst the mediæval Irish had their own characters to represent mensural music, corresponding to
the *Longa* and the *Brevis*, that is to say, practically our
modern Semibreve and Minim. Unison was called
cobhluighe, or lying together ; the fifth was termed
Tead na feithe olach, or string of the leading sinews ;
the octave below was *cronan*, etc. In fact, each string
of the harp had its own particular name; and the
ancient minstrels had an infinite variety of terms for
musical rhythm and expression.†

---

* Cambrensis, *Topog. Hib.*, Dist. c. xii.

† The following is a brief description of the dress worn by ancient
Irish harpers, as is chronicled in the "Bruidhean da Derga," one of
the oldest Irish sagas now known, and contained in *Leabhar na
hUidhre*: " I saw another row of nine harpers. Nine branching,
curling heads of hair on them : nine grey winding cloaks about
them : nine brooches of gold in their cloaks : nine circlets of pearls
round their hands : nine rings of gold around their thumbs : nine
torques of gold around their ears : nine torques of silver round their
throats : nine bags with golden faces in the side-wall : nine wands
of white silver in their hands." Dr. Hyde dates this saga as of the
seventh century if not earlier.

In regard to the old Irish form of "organising," O'Curry writes: *Rind* was music consisting of full harmony, while *Leithrind*, or half Rind, was one or other of the two corresponding parts which produced the harmonious whole and these parts were the bass and treble notes, or the bass and treble strings—the *Trom Threda* and the *Goloca*, or the heavy and the thin strings. *Coir* is another Irish term for harmony, and is mentioned in the Brehon laws * From a passage in the Life of St. Brigid by Anmchad, Bishop of Kildare, who died in the year 980, it is evident that the harp was at that period employed as a favourite accompaniment for part-singing.

The commentary on the Elegy on St. Columba, which was certainly written before the year 1100, contains musical allusions, including the *ceis* and the "*bass* chord in the harp of Crabtene.'' From the well-known passage of our Irish John Scotus Erigena, in his tract *De Divisione Naturae*, written about the year 864, it is perfectly clear that the free Organum of the Fourth, or of the *Diatesseron*, was well known to the Irish of the ninth century—that is to say, a hundred and fifty years before the appearance of the *Scholia Enchiriadis* and the *Musica Enchiriadis*. Professor Wooldridge, in the *Oxford History of Music*, says that "Erigena's description of the alternate separation and coming together of the voices quite admits of application to this method." For the benefit of the musical student, I give the Latin passage of Scotus:—

"Organicum melos ex diversis qualitatibus et quantita-

---

* The seven Irish words for concerted music are :—*cómseinm, cóicetul, aidbse, cepóc, claiss, clais-cetul,* and *foacanad*. In *Cormac's Glossary* (p. 43) *cómseinm* refers to instrumental harmony, whilst *cóicetul* is given as "singing together"—*clais-cetul* signifying "choral singing."

tibus conficitur dum viritim separatimque sentiuntur
voces longe a se discrepantibus intensionis et remis-
sionis proportionibus segregatae dum vero sibi invicem
coaptantur *secundum certas rationabilesque artis musicae
regulas per singulos tropos naturalem quandam dulcedinem reddentibus*."

From Coussemaker it appears that a monk who wrote
soon after the death of Charlemagne alludes to the art
of "organising," and he concludes that the practice of
harmony was certainly known in the early part of the
ninth century.*

Brompton, writing in the reign of Henry II., waxes
enthusiastic over the very advanced skill of Irish
musicians in the twelfth century on the cᴘuɪᴄ, timpan,
and bagpipe ; and he extols "*the animated execution, the
sweet and pleasing harmony*, the quivering notes and
intricate modulations of the Irish "—"*crispatis modulis
et intricatis notulis, efficiunt harmoniam*" (Hist. Anglic.
Script., p. 1075).

In justice to Tom Moore it must be acknowledged that
he pointed out the ridiculous error into which Walker
and Bunting had been led, quoting from Beaufort,
owing to a mistranslation of Brompton. Walker makes
the foregoing extract as signifying that the Irish had
"*two sorts of harps, the one bold and quick, the other soft
and pleasing*"!!!

This brings us to the epoch of the Anglo-Norman
invasion ; and, as contemporary evidence is always of

* There is a manuscript translation into English of Erigena's
valuable tract, made by the late William Larminie (whose death,
in 1900, was a great loss to Irish studies), which is now in the
National Library of Ireland, Kildare-street, Dublin. It is said to be
the only English version of Erigena's work. The translation is in
two quarto volumes, and was presented to the library by the author's
brother.

the first importance, I cannot conclude this chapter better than by quoting the following eulogy on the Irish school of harpers from the pen of Gerald Barry, better known as Giraldus Cambrensis, Archdeacon of St. David's, who came to Ireland in 1183 :—

" They are incomparably more skilful than any other nation I have ever seen. For their manner of playing on these instruments [cruits, clairseachs, and timpans], unlike that of the Britons to which I am accustomed, is not slow and harsh, but lively and rapid, while the melody is both sweet and pleasing. It is astonishing that in such a complex and rapid movement of the fingers the musical proportions [as to rhythm] can be preserved, and that throughout the difficult modulations on their various instruments the harmony, notwithstanding shakes and slurs, and variously intertwined organising, is completely observed."

The Latinity of Giraldus is not easy to give in an English dress, but he wishes to display his knowledge of musical technicalities as then in vogue. He describes " the striking together of the chords of the *diatesseron*[the fourth degree of the scale], and *diapente* [the fifth] introducing B flat, and of the " tinkling of the small strings coalescing charmingly with the deep notes of the bass " —clearly pointing to the Irish free organum of the fourth, and that of *diapente*, including the discord of the Imperfect Fifth interval. He concludes as follows :—" They delight with so much delicacy, and soothe so softly, that the excellence of their art seems to lie in concealing it."*

* *Topographia Hiber.*, Disp. iii., cap. xi. In the original Latin, the terms *proportio, crispatos, modulos, organa, dispari paritate discordi, concordia, consona*, etc., can only mean, as Renehan writes, " the rhythmical measure of time, the slur and graces, the organizing or counterpoint, the harmony of discords, and all the then latest inventions of modern musie." (Renehan's *History of Music*, p. 163.)

Not even a professed panegyrist of our twelfth-century
Irish musicians could use more flattering language than
the foregoing, and, therefore, such testimony from the
prejudiced bishop-elect of St. David's should be highly
valued.   Rev. James F. Dimock, who has edited
Giraldus, under the direction of the English Master of
the Rolls, says :—" Giraldus had not an idea that anything he thought or said could by any chance be
wrong " ; and " he was replete with the exact qualities,
the very reverse of what are needed to form an impartial
historian."   For all that, the observant Archdeacon was
completely captivated by the charm of Irish music, and
he has left us the above imperishable record.   Well does
Moore sing :—

> " The stranger shall hear thy lament on his plains :
> The sigh of thy harp shall be sent o'er the deep.
> Till thy masters themselves, as they rivet thy chains,
> Shall pause at the song of their captive, and weep."

CHAPTER VIII.

IRISH MUSIC IN THE MIDDLE AGES.

THE year 1216 is remarkable for an incident from which we get a clue to the origin of the so-called " Brian Boru's Harp." So much legend has attached to the historic instrument of that name (now housed in Trinity College, Dublin), said erroneously to have belonged to King Brian, that a sketch of the real facts will not be unwelcome to critical readers.

Muiredach O'Daly, of Lissadil, Co. Sligo, was a famous Irish minstrel at the opening of the thirteenth century.   In 1216, Donal *mor* O'Donnell, Prince of Tyrconnell, sent his steward (Finn O'Bradley) into Connaught, to collect tribute, who was slain, in a fit of anger, by O'Daly, for a supposed insult to the bardic profession.   The bard fled to Athenry (where, for a while, he was protected by Richard de Burgo), and thence to Thomond and Dublin, pursued by O'Donnell himself, and finally escaped to Scotland, where he remained for some years [1217-1222].

Whilst in Scotland, O'Daly wrote three celebrated poems to O'Donnell, " who permitted him to return unmolested to his native country, and even restored him to his friendship."   These Irish poems were fortunately preserved in Scotland, in the Dean of Lismore's Book ;* and O'Daly was known as *Albanach* that is, the Scotchman, from his residence in Albania, or Alba.

* The editor (Rev. Mr. MacLachlan) of this valuable Gaelic MS. says that O'Daly " was the ancestor of the MacVurricks, bards to the MacDonalds of Clanranald."

Meantime, Donnchadh Cairbre O'Briain, King of
Thomond, *sent his own harp*—"the jewel of the
O'Briens"—as a pledge, to Scotland (for the ransom or
return of the bard O'Daly), where it remained for over
80 years.   Thus, we can accurately trace the history of
a rare harp of the O'Brien sept, sent to Scotland, about
the year 1221, as a forfeit, by the valiant King of
Thomond, whose death took place on March 8th, 1243.

About the year 1229, Gillabride Mac Conmidhe [Mac
Conmee, Mac Namee, or Conmee], a famous Ulster
bard, was commissioned by King O'Brien to endeavour
to ransom the much-prized harp.   In response to this
request Mac Conmidhe—also known by the soubriquet
of *Albanach* on account of his many visits to Scotland—
composed the well-known "Ransom song," in commemoration of his playing on its chords for the last
time.   At that time, the power of a bard was very great,
and even a song fetched a high price; but, alas! the
lovely harp of the O'Briens—the so-called harp of Brian
Boru—would not be restored for "whole flocks of
sheep," and so, as O'Curry considers, it remained in
Scotland until Edward I. took it with him to Westminster.   Finally, on July 1st, 1543, when Henry VIII.
created Ulick Mac William de Burgo Earl of Clanrickarde, he presented the Earl with this Irish harp,
which had belonged to Donnchadh Cairbre O'Briain.

Vallancey says that this harp, having reverted to the
Earl of Thomond, was purchased by Lady Huxley, for
"twenty rams and as many swine of English breed,"
and "bestowed by her to her son-in-law, Henry Mac
Mahon, of Clenagh, County Clare,* who about the year

* The husband of Lady Elizabeth de Burgh.

1736, bestowed it on Mat MacNamara of Limerick, Esq., Counsellor-at-Law, and some years Recorder of that city." In the year 1760, Arthur O'Neill, the great harpist, played on this venerable instrument, newly strung for the occasion, through the streets of Limerick. It was bequeathed by Mr. MacNamara in 1778 to Ralph Ouseley, Esq., of Limerick, who, in 1781, presented it to the Right Hon. Colonel Conyngham, and, at length, in 1782, Conyngham donated it to Trinity College, Dublin.*

The following is Petrie's description of the O'Brien harp :—

" From recent examination, it appears that this harp had but one row of strings; that these were 30 in number, not 28, as was formerly supposed, 30 being the number of brass tuning pins and of corresponding string holes. It is 32 inches high, and of exquisite workmanship ; the upright pillar is of oak, and the sound board of red sallow ; the extremity of the fore-arm, or harmonic curved bar, is capped in part with silver, extremely well wrought and chiselled. It also contains a large crystal set in silver, under which was another stone, now lost. The buttons or ornamental knobs at the side of the curved bar are of silver. The string holes of the sound board are neatly ornamented with escutcheons of brass carved and gilt. The four sounding holes have also had ornaments, probably of silver, as they have been the object of theft.† The bottom which it rests upon is a little broken and the wood very much decayed. The whole bears evidence of having been the work of a very expert artist."

There is a remarkable entry in connection with the year 1225 in the *Annals of Lough Cé*, amply demonstrat-

* Egerton MSS., No. 74.
† In 1876 one of these ornaments was found in the Phœnix Park. (See *Journal R.S.A.*, for October, 1878.)

ing the progress of instrumental music at that period, especially the cultivation of the harp :—"A.D. 1225. Aedh, the son of Donlevy O'Sochlann, Vicar of Cong, a master of vocal music and harp making, the inventor of a new method of tuning, a proficient in all arts, poetry, engraving, and writing, and other arts, died this year."

Apropos of harp-tuning, I may here repeat what has been incidentally mentioned in Chapter II., that this was effected by means of the ceɼ or harp fastener. Furthermore, ᵹleɼ is the Irish term for tuning; and we find in the Brehon Laws an allusion to the Cɼann ᵹléɼa, that is, tuning-tree or key. But, as has so frequently been insisted on, the theory of music and the rules of the minstrel's art were the outcome of many years of weary study. Blessed Edmund Campion, S.J., in his *Account of Ireland* written in 1571, tells us that he himself had seen the Irish students "chanting out their lessons piecemeal," which they were wont to "conn by rote."

" Sumer is icumen in "—the earliest known version of a double canon with a ground bass, in England—is merely a harmonised arrangement of a phrase taken from the old Irish tune : " Cá an Saṁɼaḋ aᵹ ceaċc," which may be Englished : "The Summer is Coming," sung time out of mind in ancient Erin to usher in the summer season. This Irish air, wedded by Moore to his lyric " Rich and Rare," was copied by John Fornsete, a Benedictine monk, of Reading, about the year 1230, and, "though animated in its measure," as Lady Morgan writes, " yet, still, like all the Irish melodies, breathes the very soul of melancholy." Its Irish origin was clearly proved by Dr. Young, Protestant

Bishop of Clonfert, at the close of the eighteenth
century, who ably refuted the English claim to it, as
advocated by Dr. Burney, in his *History of Music.**

In this connection, Ireland can justly claim the invention of what is now called "ground bass" or "pedal
point," as its origin must be sought in the old Irish
cronan, an allusion to which is to be found as far back
as A.D. 592, when it is described as "the most excellent
of music." St. Colman Mac Lenan, founder of the See of
Cloyne, gives us to understand that the ⰀⰭⱁⰱⱃⰵ (Ⰲⱁⱂⱆⱃ
Ⱈⱃⱁⱀⰰⰺⱀ) was the most favourite form of part singing
with the educated musicians of the sixth century.†
O'Curry calls it "a low murmuring accompaniment or
chorus, which, from its name Ⱈⱃⱁⱀⰰⱀ must have been
produced in the throat, like the purring of a cat"; and
he adds that the word "croning" [crooning] is an
abbreviated anglicised form of "cronaning"—not
humming, but purring—a corruption of which has resulted in the calling an old woman a "crone."

Not so long since, it was generally believed that the
inclusion of the *harp* in the arms of Ireland only dated
from the reign of Henry VIII., but the fact is that our
national instrument appears on coins issued by King
John and King Edward I.; and, in 1251, we read that
"the new coinage was stamped in Dublin with the
impression of the King's head in a triangular harp." A
harp was originally the peculiar device of the arms of
the Leinster province, and it was subsequently applied

* Bishop Young died on November 28th, 1800.
† There are seven Irish words to designate various forms of
Harmony—in particular *foacanim*, which is glossed by Zeuss as
succino or "singing under."

to the whole kingdom of Ireland, namely, in heraldic
language, " on a field *vert*, a harp *or*, stringed *argent*."

Under date of 1269, in the *Annals of Clonmacnoise*,
is recorded the death of Aedh O'Flynn, " a good musician. A similar entry occurs in the *Annals of Ulster*
but the surname is given as " O'Finn," and he is
described as a "master of minstrelsy." [ᴦᴀɪ oɪᴦ-
ᴦɪᴏɪᵹ.]

The European fame of the Irish harp was at this
epoch well sustained, as is best attested by the following quotation from Dante (1265-1321) :—

" This most ancient instrument was brought to us
from Ireland, where they are excellently made, and in
great numbers, the inhabitants of that island having
practised on it for many ages. Nay, they even place it
in the arms of the kingdom, and paint it on their public
buildings, and stamp it on their coins, giving as a reason
their being descended from the Royal Prophet David."*

Ralph Higden, a distinguished historiographer, at the
beginning of the fourteenth century, describes the music
of the Irish harp as "musica peritissima." John de
Fordun, a Scottish priest, who wrote in the same cen-
ury, expressly says that " Ireland was the fountain of
music in his time, whence it then began to flow into
Scotland and Wales."†

In 1329, the annalist, Clyn, has the following entry
concerning the massacre of Sir John Bermingham, Earl
of Louth, at Bragganstown, near Ardee, on June 10th
of that year :—

---

* *Dialogo di Vincenzo Galilei*, A.D. 1589 (not 1581 as stated by
Bunting).
† Walker's *History of the Irish Bards* (1786).

" Maelrooney Mac Cerbhaill [O'Carroll], chief musician of the kingdom, and his brother Gillakeigh—
a famous timpanist and harper, so pre-eminent that he
was a Phœnix in his art—were killed in that company,
and with him fell twenty timpanists who were his
scholars."

The *Annals of Ulster* particularly praise the musical
powers of Mac Cerbhaill, whom they describe as " the
blind Cerbhail, namely, Maelruanaigh, the most eminent
timpanist in Ireland and of Scotland, and of the whole
world." The cognomen *caoch* was given to him " because his eyes were not straight, but squinted " ; and,
Clyn adds, " if he was not the inventor of chord music,
yet, of all his predecessors and contemporaries, he was
the corrector, teacher, and director." The author of the
Annals of Clonmacnoise further informs us that " no
man in any age ever heard or shall hereafter hear a
better timpanist."

According to Hardiman, this harper, O'Carroll, composed the lovely song : " Eleanor Kirwan," but " every
effort," he adds, " to recover the music has proved fruit-
less, although it was well known in Galway in the last
[eighteenth] century." The air " is supposed to have
died out with an old musical amateur of the name of
French, who resided in Galway a few years ago ; and
thus perished, perhaps, the last known relic of the genius
of O'Carroll." *

It must, however, be borne in mind that the battle of
Bragganstown was in reality an Anglo-Irish feud ; and
an ancient chronicler relates that an old nurse distinctly
gave warning to the Earl of Louth and his attendants

* Hardiman's *Irish Minstrelsy*, vol. i., p. 361.

of their approaching doom, in a song commencing :
" All the joy of my heart is the hearing." I may add
that on the Patent Rolls of Edward III., a pardon,
dated May 31st, 1330, was granted to those Anglo-Irish
who took part in the conflict, and, amongst others, to
John the harper, of Ardee, Co. Louth.*

A charming legend is told in connection with the
founding of the Franciscan Friary at Irrelagh—better
known as Muckross Abbey, Killarney—in the year 1340.

MacCarthy Mor, *i.e.*, Donnell, son of Tadhg, had
vowed to build a monastery for Franciscans in thanks-
giving for his delivery from a great danger. He found
it difficult to select a suitable locality. While he hesi-
tated a vision appeared to him, warning him to erect the
convent nowhere but at *Carraig-an-chiuil* (the Rock of
Music). He knew of no such place, and dispatched a
number of his followers in various directions to make
inquiries. The search was unsuccessful; no one had
even heard of the name. They were returning in despair
when they heard the most enchanting music issuing
from a rock in OꞮꞮꞰꞙꞀꞆꞐꞨ [Irrelagh]. They hurried
home in all haste, and related their experience to Mac-
Carthy. He concluded that this was *Carraig-an-chiuil*
—the Rock of Music spoken of in the vision—and
commenced to build the monastery without delay."†

Under date of 1345, an Irish musician appears in the
dual capacity of bard and minstrel. In the celebrated
Leabhar na h-Uidhre, or Book of the Dun Cow (compiled
and transcribed, in the year 1100, by Maelmuire Mac
Kelleher), there is an entry, at page 37, from which we

---

* *Calendar of Patent Rolls*, 4 Edward III., p. 532.
† *History of the Franciscan Order in Ireland, sub.* " Irrelagh."

learn that Sigraidh O'Cuirnin, who had carefully perused
said volume, in the year 1345, begged a prayer for the
writer of the book.   This Sigraidh O'Cuirnin, hereditary
poet and ollav of the O'Rourkes, therein described as
"poet and musician," died on a pilgrimage to Clonmacnoise in 1347.*

In reference to the hospitality extended by the Irish
people of all classes to minstrels and bards, we read in
the *Annals of Clonmacnoise,* under date of the year
1351 :—

"William MacDonogh *maenach* O'Kelly invited all
the Irish poets, brehons, bards, harpers, etc., in Ireland
to his house, upon Christmas of this year, where every
one of them was well used during the Christmas holidays, and gave contentment to each of them at the time
of their departure, so as every one was well pleased, and
extolled William for his bounty."

Thierry thus writes :—"Every house preserved two
harps, always ready for travellers, and he who could
best celebrate the liberties of former times, the glory of
patriots, and the grandeur of their cause, was rewarded
with a more lavish hospitality."

For the year 1357, there is a record of the demise of
Donlevy O'Carroll, "an excellent musician," and "a
noble master of melody, the person that was best in his
own art in Ireland."   Three years later, according to the
Annals of Ulster, died Gilla-na-naem O'Conway, "ollam
of Thomond as Timpanist," whom other annalists
describe as "chief professor of music in Thomond."

In 1361, the obit is chronicled of Magrath O'Finn,
"chief professor of Siol Murray (Sligo) in music and

* *Facsimiles of National MSS. of Ireland* by Sir John T. Gilbert.

minstrelsy," followed, three years later by that of Bryan
O'Brien—also called Bran Ua Briain—an eminent timpanist—or performer on the ᴄιοmpᴀn.

A terrible blow was given to music in Ireland by the
passing of the iniquitous Statute of Kilkenny, ιn 1367,
which made it penal to receive or entertain Irish bards,
pipers, harpers, minstrels, rhymers, etc., the ostensible
reason being that "these and such like often came as
spies on the English." However, as Dr. Joyce writes,
"it was intended to apply only to the English, and was
framed entirely in their interests—its chief aim being to
withdraw them from all contact with the ' Irish enemies,'
and to separate the two races for evermore."*

From the *Annals of Clonmacnoise,* we learn that John
Mac Egan and Gilbert O'Barden, two most famous
harpers of Conmaicne (Ardagh), died in 1369 ; and
Andrew Mac Senaigh, " master of melody," died of the
plague, at Tuam, in 1371—whose name is given as
"Amhlaim Mac Senaigh, accomplished emperor of
melody," by the Ulster Annalists.

On the Patent Rolls of the year 1375 (49 Edw. III.),
we find a license granted to Donal O'Moghan, an Irish
minstrel [Ministrallus Hibernicus], "for that he not
alone was faithful to the King, but was also the cause
of inflicting many evils on the Irish enemies," permitting
him, contrary to the *Statute of Kilkenny,* to dwell within
the English Pale.† Hardiman adds: " This recreant
bard was one of the very few traitors of his Order, of
which Patriotism was the motto and ruling principle.
Like Alfred, the Irish bards went amongst the enemy to

* Joyce s *Concise History of Ireland* (1895), p. 108.
† Hardiman's *Irish Minstrelsy,* vol. i., p. xviii.

learn their situation, strength and intentions, which they never failed to report to their countrymen "

Under date of 1379, the Four Masters chronicle the obit of Gillacuddy O'Carroll, "the most delightful minstrel of the Irish," who is called by the Ulster Annalists, "William, son of Gillacuddy O'Carroll." Evidently the musical abilities of the O'Carroll family had not diminished since the days of Maelroony O Carroll— so lauded by the Irish chroniclers, as also by the Anglo-Irish annalist, Clyn, who died in 1349, as Guardian of the Franciscan Friary, Kilkenny.

One of the many legends that for long obtained currency was the ascription of the song, " Eıblín ᴀ Rúın." – *vulgo* "Aileen Aroon"—to Donogh *mór* O'Daly, of Finvarra, Cistercian Abbot of Boyle, who was called "the Ovid of Ireland,' and who died in the year 1244. Most writers concur in dating the music and words as from " the first half of the thirteenth century," whilst the more sceptical tell us that it was composed in " the latter portion of the sixteenth, or the first half of the seventeenth century." The sober truth is that this exquisite melody, so admired by Handel (as we learn on the unimpeachable testimony of the Venerable Charles O'Conor, of Belanagare), was written in the last quarter of the fourteenth century. It was composed by Carrol *mór* O'Daly, about the year 1390, in honour of Eibhlin Kavanagh, of Polmonty Castle, near New Ross, Co. Wexford; and all readers are familiar with the romantic story of how our Irish harper and composer successfully won the hand of Kavanagh's fair daughter.•

* Cormac Comyn (Cormac *dall*) was the first to furnish an account of the circumstances under which "Eıblín ᴀ Rúın" was

The minstrel O'Daly, who is described by the old annalists as "chief composer of Ireland, and Ollav of the country of Corcomroe," died early in 1405.

As a proof of the estimation in which Irish minstrels were held at this epoch, we learn from Froissart that, during the Christmas and Spring of 1394-5, at the sumptuous banquets given by King Richard II. to the Irish chieftains who visited him, these princes, contrary to English ideas, "had their minstrels and principal servants sitting at the same table, and eating from the same dish as they themselves."

In connection with the year 1399, the death is chronicled of Conla Mac Neal O'Neill, "a great benefactor of the professors of Irish poetry and music."[*] During the same year died Boetius Mac Egan of Breffni, "a learned man in laws and music," who is described in the *Annals of Ulster* as "ollav in jurisprudence."

It scarcely comes within the scope of this work to touch on literary Irish personages, yet I cannot well resist the temptation of citing a little-known item of information, namely, the appointment of an Irishman as Lecturer in Oxford University. This eminent divine— Matthew O'Howen (Owens), son of the A1ριόinneιό of Inishkeen on Lough Erne—lectured continuously at Oxford for fourteen years, and died on September 4th, 1382. His son, Matthew, was chaplain of Inishkeen, whose death occurred on October 11th, 1393, as is recorded in the *Annals of Ulster*.

composed. This he did in 1750; and it will be found in Walker and Hardiman. O'Conor's testimony, quoting Handel, may be found in his *Dissertations*, p. 58. From the concluding stanza the Irish motto: Ceυυ míle ράιιτε has been taken.

[*] *Annals of Clonmacnoise*, p. 322.

On February 8th, 1396, died Matthew O'Luinin, "Herenach of the Ards [near Enniskillen], namely, an expert, learned man, both in poetry and history and *melody* and literature and other arts "—(*Annals of Ulster*).

The advent of Sir John Stanley as Lord Lieutenant of Ireland, in December, 1399, is memorable for renewed hostility to Irish Bards and Minstrels, and as a consequence, his Viceroyalty was most unpopular. He left the country in May, 1401, and in the August following he was succeeded by Stephen Scrope, Deputy for the Duke of Clarence. This brings us to the fifteenth century, which demands a chapter all to itself.

CHAPTER IX.

Irish Music in the Fifteenth Century.

ALTHOUGH the first quarter of the fifte enth century was a most troubled period in Ireland, yet there were not wanting many learned men and musicians. In 1405, the *Annals of Ulster* chronicle the death of Gilladubh Mac Curtin, who is described as " Ollav (Doctor) of Thomond in Music," and who was also distinguished as an historian and writer. The same year is memorable for the demise of Carrol O'Daly (Cerbhall Ua Dalaigh), composer of " Eiblín ᴀ Rúin," whose obit is thus quaintly given by the annalist of Clonmacnoise :— " Keruell O'Daly, chief composer of Ireland, dane of the country of Corcomroe, died."

A great benefactor of the Irish minstrels—Tadhg O'Carroll, Prince of Ely O'Carroll—was gathered to his fathers in 1407. Conal Mac Geoghegan thus writes of him :—" This Teige was deservedly a man of great account and fame with the professors of poetry and music of Ireland and Scotland, for his liberality extended towards them, and every of them in general." According to the *Annals of Ulster*, Tᴀᴅᵹ Uᴀ Cᴇᴘʙᴀɪʟʟ was defeated and slain by the Lord Deputy Scrope, who himself died of a pestilence in May, 1408.

The lovely song " Deiᴘᴏᴘᴇ ᴅᴇᴀᵹ-ᵹnúiᴘᴇᴀċ "— Englished " The Blooming Deirdre "—was composed, in 1409, for the marriage of Thomas Fitz John, 6th Earl of Desmond, to Catherine, daughter of William Mac Cormac Mac Carthy, a romantic wedding which cost the bridegroom his inheritance. Certain it is that the unfortunate Earl, in whose honour the song was written, was compelled by his own family to surrender his title and possessions, and he died an exile at Rouen, on August 10th, 1420. Deirdre is used by the Earl's bard as representing the ancient Irish heroine of that name, who is the central figure of the "Fate of the Children of Usnach." Founded on the same story is Moore's lyric : "By the Feale's wave benighted."

As illustrating the satirical powers of the bardic family at this period, it is recorded by the Four Masters, in January of the year 1414, that the bard Nial O'Higgins satirised Sir John Stanley, Lord Lieutenant of Ireland, for having plundered his property, and so fierce and stinging was the satire that the English Deputy died from the effects of it. In a word, O'Higgins literally rhymed him to death : and we know from the chronicles of Henry of Marlborough that Sir John Stanley, who had landed at Clontarf, in October, 1413, died at Ardee, Co. Louth, in January, 1414. The same annalists chronicle a second "poetical miracle" performed by the same family of rhymers against a hostile tribe. By way of retaliation, Sir John Talbot, Lord Furnivall, despoiled many of the Irish rhymers, as is recorded in the *Annals of Ulster*.

Under date of 1429, the Four Masters give us the obit of a distinguished Ulster musician, as follows :— Matthew, the son of Thomas O'Kiernan, Ollav of Breffni, and universally learned in history and music, died in his own house."

In 1433, as appears from the *Annals of Ulster*, occurred the death of Aedh O'Corcrain, a remarkable harper; and, early in 1435, Seanchan Mac Curtin, "historian, poet, and musician," was gathered to his fathers. From the MS. Annals of Ireland, by Duald MacFirbis, we learn that the year 1433 was memorable in Irish musical history by reason of the "two general invitations" given by Dame Margaret O'Carroll, wife of Calbach Ua Concobair, Prince of Offaly, to bards, minstrels, and learned men. The first general invitation (reception) took place on March 25th, at Killeigh, King's County, when 2700 persons assembled—"besides gamesters and poor men "—and each person was given a generous gratuity before dinner. The second reception was given on August 15th, at Rathangan, which was equally well attended.[*]

At this epoch, the enactments of the Statute of Kilkenny were utterly ignored, and this is confirmed by the Patent Rolls of the 15th of Henry VI. (1435) From this State Paper, it is quite apparent that the provisions of the statute were practically inoperative. It is distinctly stated " that Mimi, [Comedians], Irish Clarsaghours [Harpers], Tympanours [Timpanists], Crowthores [performers on the cṗuιc], Kerraghers [Chess-players], Rymours [Rhymers], Skelaghis [Story-tellers], Bardes, and others, contrary to the Statute of Kilkenny, went amongst the English, and exercised their arts and minstrelsies, and afterwards proceeded to the Irish enemies, and led them upon the King's liege subjects."[†]

Henry VI., as Renehan writes, "finding such laws

* Miscell. Ir. Arch. Soc. i,, pp. 227-8.
† The Mimi mentioned in above Patent Roll were Irish Mummers, a survival of the Druith Righeadh, or Royal Comedians, in the Irish Court train since the days of the Ḟeιṙ of Tara.

ineffectual, and his lieges habitually paying *grandia bona et dona*, in exchange for Irish music, commissioned his Marshal in Ireland to imprison the harpers ; and, in order to stimulate his activity, authorised him to appropriate, to his own private use, their gold and silver, their horses, harnesses, and instruments of minstrelsy."*

From the *Annals of Ulster*, under date of 1448, we learn of the death, at Kilconly, Co. Galway, of a munificent patron of minstrels, namely Tadhg O'Higgins, who is described as "preceptor in poetry and erudition of schools in Ireland and Scotland, and general entertainer of the litterati and pilgrims of Ireland."†

In striking contrast to the world-renowned fame of Irish musicians, England had no music-school of the least importance, even in the first decade of the fifteenth century. We have it on the authority of the late Rev. Sir Frederick Gore Ouseley, Bart., Mus. Doc., Professor of Music in Oxford University, that, of the English compositions which have survived, ranging from 1300 to 1510, "none seem to be of any great merit," and all betray "much crudeness and a sad lack of regular melody." Even Davey, the avowed eulogist of English music is forced to admit that "its condition in the fourteenth century was more barren than the thirteenth," and he adds: "Not a piece of music endurable by modern ears existed in England before 1400." In fact, the so-called "English School of Music" only dates

---

* Renehan s *History of Music*, p. 164.

† Another bard named O'Higgins, *i.e.* Bryan mac Fergal ᚱuᚪiᚑ Ua Uiccinn, named by the Four Masters as "Superintendent of the Schools of Ireland, and preceptor in poetry," died on Holy Thursday of the year 1477.

from 1425, with John Dunstable as its founder, who died December 24th, 1453.

The wars of the Roses, which commenced in 1455, added materially to the existing strife in Ireland.   We find the Geraldines of Kildare and Desmond, taking sides with the Yorkists, whilst the Ormondists threw in their lot with the Lancastrians, and of course, the Anglo-Irish and Celts participated in the general *mêlée.* Three-fourths of Ireland still belonged to the natives, and the English were obliged to pay heavy tribute to the Irish chiefs as a guarantee for peace.   Thus, the barony of Lecale disbursed £20 a-year to O'Neill of Clanaboy; the county of Uriel £40 to the O'Neill; the county Wexford, £20 to Mac Murrough; the county Limerick £40 to O'Brien; the county Cork £40 to Mac Carthy of Muskerry; the counties of Kilkenny and Tipperary £40 to O'Carroll; the county Kildare £20 to O'Conor, etc., etc.

About the year 1455 flourished an Irish Cistercian monk, Brother Aengus, of Holy Cross Abbey, Co. Tipperary, who was a harper, organist, organ-builder, and composer.   He joined the community of Duiske (Graignamanagh, Co. Kilkenny), in 1460, and was welcomed, notwithstanding the Statute of Kilkenny. The *Annals of Duiske* describe him in the most eulogistic terms.   He especially won the favour of the then English Abbot of Duiske, by repairing the abbey-organ which had been, for many years, discarded owing to its bellows having proved a prey to damp and rats.   The Anglo-Irish annalist adds :—" In truth, Brother Aengus excels in music any citharist (harper) ever heard in these parts; for not alone is he a master of psalmody and *faux bourdon*, as is evidenced by his setting of ' Benedicam Dominum,' but he is even a cunning performer on the *cruit*." In 1461, died Felimy O'Neill, described as " a man of hospitality and prowess, and head of the bardic bands and pilgrims of Ireland, and one that was a most extensive purchaser of poetic and erudite compositions, and was the greatest *rhymer* that was in Ireland in his time."—(*Annals of Ulster*.)

The Statute of Kilkenny, forbidding the English or Anglo-Irish of the Pale to receive or entertain Irish minstrels, was put in force by a new act, passed in 1481. Six different classes of bards are enumerated, and the strictest orders were given not on any account to permit harpers as guests.

In 1482 we meet with an interesting side-light of history in connection with the city of Waterford, showing clearly how the Urbs Intacta had resolved to maintain its " loyal " reputation, and uphold the penal enactments of the Statute of Kilkenny even against a Bishop who was a " mere Irishman." Nicholas O'Hennessy, Cistercian Abbot of Fermoy, had been " provided " by Pope Sixtus IV., on May 20th, 1480, to the united Sees of Lismore and Waterford, and was consecrated Bishop in 1481. This appointment was freely acquiesced in by the Chapter, clergy, and people of Lismore, yet the Waterford clergy and laity objected to the new Bishop on the plea that " he was Irish spoken, and did not understand the English language." On December 30th, 1482, the Pope bade the Archbishop of Cashel " to excommunicate the Waterford Chapter and clergy in case they should still be contumacious, and, if necessary, to invoke the aid of the secular arm." But,

all in vain ; the worthy Bishop deemed it prudent to
retire to his abbey, and John, Rector of Baudrip, diocese
of Bath and Wells, was appointed his successor—being
duly consecrated on May 4th, 1483.*

Perhaps it is as well to state that (so general was the
use of the Irish language in all parts of Ireland at
the close of the fifteenth century, even in County
Dublin) Archbishop Fitzsimon, by an Act of Parliament
passed in 1484—and renewed in 1493—was permitted
"to collate *Irish* clerics to benefices in his diocese, inasmuch as the English clerks were not expert in the Irish
language, and such of them as were, disdained to
inhabit amongst the Irish people."

The Four Masters, under date of 1488, chronicle the
death of Henry Shelly, whom they eulogise as "the
best singer of the Irish of *Leath Cuinn* [the North of
Ireland]." The *Annals of Ulster* give his obit as occurring in that year, but describe him as "Henry Ua
Selbaigh [O'Selby], the best chanter of the Irishry of
the Half of Conn."

In 1489 is recorded the obituary of Arthur O Hussey,
described by the Four Masters as "a poet and a good
scholar, and a youth honoured amongst the English and
the Irish, who was distinguished for musical powers,
both vocal and instrumental.", This entry is thus given
by the Ulster annalist :—" Athairne O'Hosey, son of
John, poet, preceptor, instrumentalist, and vocalist,
died." †

During the second half of the fifteenth century Irish

---

* Theiner's *Vetera Monumenta*.
† His son Cithruadh, described as " an eminent bard and a good
teacher," died in 1518.

minstrels were frequent visitors to Scotland ; and, in Dauney's *Scottish Melodies* there are given several items regarding the visits of our Hibernian musicians to the Scottish Court, *e.g.* :—

> "April 19th, 1490. To Martin, the clairseach player, and the other Irish harper, at ye King's command, 18 shillings.
> "May, 1490. To an Irish harper, at ye King's command, 18 shillings."

For the year 1490 there is an entry in the *Annals of Ulster* recording the sad fact that Dermot O'Carbry, *harper*, slew Aengus, "the son of MacDonnell of Scotland." Apparently O'Carbry must have been on a visit to Scotland, because the annalists are careful to inform us that his victim was called "the Lord of Aag," *i.e.*, Angus Macdonald, son of Donald, son of Ranald of Clanranald. Dr. MacCarthy identifies "Aag" as "Hay," but the annalist says "Aacc," which most probably is Eigg, an island of the Inner Hebrides, of which the MacDonalds were then Lords. MacDonald, as we read, "was slain in treachery at Inverness, by an Irish harper, Diarmait Ua Cairpri." The family of Ua Cairpri, or Cairbre, supplied many musicians, but none of their compositions have come down to our time.*

At the close of November, 1494, Sir Edward Poynings, Lord Deputy of Ireland, assembled a Parliament at Drogheda, in which was passed the infamous enactment known as "Poynings' Law." Irish war-cries (such as Laṁ ᴅeᴀᴘ5 ᴀbu) were forbidden, as also the exaction

---

* In 1495, "a month before Lammas," our Irish annalists chronicle the visit of Hugh Roe O'Donnell to James IV., King of Scotland, who received the Irish prince with much distinction. O'Donnell returned to Donegal on Friday, August 7th, of same year.

known as "coyne and livery;" and the Statute of Kilkenny was confirmed, with the exception of the unwork-
able ukase against the Irish language. But, as often
happened before, these enactments were so much
stage-thunder, and the great Hiberno-English Lords of
the Pale openly set them at naught, retaining Irish
brehons, bards, harpers, pipers, etc., whom they patronised in the most lavish style.

According to the *Annals of Uster*, in the year 1496 is
placed the obit of " Florence O'Corcoran, player on the
harp and other stringed instruments, and a distinguished
vocalist;" and, in 1497, there is mention of the death
of William MacGilroy, "a master of stringed instruments " [ᚱᚨᚔ ᚠᚔᚹ ᚈᚓᚋ].

The peaceful condition of Leinster and Munster from
1498 to 1501 contributed not a little to the cultivation
of Irish Music, but it was merely the calm before the
storm, and already the days of mediævalism were
nearly over, with the "new learning" making its way,
and the traditional folk songs gradually giving place
to Anglo-Irish music.

CHAPTER X.

ANGLO-IRISH MUSIC FROM 1200 TO 1400.

Up to the present we have been treating of Irish musical history in its true acceptation, that is Celtic-Irish music, but from the year 1200 Anglo-Irish music has to be reckoned with, as a distinct factor in the social life of Erin. Between the years 1180 and 1280 there was a fusion between the invaders and the native Irish, and some years subsequently, as Dr. Joyce writes, "the English all over the country were fast becoming absorbed with the native population."   In the first decade of the thirteenth century many of the colonists had adopted the language, dress, and habits of their adopted country, and, in 1206 (among the deeds of Christ Church, Dublin), there is mention of "Geoffrey the Piper."

· One of the greatest musical theorists of the thirteenth century was John Garland, of County Louth, known variously as De Garlande and Gerlandus. Born about the year 1190, he was sent to Oxford to be educated, as was generally the case with the Anglo-Irish nobles,* and, in 1212 or 1213, he went to finish his studies at Paris. In 1218 we find him taking part in the crusade against the Albigenses at Toulouse, where he wrote his famous treatise on music, *De Musica Mensurabili*

---

* In 1255, owing to "the noisy Hibernian element" in Oxford, there was much disturbance, and among the students were John Barry, William Power, and 28 other Anglo-Irish. The Irish students were very numerous in 1267, and occasioned much trouble.

Positio, and then returned to Paris. So great was his fame as a grammarian and poet, that he was selected to assist at the foundation of the University of Toulouse in 1229, but he had to leave, in 1232, owing to friction with the Dominicans. We again find him in Paris, in 1234, where he was still living, in 1264, according to Roger Bacon. The street in which he lived and taught was called the " Clos de Garlande," afterwards known as " Rue Gallande."

John Garland gives ample evidence of the musical principles he had imbibed in Ireland by his strong insistence on the rhythmical test in Organum. He divides Organum into two kinds, namely, *Rectum* and *non rectum,* and he tells us that the Long and the Breve are to be strictly taken in the first regular mode—the plain chant being notated in symbols of equal length. To him is due the invention of the *copula* and the figures *sine proprietate.* But he also shone as an original composer, and gives some admirable lessons in double counterpoint.

Not alone did Garland excel all his fellows as a musician, but he was a distinguished literary man, as appears from his *De Triumphis Ecclesiae* which he finished at Paris, in 1252, and of which the British Museum possesses a MS. copy, which has been printed by Mr. Thomas Wright.

Among the deeds of Christ Church, Dublin, there is mention, under date of 1260, of " William the piper ; " * and, in 1287, there is a record of a grant of land to " Roger the harper." In addition to players on the pipe

---

* Geoffrey Chaucer (1328-1400) says of his Miller:—

     " A baggé-pipe coude he blowe and soune."

and harp, there is ample evidence to prove that the Anglo-Irish of this period were also conversant with the flute and the recorder.

Lovers of Shakespeare do not need to be told of the skilful manner in which the bard of Avon introduces the "recorder" in Hamlet, but it is not generally known that the earliest mention of the instrument of that name is in the *Manipulus Florum*, begun by John Walsh, in 1280, and finished by Thomas Walsh, of Palmerstown, Co. Kildare, in July, 1306. Both these learned men were Anglo-Irish Franciscan Friars, and their conjoint book was printed at Venice in 1492. Dr. John Walsh was regent of Oxford in 1258, and subsequently taught in Paris, where he died in 1284. His fellow-countryman, Dr. Thomas Walsh, mostly lived at Naples, where he ended his days, and is better known as Thomas *Hibernicus*.

In the Anglo-Norman ballad entitled "Rithmus facture ville de Rosse," or "The Entrenchment of New Ross"—describing the building of the walls of Ross, Co. Wexford, in 1265,—written by Brother Michael FitzBernard, a Friar of Kildare, allusion is made to tabors and flutes, also to carols.

It is probable that the lovely air "An Cúilḟionn," anglicised as "The Coolin," dates from the year 1296 or 1297, inasmuch as it must have been composed not long after the passing of the Statute, 24th of Edward I., in 1295, which forbade "the degenerate English in Ireland" to imitate the native Irish "by allowing their hair grow in coolins"—"nec amplius praesumant avertere in *Colanum*." In the Irish song the bard makes the Irish maiden despise the Anglo-Irish who conformed

to the statute by cutting off their coolins, and prefer
the chieftain-lover who was proud of his Irish ancestral
custom. This inedited Statute, which was apparently
unknown to Moore, Moffat, and Stanford, is quoted by
Ledwich in his *Antiquities* (p. 347), and is also to be
found in the Harris manuscripts.

Some Irish and Anglo-Irish minstrels accompanied
King Edward I. in his expedition to Scotland in 1301.
From the *Annals of Ulster* we learn that John Fitz-
Thomas MacFeoris (Bermingham), and the principal
barons of Ireland were in Scotland " from a fortnight
before Lammas [August 1st] to November day of that
year," and again, in 1303. Allusion has previously been
made to the bagpipers who went to Calais in the train
of King Edward I.*

As an instance of the general use of the Irish language in speech and song by the Anglo-Normans in
Ireland at the opening of the fourteenth century, there is
an interesting item chronicled by Friar Clyn, under date
of 1326 : " A.D. 1326. The O'Carrolls killed Sir Matthew Mylborne, a trusty and prudent Knight, *English by
nation, but Gaelic by use of speech, speaking only
Gaelic.*"

Mensural music was now beginning to supersede the
old metrical measure peculiar to plain chant. The Longa
or Long Note ■ was divided into three equal or two
unequal parts, or breves, *e.g.* ■, which in turn was sub-
divided into three notes called semi-breves, ◆ ; and,
from this system was evolved the structure known to
mediæval musicians as " Cantus Mensurabilis." In the
theoretical treatises of this period, we get specimens of

* See Chapter iii.

Organum purum, Conductus, and *organum communiter sumptum;* and there are yet preserved many illustrations of Cantilena, Rondel, Ochetus, or Hoquet, and Motet, all of which go to prove that the line of cleavage with old traditions had definitely begun—soon to develop into what is now known as Modern Music.*

The adaptation of secular songs to sacred words was freely practised in the thirteenth and fourteenth centuries. William of Malmesbury tells us of Thomas, Archbishop of York (1070), that "whenever he heard any new secular song or ballad sung by the minstrels, he immediately composed sacred adaptations of the words to be sung to the same tune." Very remarkable it is that the existence of the very earliest known English folk-songs is due to a record among the archives of the Kilkenny Corporation. In the *Red Book of Ossory,* there are fifteen pages written in double columns containing sixty Latin verses, written by Richard Ledrede, Bishop of Ossory, who ruled from 1317 to 1360—best known for his connection with the heresy and witchcraft trials between the years 1324 and 1331. We may date the Bishop's verses as of about the year 1324.

These Latin verses, or *Cantilenae,* were written by Bishop Ledrede "for the Vicars Choral of Kilkenny Cathedral, his priests, and clerics, to be sung on great festivals and other occasions," as is stated in a memorandum in said book, "that their throats and mouths, sanctified to God, might not be polluted with theatrical, indecent, and secular songs." The sixty pieces are in honour of Our Lord, the Holy Ghost. and the Blessed

* See *Oxford History of Music,* Vol. I. (1901).

Virgin Mary, and the first of them is entitled : *Cantilena de Nativitate Domini*, a sort of Christmas Carol, followed by three others " de eodem festo."

To the antiquarian musician the really interesting feature of the Bishop of Ossory's verses is that six of them are set or adapted to English tunes, the names being given as follows :—

1. Alas ! how should I sing, yloren is my playing
   How should I with that old⎫
                   man   ⎬ Sweetest of all thing
   To leven and let my leman⎭
2. Have mercy on me, frere, barefoot that I go.
3. So, do, nightingale, sing full merry
      Shall I never for thine love longer Kary.
4. Have good dey, my lemen dear
5. Gaveth me no garland of green
      But it ben of wythones [withies] yrought.
6. Hey how the chevaldoures woke all night.

Two of the *Cantilenae* are set to French tunes, and may be of somewhat earlier date than the English songs. It may be added that Chappell's account of the contents of the *Red Book of Ossory*, so far as it relates to the adaptations of Bishop Ledrede, is both inaccurate and misleading. The interested reader will find an accurate description given by Gilbert in the Tenth Report of the Historical Manuscripts Commission where some of the Latin lyrics are given in their entirety.*

Another most valuable contribution to Anglo-Irish literature is the morality-play, called " The Pride of Life "—written in 1345. This play is regarded by the

* Appendix Part V.

late Professor Morley as one of the earliest known specimens of its class in the English language. It was found
among the deeds of Christ Church, Dublin, and was
written on the back of an account-roll. In this old
morality-play we have the familiar mumming characters
of King, Queen, Nuncio, Bishop, First Soldier and
Second Soldier. There are 120 quatrains, mostly in
dialogue form, one of which will suffice as an
example :—

> "Th^u art lord of lim and life
> and King w^t outen ende,
> stif and strong and sterne in strife
> in loude qwher th^u wende."

In 1360, King Edward III. issued an ordinance to
the Sheriff of Kilkenny forbidding any Englishman
dwelling in said liberty to speak *Irish*, and also ordering that "*every Englishman must learn English and must
not have his children at nurse amongst the Irish.*" Almost
needless to add that this enactment was openly violated
by the denizens of the Pale ; and the violaters, who were
termed "degenerate English" by the loyal colonists,
were regarded on a par with the "wilde Irish." In fact
many of the great nobles were said to have become
Hiberniores Hibernicis ipsis, and, in 1388, a royal license
was granted to Gerald, Earl of Desmond, "to allow his
son to be brought up as an Irishman," under the tute-
lage of Conor O'Brien, of Thomond, "for the better
preserving the peace for the future."

Sir James Ware has preserved for us the "first staffe
only" of a ballad which was composed about the year
1370, by some Anglo-Irish citizen of Waterford, to warn

the townsmen of the old city by the Suir against the
machinations of the Powers, of County Waterford, who
had become more aggressive than the natives by reason
of their many raids on the city, The original ballad
which, like its counterpart in our own time, must have
had a dozen or more verses, has long since perished
(having been torn out of the antique parchment volume
some time after Sir James Ware made an extract from
it), but we are assured that it was a regular household-
song in Munster at the close of the fourteenth century.
At page 94, of Sir James Ware's manuscript,* we
read :—

"There is in this book (*the Book of Ross or Waterford*)
a longe Discourse in meter, putting the youth of Waterford in mind of harm taken by the Powers, and wishing
them to beware for ye time to come. I have written
out ye first staffe only :—

> ' Young men of Waterford lernith now to plai
> For yur mereis plowis ilad beth a way †
> Scure yur hafelis yᵗ lang habith i lei ‡
> And fentl you of the Powers that walketh by the
>   way

> ' For rede.
> ' For if hi taketh you on and on
> From him scapeth ther never one
> I swer bi Christ and St. John
> That off goth yur hede
>   ' Now hi walkith etc.,' "

Sir James Ware's transcript was made in February,

---

* Lansdowne MS. No. 418.
† For your mares and plows are both led away
‡ Secure your oats that lieth overlong in the fields.

1608, and was acquired by Bishop More, of Norwich, who lent it to Bishop Tanner, and it subsequently passed into the library of the Earl of Oxford. As an instance of the manner in which the editing of the Lansdowne Catalogue was done by Douce, it is rather amusing to find him giving the following explanation regarding the line "in mind of harme taken by the Povers"—"The Povers," says this eminent antiquary, "seem to mean the paupers or rabble"!

Of course, it is the Powers, or le Poers, of County Waterford, who are here alluded to, and who were by far the most powerful clan in that county from the thirteenth to the sixteenth century. Crofton Croker adds:—"Mr. Lemon, of the State Paper Office, has queried, whether the common expression of 'By the powers' does not refer to the warlike strength of the Poer family, or faction, becoming proverbial?"

Anyhow, although Ware attached no importance to this ballad in his day, yet we, of the twentieth century, would gladly have wished that he had not stopped at transcribing "one staffe onely." Had he taken down the traditional folk-tune it would have been more interesting still. We possess no single example of thirteenth, or fourteenth, century Anglo-Irish secular music; and all that has escaped the vandalism of the so-called Reformation is of a sacred character, of which I shall treat in a subsequent chapter.

The history of English Music during the first half of the fourteenth century is almost a blank, and the only two names that adorn the latter half of that century are Anglo-Irish—namely John D'Exeter and Lionel Power. Of the former very little is known save that he was of the D'Exeter family, Lords of Athleathan or Ballylahan, now known as Strade, barony of Gallen, Co. Mayo, and he wrote some sacred music now preserved in the Old Hall MS. a most valuable repertory of fourteenth and fifteenth-century English composers.* Concerning the latter, we are, fortunately, in a better position. To Lionel Power, a worthy Anglo-Irishman, of Co. Waterford, is due the first English treatise on Music, about the year 1390, and his nationality is placed beyond question by another Anglo Irish contemporary who styles him *noster Lionel*.

Davey, the historian of English Music, tells us that Power appears in Coussemaker's great work as *Iconal*. His treatise on Music is included in a volume which Tallis found in Waltham Abbey, in 1537, and which is now in the British Museum, among the Lansdowne MSS. No. 763. Not only is it written in English, but it is illustrated by musical examples.

It is regrettable that we have no details regarding the early life of Lionel Power, but it is almost certain that, like many of the younger sons of the wealthy Anglo-Irish in Ireland, he went over to Oxford to study, and became a cleric.† His relative, Milo Power, was Bishop of Leighlin from 1321 to 1347, and another, Sir

---

* The Old Hall MS (so called because it belongs to the famous English Roman Catholic College of St. Edmund's, Old Hall, Ware) is a transcript made in the latter part of the fifteenth century, apparently intended for a church choir A very full description of the contents of this manuscript was given by Mr. W. Barclay Squire, of the British Museum in *Sammelbande Internationalen Musikgesellschaft*, an excellent digest of which was published by Mr. Robin Grey, in the *Edmundian* for July, 1901.

† In the fourteenth century students from Ireland were very numerous at Oxford University. However, we read that, in 1423, Irish students were expelled from England.

Maurice Power, was Knight of St. John of Jerusalem in 1415. We can unhesitatingly assign the period of his musical works as about 1380 to 1395, although Davey supposes him to have outlived Dunstable, which could only hold good unless we assume Power to have lived to the age of 120, which is improbable.

The works of Power which have come down to our own time prove conclusively that he had assimilated all that had been written by Guido of Arrezzo, Odington, Tunstede, Franco, Garland, Jerome of Moravia, and other theorists, and had materially advanced the development of harmony and counterpoint. " He certainly," as Davey admits, " establishes the use of sixths and thirds, and the distinct prohibition of consecutive unisons, fifths and octaves." Moreover, he was the first to indicate chords by figures, in other words, he was the inventor of figured bass.*

Of Power's compositions which have survived, Morley, in 1597, knew several which cannot now be traced. However, in the choir books formerly belonging to Trent Cathedral, but now at Vienna, out of forty works, mostly by English composers, eleven are by Power, eight of which were transcribed about the year 1430.

Other compositions by our distinguished countryman are in the Liceo Communale, Bologna, whilst, at Modena, eight motets of his are still to be seen, one of which is for four voices.

Between the years 1375 and 1400 improved organs were gradually being introduced into the larger churches in Ireland. In the absence of any local records, it is of

* Davey's *History of English Music*, p. 58.

interest to quote the earliest bill in existence for the erection of an organ in Ely Cathedral, in 1396 :—

Twenty stones of lead, ...	... 16s. 9d.
Four white horse-hides for four pairs of bellows,	... 7s. 8d.
Ashen hoops for the bellows,	... 4d.
16 pairs of hinges, ...	... 1s. 10d.
13 springs, ...	... 3d.
1 lb of glue, ...	... 1d.
1 lb. of tin, ...	... 3d.
6 calf-skins, ...	... 2s. 6d.
12 sheep-skins, ...	... 2s. 4d.
2 lbs. of quicksilver, ...	... 2s. 0d.
Wire, nails, cloth, hooks, staples, etc.,	12d.
The Carpenter, 8 days making the bellows, ...	... 2s. 8d.
Organ builder and his board,	... 40s. 0d.

£4 8s. 5d. [sic].

This was a "pair of organs" which had twelve notes corresponding to the twelve sounds of the plain chant and was furnished with chromatic notes—sharps and flats—in a separate row from the natural keys. The actual amount of the bill as furnished tots up to £3 17s. 8d., but we must presume that there are some items omitted. At a rough calculation, £4 8s. 5d. may be estimated as equal to £100 of to-day. At this period the organ keys were so large that the performer was termed a "pulsator," or smiter, and the keys were struck with the clenched fist. As a matter of fact, the keys of the organ built at Halberstadt, in 1361, were from two to four inches in width, with a space of two inches between some of them.

CHAPTER XI.

ANGLO-IRISH MUSIC DURING THE FIFTEENTH CENTURY.

DAVEY is forced to admit that "not a piece of music endurable by modern ears existed in England before 1400." But all this is by the way of glorifying the work of John Dunstable, whom the historian of English music claims as the inventor of polyphony and counterpoint. Professor Niecks, of Edinburgh University, very properly denies this statement; and he instances dozens of examples of two and three-part counterpoint all anterior to the birth of Dunstable, a few of which go back to the year 1300.[*] Mr. Barclay Squire, of the British Museum, shows clearly that the absurd claim for Dunstable's invention of counterpoint is owing to a misreading of Tinctoris (1455-1511).

Certain it is that the so-called "improvements," attributed to Dunstable, e.g., "the independence of his voice parts, and the use of suspensions, passing-notes, and short imitations "—were known to our Anglo-Irish composer, Lionel Power. Davey rather naively adds that " it is not easy to point out exactly in what the improvements of Dunstable consisted;" and that "the lack of older music makes it unclear whether these were known previously."

After this damning admission on the part of Mr. Davey, it is scarcely worth while to examine too closely

[*] *The Teaching of Musical History*, 1900.

the assertion that "we may take it as certain that Dunstable walked in Rouen Cathedral before Henry V., in January, 1419-20." But when we are seriously told that the great Guillaume Dufay (1370-1474) graduated at Paris, "where he learned the *English* art of composition," it is time to protest. "Paris," writes Davey, "was under English rule from 1420 to 1436, . . . and, thus Dufay, without visiting England, could learn *how immeasurably superior English music then was to all other; indeed, to any music which had ever existed.*"

No better refutation of this amazing statement need be quoted than the words of Professor Ransome, who tells us in his *Short History of England* that "*from 1424 to 1429 England had practically lost France;* and, in 1440, Paris was completely abandoned—the English with difficulty maintaining themselves in Normandy." Moreover, it is doubtful if ever Dunstable was in France; and we know that Dufay went to Rome in 1427, where he remained till 1437. Strangely enough, Davey ignores the ancestry of Dufay, who was a Walloon, and the Walloons were Celts.* It is only pertinent to add that Dunstable died on December 24th, 1453, whilst Dufay's death, at Cambrai, is chronicled on November 18th, 1474.

The Irish harp and the timpan were popular at this period with the inhabitants of the Pale, and, in 1450, there is an allusion to the Clavichord or Clavicembalo, a primitive keyboard stringed-instrument. Nor was the bagpipe, or Cornemuse, neglected. In the " Buke

* See paper on "Music and Musicians of the Walloon Provinces of Belgium," by Mr. W. W. Cobbett, read before the Musical Association, on January 9th, 1901.

of the Howlate," a Scotch MS., written *cir*. 1455, there is mention of "the trump, the tabour, the recordour, the tympane, and the lilt-pype."

In regard to the organ, it is of interest to mention that one of the earliest organ builders in England of whom there is authentic information, was Brother John Rouse, a Dominican Friar, who had learned the art in Kilkenny, in 1455. As yet, organs were not very elaborate in construction, and we read that the "noble instrument" which was presented to St. Alban's Abbey, in 1448, by Abbot Wheathamstead, only cost £18. The same year is memorable as the date of the earliest example of an organ score, namely, a manuscript autograph scored for pedals, on a staff of eight lines, with the three clefs of F, C, and G, by Adam Ileborg, Rector of the University of Stendall.

Under the date of 1460, in the MS. Annals of Duiske (Graiguenamanagh, Co. Kilkenny), we read that Brother Aengus, a Cistercian monk, of Holy Cross Abbey, Co. Tipperary, came to Duiske and repaired the "old organ" there, "which, not having been used of late years, was sadly affected by damp, and the leather of the bellows was gnawed by rats."

In the will of Michael Tregury, Archbishop of Dublin, dated December 10th, 1471, that estimable prelate bequeathed "a payre of organs" to St. Patrick's Cathedral, to be used in St. Mary's Chapel.* About this time the keys of the organ were reduced in size from two inches to 1¾ inches, and new contrivances were devised to facilitate alike the labours of the "pulsator organorum"

* MS., T.C.D., B2. See also "Register of Dublin Wills," 1457-1483.

and the blowers. Each key had its name-letter inscribed on it, namely, F, G, A, etc.

John Lawless was a most celebrated Irish organ
builder during the latter half of the fifteenth century.
Unfortunately, none of his specifications have survived,
but there is evidence that he erected twenty organs in
various parts of Ireland for cathedral and monastic
churches. He was held in such high esteem that the
Kilkenny Corporation, at the suggestion of the Earl of
Ormonde, granted him many privileges on condition of
making a permanent residence in the cathedral city of
St. Canice. Fortunately, among the deeds of the Corporation, there is still preserved a document, dated
December, 1476, "on the Monday after the Feast of the
Nativity," agreeing to the terms of the ground rent,
etc., from John Lawless, "organ maker," with the
proviso that he was " to practise his art within the said
town of Kilkenny."

In an interesting MS. account of the Dominican
Abbey, Athenry, Co. Galway, there is an entry, under
date of 1479, which proves that the Friars Preachers, or
Black Friars, availed of the king of instruments in their
musical services. We read that Thomas Bermingham,
Baron of Athenry, and his wife, Annabella, bestowed
" three silver marks towards the building of the abbey-
church organ."* The "loyal" tendencies of this munificent benefactor to Athenry Abbey may be gauged from
the fact that he repaired, at his own expense, " the
rooms of the English bachelors of theology "

Milo Roche, Bishop of Leighlin (1470-1490), was an
accomplished musician, and "a skilled performer on all

* Sloane MSS. (Brit. Mus.), 4784, p. 43, No. 4.

manner of instruments." The annalist Dowling says :—
" Inter bardos numeratur pro omnibus instrumentis";
whilst Ware adds that " he was more addicted to the
study of music and poetry than was fit."

In reference to Davey's statement that " probably
Dunstable taught Okeghem," it is only necessary to
say that the Latin original of Tinctoris from which he
professes to quote can bear no such interpretation.
The text of Tinctoris merely gives the reader to understand that the then modern school of music *followed the
example of Dunstable, Dufay, Obrechts*, etc. However,
it is satisfactory to read the following candid admission
by the historian of English music :—" Okeghem's
science brought forth the genius of Josquin des Pres,
who, as early as 1480, had produced that *Stabat Mater*
which to this day commands admiration, *while the
English were still doing what had been done before.*" Of
course this is equally true of Anglo-Irish music.

In the "Squyr of Lowe Degre,' written *cir.* 1480,
there is mention of the various instruments then popular
in England, including "harp, getron, sautry, rote,
ribible, clokarde, pypes, organs, bumbarde, sytolphe,
fydle, recorder, doucemere, trompette, and claryon."*

With the invention of music printing, in 1473, the
knowledge of the "divine art" made considerable head-
way all over the continent. It is not a little remarkable

* King Henry V. of England was a good musician, being distinguished as a harper, composer, and organist. He brought a military
band with him to France in 1415, consisting of " ten clarions and
other instruments." He married the Princess Katherine of Valois,
at Troyes, on June 3rd (Trinity Sunday), 1420, and, notwithstanding
the dreadful strife, spent not a little of his spare time cultivating
music. In October, 1420, he sent to England for a harp for Queen
Katherine; and there is an entry in the Exchequer Rolls of
£8 13s. 4d., being the amount paid to John Bore, harp-maker, London, for two new harps.

that the very first book containing plain chant in Roman notation, printed from movable types, was issued from the press of Octavianus Scotus, of Venice, in 1481, under the supervision of an Irishman, Maurice O'Fihily, a Franciscan Friar, who was subsequently Archbishop of Tuam. It was not till 1495 that Wynkyn de Worde printed the first book in England containing musical notes.

After the Lambert Simnel comedy in 1487, Sir Richard Edgecombe was sent to Ireland as Royal Commissioner to administer new oaths of allegiance, and we read that, on Monday, July 21st, 1488, he was present at St. Thomas's Abbey, in Dublin. The old record of his "progress" runs as follows :—"At the termination of High Mass in one of the oratories, the Earl of Kildare and the other magnates went into the great church ; and, in the choir thereof, the Archbishop of Dublin began the *Te Deum*, and the choir *with the organs* sung it up solemnly."*

I have dwelt at rather unusual length on the use of organs in Ireland in the fifteenth century, inasmuch as most writers, copying Walker, have asserted that organs were only introduced into this country after the period of the Reformation. A similar fiction has long obtained to the effect that Mumming and Christmas Carols only go back to the days of Elizabeth, and hence a brief refutation of such a statement is within the scope of the present chapter.

As to Mumming, we have ample documentary evidence that Mystery or Morality plays were performed

* In 1486 William Wotton, "orkyn maker," built a "payre of organs" for Magdalen College, Oxford, for £28.

in Dublin and Kilkenny in the fourteenth century, from which sprang the Mummers. Dodsley says that "the Mummers, as bad as they were, seem to be the true original comedians of England." It is quite apparent that the Buffoon who invariably accompanied the Mummers was an evolution of the Vice of the old Morality plays, subsequently represented by Punch, in the now fast disappearing Punch and Judy shows. *

Christmas Carols were popular among the Anglo-Irish in the fourteenth century, and continued in unabated favour till the reign of Elizabeth. They were mostly adaptations of secular songs, as we have seen in the case of Bishop Ledrede's Cantilenae. The word "Carol" is of the same family as "Choir"—meaning Song or Dance, or both—and is derived from the mediæval form *Corduld*, which, in turn, is derived from the Celtic. In the Coventry Mysteries there is introduced a Christmas Carol. A very natural outcome of the various hymns sung in the churches during the Christmas season was the transference of such airs to the home circle.

Naturally, the Wars of the Roses did much to retard the development of music during the second half of the fifteenth century. The Earl of Ormonde was hanged after the battle of Towton, on March 29th, 1461, but the Butlers were again taken into favour in 1468. In 1485, Henry VII. propitiated the Yorkists by appointing Gerald, Earl of Kildare, as Viceroy, and Thomas Fitzgerald as Chancellor. Seven years later, the Perkin

---

* The names "Punch" and "Judy" are corrupt survivals of *Pontius* and *Judas*, respectively intended for Pontius Pilate and Judas Iscariot.

Warbeck plot complicated matters ; but it fizzled out ngloriously in 1494, and Warbeck was hanged at Tyburn, with his friend, John Waters, Mayor of Cork, on November 16th, 1499.

England, from 1450 to 1500, can only boast a few compositions of any merit, for which Davey apologetically explains as follows:—"So much of Flemish work remains, and so little of the English work, that the English appear to be more inferior than they really were." If this apology seems satisfactory as regards music in England at this period, it is of still greater force in the case of Anglo-Irish music, both on account of the Wars of the Roses, the Lambert Simnel and Perkin Warbeck plots, and the internecine conflicts of the colonists themselves, as also the destruction of manuscripts.   In any case, practically the only secular music in Ireland at the close of the fifteenth century was the old Irish music, whilst, as regards sacred music, matters were pretty much as they had been a century previously.   But of this latter phase I shall treat in a separate chapter.

CHAPTER XII.

Irish Music in the Sixteenth Century.

MANY of our old annalists tell of the fame of harp making in Ireland during the first decade of the sixteenth century. This statement is accentuated by Dr. Petrie, who describes for us a very beautiful harp, which bore the date 1509, but which has, unfortunately, disappeared since 1810. " It was small," he writes, " and but simply ornamented, and on the front of the pillar, or forearm, there was a brass plate on which was inscribed the name of the maker and the date—1509. The poor harper [a wandering minstrel in 1809], had often expressed his intention of bequeathing this harp to his kind entertainers [Mr. Christoper Dillon Bellew and his lady, of Mount Bellew] ; but a summer came without bringing him to his accustomed haunts, and the harp was never forwarded, nor its fate ascertained."

For contemporary criticism of this period, one may adduce the learned John Major, (*d.* 1525) who gives unstinted praise to Irish music and musicians, especially to harpers : " Hibernenses . . . qui in illa arte praecipui sunt."

To those who are interested in the bag-pipes, it is worth mentioning that though we have no pipes of the sixteenth century now existing, there is, in Vienna, an excellent representation of an Irish piper, with the date 1514, from the world-famed master-brush of Albrecht Dürer ; and, in Ferguson's *Dissertation*, there are two illustrations given of a piper and pipes of this period.   Galilei, whose *Dialogue on Ancient and Modern Music* was published at Florence, in 1589, thus writes :—" The bagpipe is much used by the Irish. To its sound, this unconquered, fierce and warlike people march their armies, and encourage each other to deeds of valour.   With it also they accompany their dead to the grave, making such mournful sounds [*caoines*] as to invite, nay almost force, the bystanders to weep."

Niall *mor* O'Neill, Lord of Upper Clannaboy, who died April 11, 1512, is described by the *Four Masters* as " a man well skilled in the sciences, history, poetry, and *music*." Gerald, Earl of Kildare was paid *honorarium* of six beeves yearly by MacWards, Ulster rhymers, for protecting them. In 1518, we find Dermot O'Coffey, *rhymer*, as tenant of this Earl, holding a carucate of land in Ballysallagh, in Machairecuircne, barony of Kilkenny West, Co. Westmeath.   All readers of Irish history are familiar with the dramatic incident which happened on June 11th, 1534, when O'Keenan (some authors call him *Nelan*), harper to Silken Thomas, struck up an Irish song in praise of his lord, at St. Mary's Abbey, Dublin, with the result that the impetuous Geraldine threw down his sword of state, and went into rebellion.

The first enactment against Irish bards and minstrels, in this century, was, on the recommendation of an Anglo-Irish noble, Patrick Finglass, Chief Baron of the Exchequer, about the year 1524, who in his *Breviate* proposed as follows :—" That noe Irish minstralls rymers, ne bardes, be messengers to desire any goods of any man dwelling within the English Pale," upon pain of forfeiture of all their goods, and their bodies to be imprisoned at the King's will.   This recommen

dation was ostensibly acted on, but the magnates of
the Pale, following the example of the Earls of
Kildare, Desmond, and Ormonde, defied all such
legislation, and retained each an Irish harper. Under
date of 1533, the *Annals of Ulster* chronicle the death
of O'Sullivan Beare, who is described as exceedingly
bountiful to bards, ollamhs, pilgrims, and learned men.
Five years later, the same *Annals* have a similar entry
in connection with the death of Hugh Ò'Donnell.

In 1533, there was issued a proclamation in England
to suppress "foolish books, ballads, rhymes, and other
lewd treatises in the *English* tongue." Evidently,
Robert Cowley, Collector of Customs in Ireland, was of
opinion that seditious ballads in the *Irish* language
should be also suppressed, and, accordingly, in 1537,
he wrote to Secretary Cromwell that " harpers, rhymers,
Irish chroniclers, bards, and *isshallyn* commonly go
with praises [elegies] to gentlemen in the English Pale,
praising in rhymes, otherwise called *danes* [ᴠᴀɴᴄᴀ], their
extortions, robberies, and abuses, as valiantness, which
rejoiceth them in that their evil doing," etc.

Polydore Vergil (Virgilius) in his *History of
England* (published in 1534) writes thus of our Irish
minstrels :—Cujus Musicae peritissimi sunt : canunt
enim *tum voce tum fidibus eleganter*, sed vehementi
quodam impetu, sic ut mirabile sit, in tanta vocis
linguaeque atque *digitorum velocitate*, posse artis
numeros servari, id quod illi ad unguem faciunt." *

Inasmuch as the people of the Pale adhered to
Irish customs as well as music and language, a
statute was passed, in 1537, by the obsequious Irish

* *Angliae Hist.* lib. xiii.

Parliament, enacting: "That *no person* or persons, after the 1st of May, 1539, shall be shorn or shaven above the ears, or use the wearing of hair upon their heads, like unto long locks called *glibbes*," etc. This statute expressly forbade the wearing of *Crommeals* or *glibbes*, or flowing locks of hair, by any resident whatever in Ireland, whether Palesman or native born; and is the celebrated enactment which Moore erroneously supposed to have called forth the exquisite melody and words of *An Cuilfhionn* or *The Coulin*—printed by Walker in 1786.

Chappell tells us that in 1537, John Hogan was arrested in London, for "singing with a *crowd* or a *fyddyl*" a political song to the tune of "The Hunt is up"—an old dance tune mentioned by Shakespeare. In the same year the *Annals of Ulster* place the death of O'Keenan, a famous instrumentalist—namely, Bryan son of Cormac O'Keenan—who is said to have composed the charming melody, *Cailin og a stuir me.*

From the Patent Rolls we learn that on January 27th, 1540·41, pardon was granted to Owen Keenan, the blind minstrel of Cappanargid, Co. Kildare, harper to Gerald, Earl of Kildare, and also to his son, Cornelius Keenan, harper.

Lord Leonard Grey, Viceroy of Ireland, who had been censured by the English Privy Council for "plundering the *rhymers* on the mountain side," was recalled on April 1st, 1540, and was replaced after a short interval by Sir Anthony St. Leger. This St. Leger, or Sellenger, was sworn into office on July 25th, 1540, and was, on the whole a tolerant ruler. He pursued a policy of conciliation towards the chief minstrels and rhymers.

At a Parliament held at Limerick on July 12th, 1541, the Royal Commissioners enacted :—" That no poet or other person whatever shall make verses called *auran* [ᴀᵬⱤᴀɪn] to anyone after God on earth except the King, under penalty of forfeiting all his goods." This decree, as is evident, was aimed at rhymers and wandering minstrels who "made songs" on those whom they visited, being paid liberally for such poetic expressions.

In 1541, we meet with an interesting entry in the State Papers, from which it appears that the doughty warrior Cahir Mac Art Kavanagh, Tanist of Leinster* gave a guarantee to Sir Anthony St. Leger, for the loyalty of his *rhymers*, " so as parcels of their land shall rest with the King for their offence." This agreement affords evidence that even in the sixteenth century it had been the custom to give fee-farm lands to harpers, rhymers, brehons, etc.

We learn of the existence of Tuathal Maelmuire Mac Keogh of Rathtorkill, Co. Kildare, *rhymer*, from a brief reference to him in the State Papers, where it is mentioned that he was indicted, in 1542, for stealing "one pork, of the price of five shillings," belonging to a brother rhymer named Patrick Mac Hugh of the same village. It is satisfactory, however, to learn that Mac Keogh was pardoned for this offence on May 11th, 1549, as is recorded in the same official sources.

Among the *fiants* of Edward VI. we meet with a pardon to Fergal Mac Thomas Mac Keogh, of Donard,

---

* In 1544, Cahir Mac Art of Polmonty, Lord St. Mullins, furnished nineteen kerne for the French wars under the command of Captain Redmond MacCahir, " with Edmund *the Piper* as leader."

Co. Wicklow, *rhymer*, on April 16th, 1549; and to Owen *oge* Mac Crossan, of Ballymacrossan, *rhymer*, on June 10th, 1550. Hugh *boy* (buıɖe, the yellow complexioned) of Ballyedmond, Co. Wexford, *piper*—one of the retainers of Mac Edmund *duff* of Hy Kinsellagh—received a pardon on February 10th, 1552; and another performer on the bagpipes, known as "Cormac the piper," was accorded a similar mark of clemency in the autumn of the same year.

One of the most distinguished harpers of this epoch was Edmond O'Flynn, of Meylerstown, Co. Kildare; and his compositions are said to have been numerous, but, none of them have come down to our time. He was chief harper to an Anglo-Irish nobleman, Walter Bermingham, and received a royal pardon on February 8th, 1553. (Fiants of Edward VI.)

In *Smyth's Information for Ireland*, dated May 5th, 1561, there is mention of four classes of rhymers, namely, brehons, shanachies, *aois-dana* (men of songs), and *fileas* or poetic story-tellers; also, female ballad singers called mná ʀıubaıl. Sir William FitzWilliam, Lord Justice of Ireland, thus writes to Cecil, on April 14th, 1562: "These rhymers set forth the most 'best-lyest' and odious parts of men's ancestor's doings and their own likewise, for whom the rhymes are made. Such be caressed and defended, even with their priests, and rewarded with garments till they leave themselves naked [metaphorically], besides the best piece of plate in the house, and chiefest horse away with them; *not altogether departing empty-handed when they come among the Earls and others the nobility of the English race.*"

As might be expected, severe measures were now

ordered to be taken against all classes of musicians.
From 1523 to 1563, notwithstanding the ordinances
above-mentioned, wandering bards and harpers had
freely exercised their avocations, and were even
welcomed by the Lords of the Pale. "These laws,"
as Dr. Joyce writes, " were almost wholly inoperative ;
for the people went on speaking Irish, shaving, riding,
and dressing just the same as before."   In fact Irish
music was almost at the zenith of its glory at this epoch,
and was inseparably associated with the Irish language.

The first Elizabethan enactment against " Rymours,
Bardes, dice players," etc., was on December 20th,
1563 ; and the reason alleged for such legislation was
because " under pretence of visiting, they carry about
privy intelligence between the malefactors in the dis-
turbed districts."   From this enactment, which is to be
found in the Patent Roll, 6th Eliz., it appears that the
nobles of the Pale often gave as much as 100 marks " as
a reward for *lewd* rhymes," *i.e.* rhymes of a *deluding*
nature, viewed politically.   It was decreed that " if anyone in future gave a reward for such rhymes, a fine
would be exacted of double that amount to the Queen,
and the poet was to be fined at discretion."   Some
readers of the twentieth century will doubtless marvel at
the interesting fact here disclosed, namely, that over £500
of our present money had been then frequently given in
return for a song.   A song writer was surely a person
to be envied in those days—" 'twas something then to
be a bard,"—but, alas ! the professional rhymer could
scarcely have foreseen that in days to come " the price
of a song" would be synonymous with the merest trifle.

In connexion with the above statute, let me explain

that as the person of a bard, harper or rhymer, was deemed sacred, these worthies were, in consequence, enabled to act, as a sort of intelligence department for the Irish chiefs, whilst often accepting largesse from the English enemy. The English themselves made use of bards or rhymers as spies, and in 1561, Fardoragh Mac Namee is mentioned in a State Paper as conveying " secret information " to Captain Piers, Governor of Carrickfergus.

Father William Good, an English Jesuit, who taught a school, at Limerick, in his " Description of the Manners and Customs of the Wild Irish "—written in 1566, at the request of Camden, says : " They love music mightily and, of all instruments, are particularly taken with *the harp, which, being strung up with brass wire and beaten with crooked nails,* is very melodious." The Scotch harp of this period was exactly the same as the Irish, as may be proved by an examination of Mary Queen of Scots' Harp, still preserved. This harp is 31 inches high, and 18 inches from back to front, and was furnished with twenty-nine brass strings. It was richly ornamented, and was embellished with her portrait and the royal arms, which however were stolen in 1745.*

The first pardon to a musician under Elizabeth was in 1565, when Richard O'Malone, of Donore, Co. Westmeath, *harper*, was received with favour. In the following year, on May 31st, William the piper was pardoned. On March 4th, 1569, pardon was granted to Donogh Mac Crydan, of St. John's, Nenagh, Tipperary, *harper*, and to Thady Credan, of Drangan, Co. Tipperary, *harper*.

* On March 12th, 1904, this harp was sold by auction in Edinburgh, for 850 guineas. It was purchased by the Antiquarian Museum

Under date of August, 1570, there is a record of a pardon to John O'Doran, of Brittas, Co. Wicklow, *piper*, at the reqest of the Protestant Archbishop of Dublin.

The Elizabethan enactments against bards, minstrels, pipers and rhymers, were enforced after the promulgation of the Bull of St. Pius V. in 1569, though Elizabeth herself retained in her service, an Irish harper called Donogh. In 1570, there was a beautiful poem written by an unknown Irish bard in praise of the O'Brien harp which had, during the enforced absence of its owner, Conor, Earl of Thomond, been in temporary possession of a certain O'Gilligan, a famous sixteenth-century harper. The poet describes it as "a musical, fine-pointed, speckled harp," and though "sweet in the hands of O'Gilligan, it was sweeter by far in the halls of O'Brien." We have ample evidence that it is none other than the present " Brian Boru's Harp," which had been given to the Earl of Thomond by Lord Clanrickarde.

In the Indenture between Sir Henry Sydney and the Mac Damore Clan in County Wexford, dated June 26th, 1570, one of the principal freeholders was " *Morighane piberre*," that is Morgan the piper, of the Park, near Gorey. The appearance of this wealthy Irish piper as one of the parties to a treaty with the then Lord Deputy of Ireland is a sufficient proof of the estimation in which he was regarded; and he agreed to surrender his lands on the express stipulation of receiving them back by letters patent, " such lands to be held for ever at such rents and services as shall be expressed in the patents."

There is a letter in the State Papers written on

December 7th, 1572, in which mention is made of Feagh Mac Hugh O'Byrne, Rory O'More, and others of the Leinster clans, "who were wont to come by daylight *with bagpipes*, and by night with torch-light" on their predatory incursions.   About this time another proclamation was issued against "bardes, carroghs, and rimors"; and Conor, Earl of Thomond, displayed his loyalty by vigorously carrying out the decree, and actually hanging three bards, "for which abominable and treacherous act," as the Annalists say, "he was satirized and denounced."   A few years later this recreant Earl sent his son Donogh to England as a hostage to be educated as a Protestant.

Between the years 1570 and 1577, Henry Colley, of Carbury, Co. Kildare, and John Bourke, of Derryvicklan, Co. Clare, were appointed Seneschals of their respective counties, "with power to banish all malefactors, rebels, vagabonds, rhymers, Irish harpers," etc.; and Myler Delamere, of Ross, Co. Westmeath, was given the chief sergeantship of "Delamere's country," on condition of apprehending and committing to Mullingar jail any Irish minstrels.   On March 6th, 1571, pardon was granted to Brian Mac Mahon Fitz Philip, of Newcastle, Co. Meath, *harper*; and, on January 11th, 1572, to James O'Harrigan, *harper*.

On November 5th, 1571, Gerald, Earl of Kildare, and Piers Fitz James, of Ballysonan, Co. Kildare, were commissioned to execute martial law in said county, and to punish by death, or otherwise as directed, all harpers, rhymers, bards, etc.   A similar commission was given to Patrick Savage, Seneschal of the Ards, Co. Down, on March 22nd, 1572.

Among the pardons for the year 1572 are those of Conly Mac Fannin *fionn*, late of Dunamaggan, Co. Kilkenny, *piper*, and Manus the piper, on January 12th; and Thomas *reagh* Mac Shane, *piper*, and Brian Fitz-Patrick Mac Donegan, *piper*, of Queen's County on September 19th.*

On May 6th, 1573, Sir John of Desmond was pardoned on condition of not keeping any bard, carrogh, or rhymer in his train ; and, early in 1576, orders were issued by the Privy Council of Ireland against " rimors, harpers, and other Irishmen," prohibiting same from allowing their horses to graze without payment ["a foyning "] in the barony of Rathdown, in the marches of Dublin.

From a Grand Jury presentment of County Cork in 1576, it appears that the *Ollamh dann* and the various rhymers belonging to the lords of the soil "were wont to take the best apparel of the newly married wife of any freeholder in the county, or its value thereof " ; and, as a case in point, O'Daly *fionn*, of Slieve Luachra, in Desmond, is quoted, "he being the chief rhymer, otherwise called *ollave dane*."†

The following pardons were issued, *inter alia*, in the year 1577 : to Donal Mac Namara, of Galbally, Co. Tipperary, *harper*, on September 5th ; to Donal Mac-Rory O'Heffernan, of Shronehill, Co. Tipperary, *harper*,

* Fiants of Elizabeth.   12th Report of the D.K.I.

† O'Daly, of Muinter Bhaire, Co. Cork, was an important personage at this epoch, and, in a grant of certain lands to Thomas, Earl of Ormonde, for which a fiant was issued on December 10th, 1578, was included " a freehold, with the tithes of the same, which O'Daly the Rhymer lately held."   Dinely, in 1681, writes :—" The suit and service expected from O'Daly and his successors for all that land unto Carew and his heirs was *to be their Rimers, Poste, and Chroniclers of their actions.*"

on September 12th; to Fergall Mac Maelmurry O'Heffernan, Magrath O'Heffernan, and Aherny O'Heffernan,
of Shronehill, *rhymers*, on the same day; to Conor
Mac Loughlin, of Moher, *piper*, on November 14th;
and to Owen *the piper*, of Carrickmines, Co. Dublin,
about the same time.

We are fortunately able to give an illustration of the
Irish harpers and war pipers of 1578, as drawn by John
Derrick, in his *Image of Ireland*. This extraordinary
book, dedicated to Sir Philip Sydney, is extremely rare,
and was published by John Day in 1581, though, as
stated in the title, "made and devised anno 1578,"
The reader can judge of Derrick's artistic powers by
the subjoined sketches "of the habite and apparell" of
an Irish harper and an Irish piper :—

As is well-known, the minstrels of Erin stood bravely
by the proscribed religion, under Elizabeth; and, indeed,
it may be said that music and verse contributed not a

little to the preservation of the Catholic religion in Ireland during the last quarter of the sixteenth century. From the *Religious Songs of Connaught*, edited by Dr. Douglas Hyde, we can imagine what must have been the effect of these sacred effusions when rendered with due expression.

On March 13th, 1578, Sir Lucas Dillon, Chief Baron,

was ordered "to punish all malefactors, rebels, vagabonds, *rhymers, Irish harpers*," etc.; and, not long afterwards, Sir William Drury hanged Father O'Rourke,
O.S.F., and Rory *oge*, a brehon. In the following year,
on November 23rd, a proclamation was issued ordering
that "no idle person, vagabond, or masterless man,
bard, rhymer, or other notorious malefactor remain within the district of North Wicklow on pain of whipping
after 8 days, and of death, after 20 days." The great
victory at Glenmalure, on August 25th, 1580, when
Fiacha Mac Aodha O'Byrne and Viscount Baltinglass
utterly defeated Lord Grey de Wilton (Viceroy), and
Sir William Stanley (the English loss being estimated as
800 soldiers, including Sir Peter Carew, Colonel Moore,
and Captains Audley and Cosby), was celebrated by many
a martial lyric. In particular, the fine song " Ⓓía Líb,
ᴀ LᴀoċᴘᴀÖ ṠᴀoᴉᴠeᴀL," written by Aengus MacDoighre
O'Daly, bard of O'Byrne, dates from this period, but the
air has long since disappeared.

CHAPTER XIII.

IRISH MUSIC IN THE SIXTEENTH CENTURY—(continued).

PARDON was granted to MacLoughlin roe O'Brennan, harper, on October 4th, 1581 ; and, in 1582, there are grants of pardon to Thomas reagh (the brown), of King's County, piper, on May 8th ; Maelmurry Mac-Tuathal MacKeogh, of County Carlow, rhymer, on August 27th ; Walter Brenagh (Walsh), harper, on August 30th ; Owen MacLoughlin MacEgan, brehon, on September 19th ; and Donogh O'Creedan, of Synon, harper, on November 13th.

In the articles between the Privy Council of Ireland and Sir John O'Reilly, of Breffni, Co. Cavan, on August 28th, 1583, there was a special covenant ; " That he shall not keep any Irish brehons . . . nor keep within his house any Irish bard, carroghe, or rhymer," etc.* Subsequently, there were similar articles of agreement entered into at the Camp, near Dunluce, on September 18th, 1584, between Sir John Perrott and Donal gorme MacConnell of the Glens, the ancestor of the MacDonnells of Antrim.

Between the years 1581 and 1584, Edmund Spenser, author of the Faerie Queene, had a very good opportunity of studying Irish music, which he praises very highly, shrewdly remarking the then prevalent mode of elaborately embellishing the simplest airs.   This meretricious

* See Hardiman's Irish Minstrelsy. vol. ii., p 159.   However, Hardiman erroneously gives the date as A.D. 1584, whereas it should be 1583.

adornment of old melodies, as noticed by Spenser
(whose residence for three years at Kilcullen, New
Abbey, Co. Kildare, has, strangely enough, been overlooked by almost all his biographers), continued till
the close of the eighteenth century, with the natural
result that it is most difficult to get accurate versions
of sixteenth and seventeenth-century tunes. Petrie
collected fifty "settings" of one particular melody,
many of them widely different; and I myself, some
twenty-nine years ago, sent Dr. Joyce—one of our best
living authorities on ancient Irish music—five or six
variants of certain seventeenth-century melodies which
I had noted down in different parts of Ireland.

Spenser assures us that the bardic verses "are taken
up with a general applause, and *usually sung at all the
feasts and meetings by the racraidhe, whose proper function
that is, who also receive for the same great reward and
reputation amongst them.*" He adds:—"I have caused
divers of these [Irish] poems to be translated to me
that I might understand them; and surely they savoured
of sweet wit and good invention . . . . sprinkled with
some pretty flowers of their natural device, which gave
good grace and comeliness unto them." For the benefit
of the English reader it is as well to explain that the
Racraidhe above mentioned included those who sang to
the music of the *cruit* or harp, and who also recited the
poems of their master. Spenser instances a case he had
known where *forty cows* were paid by an Irish noble for
an effusive ode or *dan.*

The author of the *Faerie Queene* alludes to "the
wandering women called *Mona Shull.*" These female
ballad singers—*mna siubhail*—are also described by

Derrick in his *Image of Ireland* (1581), and were under the rule of a leader called *Lucas*, having only one eye. Severe enactments were passed against these mendicant women-rhymers, as also against *aesulla*, or *ishallyn*, as the name is written in the State Papers of Elizabeth. Camden thus writes in 1586:—"They [the Irish] have their *Brehons* [judges], *Historians* (who record their exploits), *Physicians*, *Poets* called *Bards*, and *Harpers*, each of whom have lands assigned them; and each of these [five] professions, in every territory, form distinct families, as Brehons of one lineage and name, Historians of another, and so of the rest."*

A Presentment of the Grand Jury of County Cork for November, 1584, gives the names of 72 persons who were then living as "poets, chroniclers, and rhymers," including O'Cuill (Quill) and O'Cahill, *rhymers*; Art *na caoine*, *bard*; Maelconry MacShane, of Castletown-roche, *harper*, Shane O'Dwyer, of Aherlow, *chronicler*, Cormac O'Daly, the Lord Barrymore's *rhymer*, etc.; also Mary ny Donoghue, a *she bárde*, and Mary ny Clancy, *rhymer*. An Inquisition of same year returns John MacDonnell as "Rhymer" or "*Ollamh re Dan* of Desmond."

Although Hardiman was of opinion that the famous Munster song, *Seaghan O'Duibhir an Gleanna*—"John O Dwyer of the Glen"—only dated from after the year 1651, in reference to Colonel John O'Dwyer, of Glynn, Co. Waterford, I am strongly inclined to the view of O'Daly, in his *Poets and Poetry of Munster* (2nd series), that it really dates from the last quarter of the sixteenth century, and was composed for the *Shane*

* Gough's *Camden*, vol. iv., p. 467.

O'Duibhir, of the Glen of Aherlow, Co. Tipperary, living in 1584, who figures in the above Presentment, as quoted in the Carew MS., No. 627. The clearing of the forests alluded to in this grand old song began as early as the fifteenth century, and was well nigh completed by the "Undertakers" under Elizabeth, who were anxious to make all the ready money they could, fearing that the Irish would soon dispossess them. Moreover, the very construction of the air seems to point to the second half of the sixteenth century, rather than the middle of the seventeenth century.

In the list of pardons issued in 1584 are the names of Morgan the piper (who made the Indenture with Sir Henry Sydney in 1570) and Alexander the piper, both of "The Park," near Gorey, Co. Wexford, on April 10th; Donal MacKeogh, of Co. Carlow, *rhymer*, on April 28th; Russell MacRussell, of Ballinacarrig, Co. Cork, *harper*, on June 4th; and John Piers, "chief musician and piper to Sir Gerald Fitzgerald," of Dromana, Co. Waterford, on July 13th.

The viceroyalty of Sir John Perrott (a natural son of Henry VIII.), who was sworn in on June 21st, 1584, proved fairly beneficial to Ireland; and he held a Parliament at Dublin, on April 26th, 1585, in which a statute was passed regarding costume, and another against sorcery and witchcraft. This Deputy ordered stocks to be made for punishing "idle persons, spies, *bards, gamesters*," etc.

Among the *fiants* of Elizabeth, the pardons for the year 1585 include:—William MacCruddan or Creedan, "*harper and yeoman*," on February 26th; Mahon O'Heffernan, *rhymer*, Eneas *roe* O'Heffernan, *rhymer*, and

Donogh O'Casey, *piper*, on May 14th ; Ulick O'Mael-conry, of Clonea, Co. Roscommon, "*gentleman and rhymer*," Gillananeave *caoch* (the blind), of Clonpluckane, *rhymer*, and Paudheen *oge* O'Mulconry, *rhymer*, on June 1st ; Melaghlin *roe* O'Brennan, of Co. Galway, *harper*, on June 27th ; Murtogh MacRory O'Heffernan, of Derrycloney, *rhymer*, Donogh MacCormac, of Co. Limerick, *piper*, and Conor O'Heffernan, of same, *rhymer*, on July 8th.

The pardons granted during the year 1586 include Gillaglass O'Shallow, *harper*, on May 29th ; Dermot MacGrath, of Hospital, Co. Limerick, *harper*, on May 31st ; and Flann MacEneas *oge* MacGrath, of Garristown, Co. Tipperary, *rhymer*, on September 20th. This is the renowned bard, Flann Magrath, who wrote a fine elegy on Thomas, Earl of Ormonde, published by O'Donovan in 1850, from the MS. of John Murphy, of Carrignavar, Co. Cork, dated 1726. O'Donovan only knew of Magrath's existence by the fact of his name being signed to some poems, about the year 1586 ; but the State Paper entry is an interesting addition to our scant knowledge of this Irish bard.

Notwithstanding all that Perrott had done for the "English interest" in Ireland from 1584 to 1587, he was a "marked" man, owing to the machinations of Loftus, Wallop, Bingham, Fenton, and Bagnall. One of the accusations against him was a leniency towards bards, minstrels, and others who had sounded the praises of the dispossessed Irish princes and nobles. Accordingly, an order was issued on March 20th, 1588, to John Kiernan, Seneschal of MacKiernan's Country (County Cavan), "to prosecute, banish, and punish by all means, malefactors, rebels, vagabonds, *rhymers, Irish harpers, bards*, etc.   From a letter written by the ill-fated Sir Brian O'Rourke, Lord of Breffney, on October 6th, 1588, to MacMahon, Lord of Oriel (Co. Monaghan), it would appear that this order was stringently carried out.   The scarcity of the Irish harp is lamented by O'Rourke, who thus writes :—" And what you request us to send you, as *a harp and a great spear*, we do assure you we cannot ; there is never a good harp in our country, but we will provide one for you, and will send two great spears, and two *skeins* of the best made in our country."*

On May 4th, 1588, pardon was granted to "Grany ny Malley, Sadh Bourke ny Davy Bourke, widow, Theobald Bourke MacRichard *enieran*, gent., Margaret O'Flaherty, daughter of Grany," and others.   This Grany ny Malley, or Grace O'Malley was none other than *Grania Maol* (daughter of Owen O'Malley, of the Owles, Co. Mayo, chieftain of Burrishoole), the widow of "Iron Dick."   About this time was composed a fine old song in honour of this Queen of the West ; and the name *Graine Maol* (pronounced *Grania Uaile*) was used

---

* Sir Brian O'Rourke was betrayed by James VI. of Scotland in 1590, and handed over to Queen Elizabeth—being sent as a convict in chains.   Elizabeth " ordered him to be hanged without even the form of a trial," and, to add insult to injury, assigned him in his last moments, by way of a ghostly father, Miler Magrath, the Protestant Archbishop of Cashel, " who exhorted him," as MacGeoghegan writes, " to conform to the religion of the Queen and of the state."   However, Lombard tells us that the ancient Prince of Breffni refused Miler's ministrations, and added : "As for *me*, I shall die in the religion which *you* have deserted."   O'Rourke's death (on November 3rd, 1591) was amply avenged by his son, at the Battle of the Curlew Mountains, on August 15th, 1599, when Clifford and his 1,500 men were utterly routed by O'Rourke's force of only 200.   Amongst the slain were Sir Conyers Clifford, Sir Alexander Ratcliffe, and others.

by the bards, in after days, to symbolize Erin—the affix *maol*, meaning "bald," personifying the desolate condition of Ireland from wars and famine. Though the original words of the song, as well as the tune of "Graine Uaile," are almost forgotten, an excellent Irish version was furnished by John *Claragh* MacDonnell, about the year 1730, which is printed in Hardiman's *Irish Minstrelsy* where the original lyric may also be found.

Sir John Perrott, fairly disgusted with the viceroyalty of Ireland, besought the Queen to recall him to England; and, on June 30th, 1588, he delivered the sword of state to his successor, Sir William Fitzwilliam. The destruction of the Spanish Armada in the late summer and early autumn of the year 1588 accentuated the strained relations existing between England and Ireland; and, on October 28th, 1589, another proclamation was issued against " rhymers, Irish harpers, idle men and women," etc. Lady Morgan writes :—" Elizabeth, jealous of that influence which the bardic order of Ireland held over the most puissant of her chiefs, not only enacted laws against them, but against such as received or entertained them; for Spenser informs us that, even *then*, ' their verses were taken up with a general applause, and usually sung at all feasts and meetings.'" The Earl of Cumberland paid a visit to Dingle, Co. Kerry, in 1589, as is recorded in *Hakluyt's Voyages* (published at London in 1599), and he gives an interesting account of the social state of the country at the period. *Inter alia* he writes :—" Here we wel refreshed ourselves whilest the *Irish harpe* sounded sweetly in our eares."

On January 28th, 1590, Patrick Fox, of Dublin, a Government spy, wrote to Walsingham that Hubert O'Ferrall, son of Fergus O'Ferrall, "had sent a harp as a token to Feagh MacHugh, by one Richard O'Quinn, a priest, well knowing MacHugh to be a bad member," and that he had stayed a week with the said Feagh "to establish friendship betwixt Feagh and O'Rourke and his own father."

Queen Elizabeth was particularly incensed against Hugh O'Neill, Prince of Tyrone, but yet, when that nobleman presented himself at court, attended by a numerous retinue, including his chief bard (O'Gnive) and piper, he was restored to favour, notwithstanding the malignant efforts of Cecil.*

The inauguration of Hugh O'Donnell as "The O'Donnell of Tyrconnell," on May 3rd, 1592, followed by the English defeat at the Ford of the Biscuits, in 1594, and the recall of Lord Deputy Fitzwilliam (who was replaced by Sir William Russell on August 11th, 1594), induced Hugh O'Neill, Earl of Tyrone, to sever his connection with the Hiberno-English faction. We read that the bards and minstrels were rejoiced at the alliance between O'Neill and O'Donnell ; and numerous harpers and pipers from Munster and Connaught flocked to the standards of the Northern Chiefs. Lady Morgan writes :—" Although Ulster was never deemed poetic ground, yet, when destruction threatened the bardic order in the southern provinces, ... hither they fled for protection, and, at different periods, found it from

---

* In 1593, Elizabeth sent an order to the magistrates of North Wales, directing them "to regulate certain abuses that had crept into the bardic profession."—(Trans., R.I.A., vol. ix., 1803.)

the Northern Princes." Various successes following on the victory of Clontibret, in 1595, induced Queen Elizabeth to come to terms with O'Neill, in April, 1596, but the Prince of Tyrone refused the conditions; and, on July 6th of that year, the Ulster chiefs wrote to their brethren in Munster to league with them in a war for religion and country.

Many fine old songs and ballads date from this epoch. The bards of County Wicklow strung their harps in praise of the noble Feagh MacHugh O'Byrne,* whilst those of Munster had for their theme the gallant deeds of the Earl of Desmond. The lovely tune known as "The Foggy Dew" is certainly as old as the year 1595, and it was used by Denny Lane for his ballad "The Irish Maiden's Lament." Who has not heard the grand air "Roisin *dubh*," which was written and composed in praise of Hugh Roe O'Donnell? "*Seaghan Ruadh*" (*Shaun Rua*) was composed for John of Desmond, whilst the Geraldines of Kildare were not forgotten by the harpers.

The English, too, availed of the services of Irish harpers as "intelligencers," and there is a report in the State Papers, under date of July, 1595, wherein a certain spy called Peter MacMahon, of Drogheda, detailed much secret information acquired in the household of Lord Louth. The better to ingratiate himself with the followers of O'Neill, he assiduously practised the harp, and was able to play well on the instrument.†

* On April 18th, 1590, Gerald Byrne wrote to the Lord Deputy that, "the son of Fergus O'Farrell, with another horseman, well furnished with horse and armour, and *a harper, riding upon a hackney with them*," had recently been on a visit to Murrogh MacEdmund, whose daughter was married to the son of the dauntless Feagh MacHugh.

† *Calendar of State Papers* (1592-1596), p. 350.

Turlogh *Luineach* O'Neill, who died early in September, 1595, was a great patron of bards and rhymers. His mansion house was at Strabane, Co. Tyrone, and it was ever open to minstrels. One of his bards, Ferdoragh MacConmidh (MacNamee), is described in a State Paper as " the richest rhymer in Ireland," and Turlogh himself —who had assumed the title of " O'Neill "—was wont to invite, during the Christmas holidays of every year, all literary and musical persons as honoured guests, " not one of them departing dissatisfied, or without being supplied abundantly."

From the State Papers we learn that on August 2nd, 1597, Sir Conyers Clifford availed of the services of an Irish harper to bring a message to O'Rourke. *

Edmund Spenser published his *View of the South of Ireland*, in 1596, in which he expresses the conviction that the Irish people, if managed on his lines, " would quickly consume themselves and devour one another." It seemed like a retribution when, on a certain October evening of the year 1598, Kilcolman Castle was attacked and burned by the Irish, and Spenser with his wife barely escaped.

Feagh MacHugh O'Byrne was at length betrayed by a relative to the Lord Deputy, and was killed on the 18th of May, 1597; and on May 22nd, Sir William Russell was superseded by Thomas, Lord Borough. A pardon was granted to Dermot MacGrath, *piper*, at the suit of the Lord of Upper Ossory, on June 6th, which was the first and last act of clemency exercised by the new Deputy. Lord Borough died on October

* On September 4th, 1597, Elizabeth, Countess of Desmond, made Sir Robert Cecil a present of an Irish Harp. (Cal. of the Salisbury MSS.)

14th, and was succeeded by Sir Thomas Norris, who resigned in a month, being replaced by Loftus and Gardiner as Lords Justices.

Early in September, 1597, was fought the Battle of Tyrrell's Pass, in which Captain Richard Tyrrell, with 400 men, utterly defeated the Anglo-Irish of Meath, under Lord Trimlestown, near Fertullagh, Co. Westmeath. MacGeoghegan writes :—" While the English were passing the place where O'Connor (Tyrrell's lieutenant) lay in ambuscade, this officer sallied forth with his troops, *caused the drums and fifes to play 'Captain Tyrrell's March,' this being the signal agreed on for an attack.* The English army, having got between two fires, were cut to pieces ; and so general was the slaughter that only one soldier escaped."

On July 6th, 1596, Lyon, Protestant Bishop of Cork, thus writes to Lord Hunsdon, Lord Chamberlain of England :—" Some strict order must be taken for idle persons, as *carroghes, hazards, rhymers, bards,* and *harpers,* which run about the country, eating the labours of the poor, carrying news and intelligence to the rebels, and bruiting false tales. Also, the *rithmers* make songs in commendation and praise of the treasons, spoilings, preyings, and thievings made. They flock to the *cuddies,* or night-suppers," etc.

The Battle of the Yellow Ford was a glorious victory for O'Neill, on August 14th, 1598, when Marshal Sir Henry Bagenal, with the flower of his army (about 2,000 troops), bit the dust ; and it was followed by the surrender of *Portmore,* concerning which so many songs were written. Had the Irish forces, under O'Neill and O'Donnell, marched on to Dublin at this crisis, the English power in Ireland would have been annihilated.

At the terrible "disaster" of Ranelagh, Co. Wicklow, on Tuesday, May 29th, 1599, in which Sir Henry Harrington, with 600 men, was utterly defeated by Phelim MacFeagh O'Byrne, we read in the State Papers that, on the evening preceding, "the rebel Phelim MacFeagh sent *a messenger of his own, being a Rymer*, to pray Sir Henry to forbear doing of any hurt to him, and that he would submit himself to the Lord Lieutenant." The Privy Council, in their letter of June 2nd, describe briefly how O'Byrne destroyed Harrington's "whole regiment, and brake them with a lamentable slaughter of the most part of the companies of foot."

On August 15th, 1599, a fiant was issued granting a pardon to Fineen FitzJohn, *piper*, at the suit of Edmund, Viscount Mountgarret. Two famous musicians of this epoch were Dermot O'Dugan, bard to the Earl of Desmond, and Rory *dall* O'Cahan, the harper and composer. Many a well-fought field resounded with the martial strains of *Lamh dearg abu* and *O'Donnell abu* ; and the close of the year 1599 found Hugh O'Neill practically King of Ireland. Perhaps nothing more signally demonstrates the absolute freedom enjoyed by the harpers, pipers, tympanists, and minstrels at this epoch than the non-appearance of any State pardons in the various official documents from 1586 to 1600—save the solitary one to Fineen FitzJohn, above mentioned.

One of the saddest pages in Irish history is the account given, both by native annalists and English writers, of the last twelve months of the career of James, Earl of Desmond—better know as the *Sugan* Earl. This great Anglo-Irish noble, who is described in the State Papers as "the most powerful of the Earls of

Desmond," fought against terrible odds, and, at length, was defeated, on September 17th, 1600, on his way to the Glen of Aherlow, by Captain Greame. Fortunately, he managed to get away, with about 400 men, and retreated for a time to the well-known fastness of Aherlow, immortalised by the lovely song Seaξán ó Ʋuıƀıχ an Ξleanna (John O'Dwyer of the Glen), which I have previously alluded to. In the following month he was joined by Dermot MacCraith, Bishop of Cork and Cloyne ; and the two "outlaws" lay concealed till the close of November in a cabin at Lisbarry, near the woods of Drumfineen.*

In all his hair-breadth escapes the Earl was assisted by his faithful harper, Dermot O'Dugan, who acted as a devoted sentinel, and gave due notice to his master of the approach of the soldiery. We read that during the Christmastide of 1600-1, the only companions of Desmond were Father John Shanahan, two of the Baldwin family, and the harper, O'Dugan. The noble Geraldine was at last captured, on May 29th, 1601, by his own kinsman, the White Knight (in a cave near Clogheen, Co. Tipperary), by whom he was given up to Sir George Thornton, receiving for his treachery the then large sum of £1,000.

Native Irish minstrelsy was now in a sore plight, and was destined to experience further persecution under James I., as we shall see in a succeeding chapter.

* At length, being discovered (through the agency of a spy) by the Earl of Thomond, Sir George Thornton, and Captain Roger Harvey, the Earl fled. Carew writes :—" MacCraith was met by some of the soldiers, clothed in a simple mantle, and with torn trousers like an aged churl, and they, neglecting so poor a creature, not able to carry a weapon, suffered him to pass unregarded."

CHAPTER XIV.

PRE-REFORMATION CHURCH MUSIC IN IRELAND.

THERE are still in existence two canons of a Synod held by St. Patrick about the year 450, relative to church music. Various Missals, Antiphonaries, and Hymn Books from the eighth to the twelfth century, attest the Irish form of the Roman Liturgy.* Tirechan, a writer of the seventh century, tells that a proper Preface was always sung for the National Apostle, in the Mass for the feast of St. Patrick ; and all liturgical scholars are familiar with the old Irish *Liber Hymnorum*. I have already treated of the great Continental schools of music founded by Irish monks, especially that of St. Gall's ; and reference has also been made to the Culdees of Armagh, who had a world-renowned music school, from the eighth to the sixteenth century.

Under date of 1224 we read of the death of " Maurice the Canonist, son of King Roderick O'Conor, one of the most eminent of the Irish for learning, *psalm-singing* and poetry."

From the close of the thirteenth century the Sarum Use obtained in the majority of the Irish churches, and continued till 1560. Inasmuch as Christ Church, Dublin, may be regarded as a typical cathedral, the following notices, from its archives, relating to music, together with other kindred matter, will supply a lacuna in our ecclesiastical annals.

In 1217, Henry de Londres, Archbishop of Dublin and

* Renehan's *History of Music*, p. 68.

Lord Justice of Ireland, convened a Synod, in which it was decreed that the singing of the canonical hours should be rendered " distinctly and clearly, with due reverence and devotion," and that " there should be no skipping or slurring of the notes of the liturgical chant." Two years later, this prelate erected St. Patrick's Collegiate Church as a cathedral, and founded the dignities of Precentor, Chancellor, and Treasurer, ordering that the Use of Sarum should be observed; and he died in July 1228. After eighty years dissension, a settlement was come to on March 2nd, 1300, whereby Christ Church, as the Mother Church (receiving three ounces of gold, annually, from St. Patrick's), was confirmed in its precedence over St. Patrick's, yet both Cathedrals were to be metropolitan, and both Chapters were to have a voice in the election of Archbishop.

Although Pope Clement V. on July 11th, 1311, issued a Bull for the erection of a University in Dublin, yet it was not till 1320 that Archbishop de Bicknor was able to formally open it, and he also framed a code of statutes for the infant University, the *studium generale* being in St. Patrick's Cathedral.*

In 1328, according to the *Annals of Clonmacnoise*, died Maurice O'Gibellan, Master of Arts, learned in civil and canon law, a philosopher, Irish poet, and exact speaker of the speech which in Irish is called Ogham ; a Canon and singer in Tuam, Elphin, Achonry, Killala, Annadown and Clonfert, as also Vicar-General. In

* William de Rudyard, Dean of St. Patrick's, was appointed first Chancellor. On August 14th, 1359. Edward III. endowed a Lectureship in Divinity in the University of Dublin; and, in 1364, Lionel Duke of Clarence founded a theological chair to be held by an Austin Friar—said lectures to be given in the vestry or robing-room of the Cathedral.

1343, according to the *Annals of Ulster*, "Donnchada O'Mael - Brenainn [O'Mulrenin] the cleric, Canon-chorister of Elphin, was killed by one shot of an arrow by the people of David Mac William de Burgh the Brown."

From the Statutes of the Provincial Council held in Dublin, in 1348, under the presidency of Alexander de Bicknor, Archbishop of Dublin, it is evident that the study and cultivation of sacred chant was insisted on as an essential part of the duties of clerics. (Can. 23). These statutes, according to Ware, are preserved in the White Book of the Church of Ossory.

John of St. Paul, Archbishop of Dublin, built the choir of Christ Church Cathedral in 1358, and subscribed to the fund for a new organ, which was presided at by one of the Canons, generally designated as "clerk of the organs." His successor Thomas Minot (a relative of Laurence Minot, the famous war-song writer), who was consecrated on Palm Sunday, 1363, almost rebuilt St. Patrick's Cathedral, and added a steeple to it.

About the year 1370 was transcribed the exquisite Psalter of Christ Church, now preserved in the Bodleian Library, Oxford. Mr. Mills, of the Dublin Public Record Office, says that "this work must be acknowledged to be the most elaborate extant work of Anglo-Norman art in Ireland."

In 1390, John de Sandale, Precentor of Christ Church, effected some improvements in the musical services. The ordinary choir dress for the Canons was the same as at Salisbury, that is, "black copes down to the feet, and surplices beneath them," whilst the choir boys wore *cottae* and *rochettae*, or shortened albs—the acolytes generally being vested in "scarlet cassocks with a scarlet hood over the surplice."

Reading between the lines of musty parchment deeds and account rolls of the fourteenth century, we get a tolerable insight into the constitution of the choir and its general economy. Music was sedulously cultivated; and several Latin treatises on musical theory were written by eminent prelates and clerics, including a valuable work by Simon Tunstede, D.D., O.S.F., who died in 1369. I have previously mentioned that the earliest *English* treatise on music was written by an Irish cleric, Lionel Power, about the year 1390. It may also be added that there is a fine Antiphonarium of this period among the manuscript in Trinity College, Dublin.*

In the *Red Book of the Exchequer* there is a very fine transcript of the Gregorian Modes, and also the hymn for the feast of the Ascension and the Latin hymn to St. Nicholas. Folios 49-64 contain an early illuminated Missal comprising the chief festivals, following, to a great extent, the Use of Sarum, whilst folio 135 has the well-known hymn to St. John the Baptist, "Ut Queant laxis," from which Guido of Arezzo evolved the names Ut, Re, Mi, Fa, etc. It also contains an early Church Calendar, with various notices of events from 1264 to 1524.

King Edward III., in 1335, as a mark of favour to the Carmelite Friars of Dublin, granted the said White Friars the sole right of performing Divine Service in the Chapel of the Exchequer in George Street (near the present South Great George's Street), who were, for

* No. 100 in Abbott's Catalogue of the MSS. in T.C.D

their labours, entitled to receive from the Court of
Exchequer an annual payment of one hundred shillings.
In 1347 or 1348 the Exchequer removed from George
Street, and its site was granted to the Austin Friars on
July 28th, 1362. Here it is as well to explain that there
was always a Chaplain of the Exchequer Chapel, and it
was a custom, from the close of the fourteenth century
to the year 1869 (when the "Church of Ireland" was
disestablished), for the choristers of Christ Church, on
the third day previous to the close of each Law Term,
four times a year, "to proceed to the Court of
Exchequer to do homage to the King before the Barons,
in open Court, in order to secure their estates and
privileges." On these visits the Chaplain recited the
Latin prayers contained in the Red Book, and the choir
sang appropriate antiphons and Latin hymns, "standing
on the green cloth," at the conclusion of which they
received a certificate that entitled them to all their
revenues. An entry was then made in the rule-books of
the Court to the effect that "the Chauntor of Christ
Church brought into Court the Vicar's Choral, and
performed their accustomed service and homage due to
his Majestie," receiving their wonted fee of ten shillings
sterling.*

In 1396, there is a record of the death of Matthew
O'Lonan, Archdeacon of Ardagh, who is described by
the old chroniclers as "a man versed in various arts

* Mr. Bumpus tells us that in the early years of the nineteenth
century "four of the chorister boys and the two clerical vicars
used to attend, escorted by the verger of Christ Church." Mr.
John Horan, the veteran Organist of Christ Church, who had been
a chorister from 1841 to 1846, is the last surviving member of the
choir that took part in this quaint ceremonial—abolished since
1869.

and sciences, in history, poetry, *music*, and general literature."

Under Nicholas Staunton, Prior of Christ Church from 1420 to 1438, the musical services were very numerous, owing to the number of anniversary Requiem Masses. In an interesting inventory of the goods of Thomas Weston, Prior of the Hospital of St. John of Newgate, Dublin, enrolled among the deeds of Christ Church, there is mention of "three capes and two hoods, worth 6s. 8d.;" "a breviary, worth 20s.;" "a mass book," etc.; and he bequeathed his breviary "to the Prior of Holy Trinity, *to be chained in the choir*."

In 1431, Richard Talbot, Archbishop of Dublin (brother to the Earl of Shrewsbury), instituted six minor Canons and six Choristers in St. Patrick's Cathedral, who were not, however, to have a stall in the choir, nor yet a voice in the Chapter. Each of the six Choristers was to receive four marks, English money, and twenty marks to the Precentor.

On February 18th, 1438, Pope Eugenius IV. granted an indulgence of four years and 160 days to "those who, being penitent, and having confessed devoutly, visited Holy Trinity Church yearly, on the Sunday on which is chanted *Laetare Jerusalem*, and bestow alms towards its repair and preservation." Among the items of expenditure recorded in the Treasurer's book at this period we find "quires of paper for copying music," "mats for the choirs," "surplices and rochets for the choristers," "sconces for the quires," "a key to the quire door," "a quire of paper for songs," etc.

On the death of Archbishop Talbot, on August 15th, 1449, John Streguthen, barber, acting as agent for the

Prior and monks of Christ Church Cathedral, pledged the archiepiscopal cross and crozier to Richard White, tailor, for five marks. These *insignia* were not released for seventy-eight years till Archbishop Allen redeemed them on payment of "almost 100 ounces of silver" out of his own substance, as he himself states in a note which is contained in the *Liber Niger*.

Nor was Dublin peculiar in upholding a good standard of sacred music. We learn that the Cashel province was equally zealous in the cause of plain chant. This is apparent from the 86th Canon of the Provincial Council of Cashel, in 1453, under Archbishop Cantwell: "Statuit Concilium, quod in civitatibus et locis in quibus cantus habetur et chorus regitur, nulli ad aliquas praelaturas nisi cantores admittantur, salvo privilegio speciali Sedis Apostolicae."

Archbishop Tregury—a skilled musician, as well as a most erudite prelate—by his will, dated December 10th, 1471, bequeathed his "pair of organs" to St. Patrick's Cathedral, "to be used at the celebration of service in St. Mary's Chapel."* He died on December 21st of same year, and was succeeded by John Walton, in 1472, during whose rule an Act was passed by the Irish Parliament, in 1474, for the regulation of St. Patrick's Cathedral.

Under Thomas Harold, Prior of Christ Church from 1474 to 1489, the Cathedral of Holy Trinity received many valuable bequests, and the excellence of the musical services was fully maintained. Richard White of Swords, by his will dated March 26th, 1476, left 12*d.*

---

* MSS., T.C.D., B. 52—see also *Register of Dublin Wills*, 1457-1483, by Berry.

to 12 choir boys to assist at the singing of a Requiem
for his soul. Similarly, by his will dated June 10th,
1476, Nicholas Delabre bequeathed the sum of four
nobles to a choir boy named Robert Plunket.

On April 15th, 1480, Thomas Bennett, ex-Mayor of
Dublin, granted the lands of Ballymore-Eustace, Co.
Kildare, to the Prior and Convent of Christ Church,
"in order to sustain four choristers, to be instructed,"
and to assist at certain specified Divine offices. However, as Johanna Sowerby, mother of said Thomas, had
a lien on the property, it was not until May 4th, 1484,
that seisin of the lands so assigned was given to Prior
Harold.*

From the *Calendar of Christ Church Deeds* we learn
that on October 8th, 1485, John Estrete, or Street,
Sergeant-at-Law, granted certain lands and other property in trust " to convey to the Prior and Convent of
Christ Church for a Canon to celebrate the Mass of the
Holy Ghost daily in the Chapel of St. Laurence O'Toole,
in the south aisle next the choir "; and, on every Thursday, there was to be a solemn High Mass, with full
choir, for the repose of the soul of said John and his
benefactors, the Earl of Kildare, Sir Rowland Fitz-
Eustace, and others; also directing that the annual
obit should be sung in Whitsun week.†

---

* The musical antiquarian may be interested to know that one of
the earliest inventories of choir music in England is that of St.
Paul's Cathedral, London, in 1445, in which for the first time we
find a separate organ score.

† On July 28th, 1488, the conditions of the various benefactions
given to Christ Church by Sergeant Estrete are recited at length
wherein the Prior undertakes to have the Mass of the Holy Ghost
celebrated daily, "between the quire Mass and High Mass; that
the entire convent and choir shall sing every Thursday a Mass of
the Holy Ghost; that Vespers, Complin, and *De Profundis* be said

In July, 1488, there was a grand celebration in Christ Church Cathedral, when general absolution was given to all those who had aided in Lambert Simnel's rebellion; and there was " joyful music on the viols and the organs," after which an oath of allegiance was signed by the Archbishop of Dublin, the Bishops of Meath and Kildare, and many others.*

David Winchester, who had been elected Prior of Christ Church on March 5th, 1489, was evidently determined to have the music a special feature of the services, and so, on August 28th, 1493, he founded a Professorship of Music in connection with the Cathedral. By the terms of the foundation, " the oblations offered to the relic of the Holy Staff of Jesus within the said church," with various rents of lands in Dublin and Ardee, were allocated to establish a music school. The " music master " was bound to teach four choristers and four probationers ; and these boys were to assist at " daily Mass of the Blessed Virgin Mary, and the Mass and Antiphons of Jesus every Friday in Lent, and at all other times when required." In addition to being instructed in music, the four choristers were provided with " meat and drink," and were clothed at the expense of the convent.

As an interesting specimen of the duties required of a church organist and choirmaster at this period, I cannot do better than quote the following Indenture,

every Sunday and Holyday for said persons; that, when dead, the souls of the various persons shall be prayed for, the *obit* of John, the founder, being kept on the Thursday and Friday of Whitsun week, the *dirge* being said and the parties treated as founders."

* At this date the compass of the organ was from B natural to *f*", two octaves and four notes, whilst the pedal keyboard was from A to *a*". (*Story of the Organ*, p. 53).

dated December 11th, 1502, which is among the Harleian manuscripts. This Indenture was made at Rushen Abbey, Isle of Man, on said date, between an Anglo-Irish musician, John Darcy, and William Parke, whereby John Darcy agreed, for certain considerations, to live in Rushen Abbey for six years, and to teach said William Parke "to sing prick song discant of all manner measures, and to sing upon a prick song faubourdon to tunes of every measure, and to set a song of three parts, four or five substantially, and also to play upon the organs, and any manner plain song or pricked song in two or three parts, and *to make plain and shew him the secrets and method of teaching and instruction of every of the premises in the best manner.*" Apparently, John Darcy was engaged for the term of six years in order to teach William Parke, a Cistercian monk, the profession of " clerk of the organs."

Among the manuscripts now housed in Trinity College, Dublin, there are Psalters, Antiphonaries, and Breviaries of the fifteenth century—catalogued respectively as Nos. 69, 77, 82, 86, 95, 101, 102, and 109 in Dr. Abbott's Catalogue—but, of all these, the most interesting from a musical standpoint is No. 82, being the *Kilcormick Missal*, with a four-lined stave notation —written by a worthy Irish scribe, Brother Dermot O'Flanagan, a Carmelite Friar of Loughrea, and finished on March 3rd, 1458. It was written for the Carmelite Friary of Kilcormick, or Frankford, King's County, at the request of the Prior, Father Edward O'Higgins. As is usual in pre-Reformation Missals, there are thirteen sequences (of course the number varied), and there is also a valuable Kalendar, containing obits of benefactors, etc. A charming sequence, "Mellis stilla," is given for the feast of the Immaculate Conception. The Mass of St. Patrick, too, has a very fine Sequence, and there is a fragment of the Sequence of St. Brigid.

Richard III. and Henry VII. were generous patrons of music and musicians, and, naturally, their Deputies in Ireland took the cue accordingly. In the privy purse expenses of Henry VII. we find that, in 1490, Arnold Jeffrey, "orgon pleyer," received his quarterly salary of *ten shillings.** Henry Abingdon, Mus. Bac., "Master of the Song," had a yearly salary of forty marks, as had also his successor, Gilbert Bannister, in 1480. However, the earliest record in Ireland of a salaried organist is that of William Herbit, who, in 1506, was appointed "pulsator organorum"—or organist—of St. Patrick's Cathedral, Dublin, with the munificent (?) stipend of £3 6s. 8d. a year.† It was, in truth, no misnomer for the organist of the fifteenth century to be called a "pulsator" or smiter of the organs, because the keys were both large and stiff, and could only be played on with the clenched fist.

Maurice Fitzgerald, Archbishop of Cashel, was not unmindful of the interests of church music in his diocese, and the fourth canon of a Synod which he held, in 1512, has reference to the cultivation of psalmody by the clergy. The Statutes of the Synod were inserted in the *Black Book of Lismore*, compiled by John Russell, Economist of Lismore Cathedral, under

---

* In the 31st of Henry VI. (1452) an "orgon pleyer," or organist, who, however was only employed for the *greater* feasts, was given a fee of 3s. 4d. for each service.

† Herbit was succeeded as Organist of St. Patrick's by William Browne.

the direction of Thomas Purcell, Bishop of Waterford and Lismore.

Archbishop Fitzsimon died May 14th, 1511, and was succeeded by William Rokeby, who held a provincial Synod in Christ Church Cathedral, on September 21st, 1512. In September, 1513, the body of Gerald, eighth Earl of Kildare, was interred with all religious and musical solemnity in the Kildare chapel of Christ Church; and, on January 16th, 1518, died Thomas Fitch, Sub-Prior, who wrote many important works, notably the *White Book of Christ Church.*

In 1518, Archbishop Rokeby held a Synod (the canons of which are extant in the *Red Book of Ossory,* published by Spelman), and many useful regulations were made, including some in reference to ritual and liturgical chant.* In the same year he confirmed the Statutes of the Collegiate Church of Maynooth, and he subsequently united the Prebend of Maynooth to the Wardenship of the College, and the Vicarage to the Sub-Wardenship.

A sidelight on the "music-makings" that were wont to be held in the greater monasteries on the double-feasts is to be found entered on the Patent Rolls. From a deposition made by Sir John Plunket (Chief Justice of the King's Bench) it appears that in 1528, on a certain festival there was a musical at-home at St. Thomas's Abbey, Dublin, in the chamber of John Brant, Abbot of St. Thomas's, "on which occasion Chancellor Fitzsimon, of St. Patrick's, with his strollers, sang ballads."†

---

* *Tin* chalices were strictly ordered to be discontinued; and, "the playing of football by clergymen was forbidden under a penalty of 3*s.* 4*d.* to the Ordinary, and 3*s.* 4*d.* to the repair of the parish church."

† *Cal. Rot. Pat. Depos.*, Feb. 7th, 1578.

William Hassard, Prior of Christ Church, resigned in January, 1537, and on July 4th, 1537, William Power, Archdeacon of Dublin, in pursuance of a mandate from George Browne, schismatic Archbishop of Dublin, installed Robert Penswick, *alias* Castell, " late canon of the monastery of Lanthony," as Prior of Christ Church —Richard Ball continuing as Sub-Prior. Geoffrey Fishe, Dean of St. Patrick's, died in January, 1538, and his successor was " the scoundrel Basnet," of whom Dean Swift wrote so savagely. This brings us to the period known as the " Reformation."

CHAPTER XV.

CHURCH MUSIC—1538 TO 1598.

By a Royal Commission dated April 7th, 1538, a clean sweep was ordered to be made of the Irish monasteries, and pensions were promised to those religious who surrendered. Lord Leonard Grey, Lord Deputy of Ireland, wrote a very urgent letter, on May 21st, 1539, to Thomas Cromwell, Vicar-General to Henry VIII., pointing out that six of the larger monasteries ought to be allowed "to stand and continue, changing their habit and rule into such sort as the King's grace shall will them," giving as a reason that not only were these houses ever accustomed to be utilised as lodgings for the Council and officers of State, but were excellent schools for "young men and children, both gentlemen's children and others, both of mankind and womankind, to be brought up in virtue and in the English tongue and behaviour, to the great charge of the said houses." *

As an evidence of the use of organs, even in the smaller religious houses, it is merely necessary to quote a State Paper dated July 26th, 1538, in which Lord Leonard Grey mentions that he had carried off a "pair of organs" from the Augustinian Priory of Killeigh, King's County, and had presented the instrument to the Collegiate Church of Maynooth. Moore, in his *History of Ireland*, gives the date as 1537, whilst

* *State Papers*, vol. viii., 1539.

Renehan, quoting from Moore, places the event as occurring in 1539.

Among the pensions given to the monks of the Abbey of St. Thomas, Dublin, for which a warrant was issued on September 10th, 1539, there was an annuity of £5 to Patrick Clinch, "clerk of the organs," or organist of said abbey.

Evidently, the suggestion of Lord Deputy Grey resulted in the preservation of Christ Church Cathedral, but as a religious community it was dissolved, and, by warrant of December 12th, 1539, the Prior and Canons of Holy Trinity were transformed into secular clergy, henceforth to be known as the Dean and Chapter of Christ Church—Robert Penswick, *alias* Castell, Prior, and Richard Ball, Sub-Prior, becoming *Dean* and *Precentor* respectively, whilst Walter White, Seneschal and Precentor, developed into *Chancellor* and Vicar-Choral, and John Moss, Sub-Precentor [Succentor] and Sacristan, into *Treasurer* and Vicar-Choral of the new foundation.*

Let not the reader, however suppose that the change of name and dress in the least affected the ancient Roman Rite according to the Use of Sarum. Neither the Ritual nor the musical services were in aught altered, and the dignitaries, like those of St. Patrick's, were bound to reside in the church. In the royal warrant, it was expressly stipulated " that, saving the Dean, one of the dignitaries shall celebrate second Mass daily, and the Mass of the Blessed Virgin, and High Mass on festivals proper to the same "; and, further, " that eight regular Canons and four choristers shall be known as the Vicars-Choral, £53 13s. 4d. being yearly

* *Calendar of Christ Church Deeds*, No. 431.

assigned for the Vicars, and £6 13s. 4d. for the choristers," that is, about £600 a year of our money. John Curragh, the first of the Vicars-Choral was named Sub-Dean, with a place and voice in the Chapter; John Kerdiffe,the second Vicar-Choral, was named Succentor, with the like privileges of Sub-Dean, "*whose office it shall be to instruct the choristers*"; Christopher Rathe, Chancellor, was to be Minor Canon, and, as a Vicar-Choral, was bound "*to correct the Latin of the choir books*"; and Oliver Grant, Treasurer, was made Minor Canon and Vicar-Choral. Finally, it was ordered that "*a clerk learned in music and organ playing shall teach the boys, perform at Mass, and have the office of beadle, with a stipend of £6 13s. 4d.*"; also, "a sacristan and a third clerk be appointed to ring the bells, etc.; and that a syndic steward or proctor be elected to manage the affairs of church and chapter." *

The musical reader, will, doubtless, note that the first recognised cathedral organist of Christ Church (no longer to be known as the Priory of the Holy Trinity) was bound to act as beadle, which office was likely performed by deputy, and his salary was equivalent to about £70 a year, not including perquisites. In June, 1540, the letters patent of Henry VIII. confirming the "new foundation" were made out, in which appear the additional names of William Owen and Nicholas Owgan, completing the number of eight secular Canons. It was also enacted that William Power, Archdeacon of Dublin, and his successors, "should have a stall in the choir and participate in the acts of the Chapter." However, it was only on July 11th, 1542, that all the formalities

* *Calendar of Christ Church Deeds* (20th Report D.K.I.), 1888.

were complied with, in favour of the Dean and Chapter of Christ Church.*

A very circumstantial account roll of the economy rents of the "Cathedral Church of the Blessed Trinity," in 1542, was furnished by the Rev. John Moss, Treasurer and Proctor, and is printed in Sir John Gilbert's *History of the City of Dublin*, copied from the *Novum Registrum*. Among the receipts entered from the Church, we find "the Knells," "the Month's Mind of Bea," the anniversary offices for the dead, " the Funerals, the Obligations, and the *Compos*." To the antiquarian, the payments are of exceptional interest, *e.g.*, the sum of 4*d.* is set forth for "a quire of paper," "rushes to Our Lady Chapel, 2*d.*"; " thirteen dozen tallow candles, 13*s.*"; " two chalice cloths and making, 10*d.*"; "*washing the choristers' surplices, 2 towels and 2 rochets, 6d.*"; " 5 girdles for albs, 4*d.*"; " a dozen of Christs, 2*s.*"; " 7 pair of gloves for the ringers, 1*s.* 9*d.*"; " *a, quire of paper for songs, 6d.*," etc., not forgetting the item : " To Sir John Moss for his pains, 40*s.*"

In the autumn of 1543, Thomas Lockwood, erstwhile Archdeacon of Meath (a see which, strange to say, never had a Dean, Cathedral, or Chapter), was appointed Dean of Christ Church, the other dignitaries mentioned above remaining unchanged, with John Kelly as Sexton.

* The Priory of the Holy Trinity was not the only establishment that was converted from its original foundation at this epoch, and on June 28th, 1543, the Cistercian Abbey of Newry was incorporated by royal charter as a secular collegiate church, as " the Warden and Vicars-Choral of the College of the Blessed Virgin and St. Patrick of Newry," John Prout, Abbot, to be first Warden. This Wardenship collapsed in 1549, when ex-Abbot Prout was given a pension of £15. Again, after the dissolution of the Collegiate Church of Maynooth, we find a lease of the College House granted to John Kelly, *Cook*, on April 20th, 1551.

Another important, albeit minor, personage connected with the Cathedral is mentioned in deeds of this period, namely, Thomas Grace of Dublin, barber, who was given certain lands on condition of " shaving, and trimming the Dean, Chapter, and Vicars-Choral when required, to come once a week for the purpose of shaving and, should some of the brethren be absent on the shaving day, to come when sent for, and also *to poll and round the choristers.*"

On March 16th, 1546, the Dean and Chapter granted to Robert Hayward, of Dublin, " singing man," an annual stipend, for life, of £6 13s. 4d., twelve pecks of wheat, and eight pecks of malt, " payable at the feasts of the Nativity, Easter, Nativity of St. John the Baptist, and Michaelmas; a livery coat, and a cartload of wood at Christmas, and the chamber [the monastic scriptorium] by the east of the churchyard; and the Vicars-Choral grant him four pecks of malt, in equal portions, at said feasts, his daily *finding*, table and board, sitting and taking same with them."

From the above *précis* of the emoluments and per-quisites of Mr. Robert Hayward, it will be seen that his was a very good position, and he was " empowered to distrain the lands of the Dean and Chapter in Dublin county and city, for his salary." His status as a " professional gentleman " was fully recognised, as appears from the proviso that he had daily table and board in the common hall of the reverend Vicars-Choral; whilst, at the " festive season," there was no danger of his running short of wood for the Yule log, not forgetting the " peck of malt," which was not improbably " brewed." In addition, the " livery coat," which, we may presume, was a splendid specimen of sartorial art, must have added to the dignity of his presence on all occasions. Surely, a musician to be envied !

But the reader may possibly be desirous of learning what were the duties of this first "professional" organist of Christ Church Cathedral. They are explicitly set forth in the original document, of which the following is a *résumé* :—

The said Robert Hayward was bound " to play the organ, to keep Our Lady's Mass and Anthem daily, Jesus' Mass every Friday, according to the custom of St. Patrick's, and Matins when the organs play on the eight principal feasts, as well as on a greater feast day, or Major Double, *grantors finding an organ blower.*" Moreover, he was to supply, at the expense of the Cathedral, " suitable church music," and " to behave humbly and well " to the Dean and Chapter. As soon as he was put in possession of his residence, he was " to instruct the choristers in *prick song and discant to four minims,* and to play at Our Lady's Mass." In regard to the choristers, it was the office of the Organist " to present them to the Precentor to be admitted, and they were found in all requisites *during the time of their child's voices.*"

This deed was signed by Thomas Lockwood, Dean ; Richard Ball, Precentor ; Walter White, Chancellor ; John Moss, Treasurer ; John Curragh, John Kerdiff, and Christopher Rathe, Prebendaries ; and William Lynch, William Owen, Robert Lloyd, and John Dillon, Vicars-Choral, and John Dorning.*

* *Calendar of Christ Church Deeds*—No. 1201.

Between the years 1539 and 1545 the Irish monasteries and nunneries were dissolved, and the church furniture, including many valuable organs, were sold "for a song." Some of the prices given for precious relics were only a few shillings. On November 8th, 1546, Henry VIII. issued a commission to sequestrate the property of St. Patrick's Cathedral, with a view of dissolving the metropolitan dignity of said church, and having Christ Church as the State Cathedral of Dublin, which surrender was formally made in the following January.

We learn from one of the Christ Church deeds that the English monarch "died on Thursdaie the xxviiith of January," 1547.

Under the boy king, Edward VI., St. Patrick's Cathedral was formally suppressed, and, on April 25th, 1547, a pension of 200 marks sterling was assigned to "Sir" Edward Basnet, the Dean, followed, some months later, by pensions of £60 each to Chancellor Allen and Precentor Humphrey, and £40 to Archdeacon Power. The silver, jewels, and ornaments, were conveyed to the Dean and Chapter of Christ Church.

By King's letter, dated Westminster, March 24th 1547, the residence of the Vicars-Choral of St. Patrick's was assigned for a Grammar School, with Matthew Talbot as schoolmaster, at a salary of £20, and William Talbot as Usher, at a salary of £10 a year; but it is certain that no such school was established for years afterwards. In fact, it was only on October 28th, 1552, that the residence of the Vicars-Choral in St. Patrick's Close was given over for the purpose of a School.

By King's letter of March 24th, 1547, pensions of ten

marks each annually were assigned to Christopher Rath,
John Herman, Nicholas Dardis, William Walshe, Richard
Betagh, and John Claregenete, priests, "for performing
Divine Service in Christ Church Cathedral"; and pen
sions of four marks a year were given to John Golding
and Leonard Fitzsimon, choir boys, as two additional
choristers.

During the years 1548 and 1549 strenuous efforts
were made to propagate the reformed doctrines in Ireland, but all to no purpose. Even the year 1550 passed
by without any development of the schism, and the
Roman Ritual continued to be used throughout the
country.

Easter Sunday of the year 1551 is memorable in the
annals of Christ Church, as, on that day, the "reformed"
liturgy of Edward VI. was used for the first time, under
the auspices of Archbishop Browne, who had been
accused of "gluttony and drunkenness," and called a
"brockish swine," from whom "all virtue and honesty
were almost vanished." The learned Archbishop of
Armagh, George Dowdall, openly repudiated the innovation of an English liturgy, and boldly proclaimed
that "henceforth any illiterate layman would have the
power to say Mass."*

To stimulate their loyalty Patrick Clinch and Robert
Hayward, organists, were given valuable leases early
in 1552. However, the English services do not seem
to have been received favourably, and, as yet, only the
Litany and the Book of Common Prayer were set to

---

* In 1551, the "Book of Common Prayer" was printed in
Dublin, by Humphrey Powell "in the great toure by the Crane"—
being the first work printed in Ireland. Only two copies of this
book are known to exist, of which one is in Trinity College, Dublin.

music. The Sarum Rite was in full swing, and the figured Masses of Taverner, Aston, and Fairfax were in use. Neither the first nor second edition of Sternhold and Hopkins—issued in 1549—nor the Supplement, of 1550, contains music.

With the death of Edward VI., on July 6th, 1553, ended the brief reign of the English liturgy, and almost immediately, on the accession of Queen Mary, Dean Lockwood, of Christ Church, was quite assiduous in destroying any evidences of the "reformed" tenets. On March 25th, 1555, St. Patrick's Cathedral was restored as a metropolitan church, with Bishop Leverous, of Kildare, as Dean, and William Browne,*as Organist. At the Provincial Synod held by Archbishop Curwen, of Dublin, regulations were made for restoration of the ancient creed, in which year a Jubilee was proclaimed.

On May 20th, 1555, Philip and Mary confirmed the grant of Edward VI. in regard to the increased number of priests and choristers of Christ Church—the six additional priests receiving ten marks each, and the two "chorister boys" four marks each—whose nomination was vested in the Dean and Chapter. Thomas Radcliffe, Viscount FitzWalter, took the oath of office as Lord Deputy during Whitsun week of the year 1556, in St. Patrick's Cathedral, according to the old Catholic ceremonial; and Parliament assembled on June 1st, by the acts of which the Roman Catholic religion and ritual were formally restored, heresy was ordered to be suppressed, and the "first fruits" were again given to the Church. The principal officials of Christ Church at this date were:—Thomas Lockwood, Dean; Christopher

*Browne was organist of St. Patrick's Cathedral from 1555 to 1559.

Rathe, Precentor; John Herman, Chancellor; John Kerdiff, Treasurer; Christopher More, Robert Lloyd, and Thomas More, Prebendaries ; and Robert Hayward, Organist.

Almost the last official document of Queen Mary's short reign is a deed, dated April 27th, 1558, in which there is a release by Thomas Leverous, Dean, and the Chapter of St. Patrick's, of the " goods, chattels, *musical instruments*, etc.," belonging to said Cathedral, and which had been in the possession of the Dean and Chapter of Christ Church.*   The lands of the various abbeys and monastic establishments were permitted to remain in the hands of lay impropriators, except the Priory of St. John of Jerusalem, which was confirmed to the Hospitallers, and of which Sir Oswald Massingberd was appointed Prior.

Primate Dowdall died in August, 1558, and with him expired the project of completely restoring the Catholic religion in Ireland, and of re-integrating the 380 dissolved religious houses, the revenues of which amounted to £35,000 yearly.   The intended restoration of Dublin University also came to nothing.   Three months later Queen Mary departed this life, and Queen Elizabeth was crowned, according to the accustomed Catholic ritual, on the 25th of January, 1559, after which the mask of fidelity to Rome was thrown off.

---

* On August 30th, 1559, when Thomas, Lord Sussex, was sworn Lord Deputy in Christ Church, the Prebendaries, Vicars, Choral, and Organist absented themselves.   We read that the Rev. Nicholas Dardis "*recited* the Litany in the *English* Language, after which the Deputy took the oath, and the *Te Deum* was sung in the same language *to the sound of trumpets*."   From the Fiants of Elizabeth we learn that Christopher Rathe (precentor), John Herman (chancellor), and John Cardiff (treasurer) refused the oath of supremacy.

In Reeves' great work on the *Culdees* the following entry occurs :—" A.D. 1574, September 26th, died Nicholas MacGillamurry, late Master of the Works, and Culdee of the metropolitan church of Armagh ; *he was a blameless priest, and a great proficient in the art of music.*"

It is certain that the Roman Catholic ritual was observed in Armagh till 1598, as Ussher admits.

CHAPTER XVI.

Anglo-Irish Music in the Sixteenth Century.

In the first half of the sixteenth century there is very little to chronicle, save what has already been quoted in the preceding chapter in connection with sacred music. What we would now call " scientific music " had made very little headway in Ireland until the reign of Queen Mary, when di Lassus visited England.

Between the years 1505 and 1535 there are evidences of clavichords, harpischords, and spinets or virginals, having been introduced into Ireland. The name " Virginals " was given to the Spinet as being the favourite instruments for ladies or " virgins," and Henry VIII. is said to have been a good performer on the Virginals.

Music was regarded as an important accessory to the Mystery or Morality plays, and, in 1509, there is a record quoted by Sir John Gilbert in reference to Dublin. The historian of the city of Dublin tells us that, in the year 1509, " a sum of 3s. 1d. is charged for Thomas Mayo acting with seven lights at Christmas and Candlemas, and 4s. 7d. for the Players with the great and the small Angel and the Dragon, at Whitsun-tide."

From the opening years of the sixteenth century it was customary for the several Corporate guilds of the city of Dublin to invite the Chief Governor to a play at St. George's Chapel, on the anniversaries of their patron saints. Stanihurst, writing in 1584, thus laments the fate of St. George's Church in South Great George's

Street:—"This chappell hath beene of late razed, and the stones thereof, by consent of the assemblie, turned to a common oven, converting the ancient monument of a doutie, adventurous, and holie knight to the cole-rake sweeping of a pufloafe baker." *

In 1528, during the Christmas holidays, plays were acted every day on College Green, before Piers Butler, Earl of Ossory, Lord Justice of Ireland, wherein the tailors acted the part of *Adam and Eve*; the shoemakers represented the story of *Crispin and Crispianus*; the vintners acted *Bacchus* and his story; the carpenters that of *Joseph and Mary*; the story of *Vulcan* was represented by the smiths; and the comedy of *Ceres*, the goddess of corn by the bakers. † An entry in the chain-book of Dublin Corporation supplies the information that the music consisted of four trumpets.

Sir James Ware, writing of the rejoicings got up by the Palesmen in Dublin after the proclamation of King Henry VIII. as King of Ireland, in June, 1541, enumerates *comedies* as having been performed on that occasion. However, it is more than probable that the so-called comedies were merely the morality plays given, as customary, during the octave of the Feast of Corpus Christi, as said Parliament formally opened on the day following the great festival of the Blessed Sacrament—the proclamation formally taking place "on the Sunday within the octave," in St. Patrick's Cathedral.

On Sunday, August 20th, 1552, a performance was given by the schismatic Bishop Bale of Ossory, at the

* Stanihurst's *Description of Ireland* (*Holinshed's Chronicle*). p. 23.
† Robert Ware's MSS., quoted by Walker in his *Essay on the Irish Stage.*

Market Cross of Kilkenny, of a tragedy, "God's Promises in the olde lawe," and a comedy, "St. John Baptiste's Preaching"—both written by Bale himself— "which were *accompanied with organe plainge and songes very aptly*." After each act there was a choral arrangement of the Advent Antiphon *O Sapientia*, to the accompaniment of a positive organ.

In a manuscript in Trinity College, Dublin, it is stated that in August, 1557, after the return of Lord Deputy Sussex from a successful expedition against James MacDonnell, "the *Six Worthies* was played by the city, and the Mayor gave the public a goodly entertainment upon the occasion, found four trumpeters's horses for the solemnity, and gave them twenty shillings in money."

Four years later, namely, in June, 1561, when Lord Sussex was sworn in Lord Lieutenant of Ireland, he was invited to dinner by the then Mayor (Thomas Fitzsimon), at the conclusion of which the play of the *Nine Worthies* was acted. At the evening entertainment the Corporation band discoursed music, "after which the Mayor and his brethren, with the city music, attended the Lord Lieutenant and Council to Thomas' Court, by torchlight." *

Under date of 1566, there is a manuscript "Love Song" (without music however), written by Donal, first Earl of Clancarty. A few years previously, an Anglo-Irish Song was written to the tune of "Greensleeves." In a Morality play by William Bulleyn, in 1564, a minstrel is decribed as "dancing Trenchmore and Heie de

---

* Harris's *History of the City of Dublin*, sub. an. 1561. The Earl of Sussex, writing to the Secretary of State, in October, 1561, quotes a "ditty," then popular, condemning his government, called "The Land of Perdition."

Gie," that is, the Hey of the arms, or, as the Italians call it, *da braccio*, as in the case of the *Viola da Braccio*. Thus, as early as the year 1564, two Irish dances—popular in the pale—anglicised as "Trenchmore" and "Hey," had found their way to England, just as the Irish coᴘᴘ had become known as the Reel. *Trenchmore* is introduced by Fletcher into his *Pilgrim*, and it is referred to by Stanihurst, in 1584, as follows : " And truly they suit a Divine as well as for an ape to frisk *Trenchmore* in a pair of buskins and a doublet." I shall merely add that the music of this dance tune was printed in *Deuteromelia*, in 1609.

In the notes appended to Spenser's *Shepherds Calendar*, by a certain Mr. E. K., in 1579, the Hey is explained as " a country dance or round." The Irish Hey, or Hay, is, therefore, the origin of the English Round or Country Dance. We are the more certain of this, as one of the earliest Rounds known is stated by Sir John Hawkins to be " Sellenger's Round," which Sir Anthony St. Leger saw danced in Ireland, in 1540, and which, on retiring from the Viceroyalty in 1548, he brought back with him to England, where its popularity was so great that it was arranged by the famous master, Dr. William Byrd. *

"Trenchmore" is an Anglicised corruption of *Rinnce Mor* or the *Rinnce Fada*, that is, the Long Dance, whilst the Hey was danced in a circle. Allusion is made to both these Irish dances in *The Complaint of Scotland*, in 1549.

---

* A copy of Byrd's arrangement is in Lady Neville's MS. music book, dated 1590, and it also appears as No. 64 in the Fitzwilliam Virginal Book. See also Chappell, page 69, where the melody is printed.

Nor must we pass over the antiquity of the Irish poƿc or Jig. Strangely enough, many writers, including the late Sir Robert Stewart, only regard the Jig dance as borrowed from the Italians, in the latter half of the seventeenth century. However, there is ample evidence of its existence in Ireland in the middle of the sixteenth century, at least in 1550. Sir Henry Sydney, in a letter to Queen Elizabeth, in 1569, waxes enthusiastic over the dancing of Irish jigs by the Anglo-Irish ladies of Galway, whom he describes as "very beautiful, magnificently dressed, and first-class dancers." Indeed, the Irish Jig is distinctly *sui generis*, but is so named from the *Geige* (or Fiddle) just as in the case of the Hornpipe.

From 1560 to 1580 appeared a class of Anglo-Irish ballads, of which Stanihurst, in 1583, published a good imitation, which he styled : "An Epitaph, entitled Commune Defunctorum, such as our unlettered Rithmours accustomably make upon the death of everie Tom Tyler, as if it were a last for every one his foote, in which the quantities of sillables are not to be heeded." In 1576, a ballad on the death of the unfortunate Walter Devereux, Earl of Essex, in Dublin, was sung to the Irish tune of "Fortune my Foe," under the title of "Welladay, or Essex's Last Good-Night."

I am the more particular in mentioning this "lamentation song" on Essex (who died on September 22nd, 1576), as he was a generous patron of music. From a State Paper we get a fair indication of his musical proclivities, in the account of his expenses as "Lord General of Ulster," in 1574 and 1575. To the "singing men" of Mellifont, then tenanted by Sir Edward Moore, he gave ten shillings ; to the Earl of Ormonde's musicians, twenty shillings; whilst a harper at Sir John Bellew's received three shillings. However, a princely largesse was bestowed on "Crues, my Lord of Ormonde's harper"—namely, forty shillings, equivalent to £35 of our present money. This Anglo-Irish harper is thus praised by Stanihurst, in 1584:—

"In these days lived Cruise, the most remarkable harper within the memory of man. He carefully avoids that jarring sound which arises from unstretched and untuned strings; and, moreover, by a certain method of tuning and modulating he preserves an exquisite concord, which has a surprising effect upon the ears of his auditors, such that one would regard him rather as the only, than the greatest harper." *

But a more famous lamentation song was written in June, 1584, on the martyrdom of Archbishop O'Hurley of Cashel, dealing in a special manner with the perfidy of Thomas Fleming, Baron of Slane, who had arrested the saintly prelate. It was entitled: *Slane's Treason; or, the Fall of the Baron of Slane*, set to music by Richard Cruise, the distinguished harper above-mentioned.†

We now come to an epoch-making event in the musical world, namely, the publication of the first printed book on musical theory in English, by an Anglo-Irishman, William Bathe, in 1584. Ireland has every reason to be proud of the fact that the first published theory book on music in the English language was due to a young Dublin man, who was then studying at Oxford University. Its title was as follows :—

"A brief Introduction to the art of Music, wherein

*Stanihurst's *De Rebus in Hibernia Gestis*. 4 Books. Antwerp, 1584. 4to.
† O'Sullivan's *Catholic History* (Chap. xix.). published, in 1621 at Lisbon.

are set down exact and easy rules for such as seek but to know the truth, with arguments and their solutions for such also as wish to know the reason of the truth. Which rules be means whereby any of his own industry may shortly, easily, and regularly attain to all such things as to this art do belong. To which otherwise any can hardly attain without tedious, difficult practice, by means of the irregular order now in teaching, lately set forth by William Bathe, student at Oxenford. Imprinted at London by Abel Jeffes, dwelling in Sermon Lane near Paule's Chain, anno 1584."

This extremely rare work, in small oblong quarto, black letter, was dedicated by Bathe to his grand-uncle, Gerald FitzGerald, Earl of Kildare. However, the author was not satisfied with this treatise, and so he thoroughly revised it, such that it may be regarded as almost a new book, which, however, was not published till the year 1600, entitled:—

" A brief Introduction to the Skill of Song, concerning the practice, set forth by William Bathe, gentleman. In which work is set downe ten sundry wayes of two parts in one upon the plain song. Also, a table, newly added, of the comparisons of cleffs, how one followeth another for the naming of notes, with other necessarie examples to further the learner. London : Printed by Thomas Este, 1600." *

The following extract from the latter work, written in 1587, will be of interest:—

" Wherefore, seeing sufficiently others to labour and travail in other sciences, I thought good to bestow my labour on music, seeing that pains might so much prevail, as by the fruit of my labour may plainly appear.

" I took the matter in hand upon this occasion, though it were far distant from my profession, being

* There are copies of this book in the British Museum, the Bodleian Library, and Sion College. The British Museum copy was presented to that library by Sir John Hawkins, May 30th, 1778.

desired by a gentleman to instruct him in song. I gave him such rules as my master gave me; yet could I give him no song so plain, wherein there chanced not some one thing or other to which none of those rules could directly lead him. . . . .

"In a month, or less, I instructed a child about the age of eight years to sing a good number of songs, difficult, crabbed songs to sing at the first sight, to be so indifferent for all parts, alterations, cleves, flats, and sharps, that he could sing a part of that kind of which he had never learnt any song; which child for strangeness was brought before the Lord Deputy of Ireland to be heard sing, for there was none of his age, though he were longer at it, nor any of his time, though he were elder, known before these rules to sing exactly. There was another, who had before often handled instruments, but never practised to sing (for he could not name one note), who, hearing of these rules, obtained in a short time such profit by them that he could sing a difficult song of himself without any instruction.

"There was another, who, by dodging at it, harkening to it, and harping upon it, could never be brought to tune sharps aright, who, as soon as he heard these rules set down for the same, could tune them sufficiently well. I have taught divers others by these rules in less than a month what myself, by the old method, obtained not in more than two years. Divers other proofs I might recite which here, as needless, I do omit." *

Briefly, William Bathe, the young Irish student at Oxford, was not only the first to print an English treatise on music, but he actually formulated methods of transposition and sight-reading that may still be studied with profit. Davey, in his *History of English Music,* thus writes of Bathe's *Brief Introduction*: "It is remarkable in its *perception of the octave, instead of the hexachord, as the foundation of the scale, and for its rules*

---

* British Museum copy: a small unpaged octavo of 25 pages, of which six pages have musical notation.

*regarding accidentals. These merits would require fuller
notice in a work on general musical history."* However,
like most other biographers, Davey is in error when he
says that "Bathe subsequently became head of the
Jesuit College at Salamanca, where he died in 1614."

William Bathe was born in Drumcondra Castle, Dublin, on Easter Sunday, 1564, his parents being John
Bathe (appointed Chancellor of the Exchequer in 1579)
and Eleanor Preston, daughter of the 3rd Viscount Gor-
manston, and niece of the Earl of Kildare. He studied
"humanity" in Ireland, and evinced a great taste for
music, but was always of a religious turn of mind. In
1582, he was sent to Oxford, where he studied for four
years, during which, in October, 1584, he was introduced
to Queen Elizabeth by Sir John Perrott, Viceroy of Ireland. His earliest biographer, Fr. Paul Sherlock, S.J.,
tells us that Bathe became a great favourite of the
Queen, "whom he delighted by his wonderful skill in
playing *all kinds of musical instruments*, and amused by
teaching her mnemonics, whilst his many other brilliant
parts won for him universal estimation."

We have the clearest evidence that William Bathe was
a prime favourite with Queen Elizabeth, from several
entries in the State Papers between the years 1587
and 1591 ; and the Lord Deputy of Ireland wrote to
Burghley that this young gentleman of the Pale was
especially known at Court "for his skill in music, and
for *his late device of the new harp which he presented to
Her Majesty."*

His father died at the close of July of the year 1586,
whose successor, Sir Edward Waterhouse, was appointed Chancellor of the Exchequer on October 19th, 1586.

Bathe then returned from Oxford and stayed for some time in Dublin, but again came back to England in the train of his friend, Sir John Perrott, who was recalled in June, 1588. He got livery of his property on September 24th, 1590; but, having made over his inheritance to his brother John, he set sail for Spain, in October, 1591, when he went to Flanders, with a view to entering a religious order.

William Bathe became a Jesuit, at Tournai, on September 21st, 1596, and continued his theological studies at St. Omer's and Padua where he was ordained in 1601. We next find him at Valladolid, and, in 1604, he was made spiritual director of the Irish College at Salamanca. In 1611, he published his *Janua Linguarum* in Latin and Spanish, which went through an endless number of editions, being issued in eleven languages, of which the English version appeared in 1615. At Salamanca he taught church music and liturgy with conspicuous success for ten years, and, in 1614, he was invited to conduct spiritual exercises at the Court of Madrid. Father Bathe died at Madrid, on June 17th, 1614—one of the most learned men of his day.

In the same year (1584) which is memorable for the printing of Bathe's *Brief Introduction* was issued *A Handful of Pleasant Delites*, by Clement Robinson and others, "containing sundrie new sonnets newly devised to the newest tunes." This rare little book has a few Irish tunes, including the familiar "Cailín óg a'ᵴτιυιᵱé me" under the corrupt anglicised form of "Calen o custure me," quoted by Shakespeare in "Henry V." In Playford's *Musical Companion*, printed in 1673, this air is set in four parts, and is expressly headed: "An Irish Tune."

On the feast of Corpus Christi, 1598 (as appears from
a letter written by Father P. Hamill, on July 12th of that
year), Father Henry Fitzsimon, S.J., of Dublin, had a
Solemn High Mass celebrated in the house of a nobleman, "with full orchestra, composed of harps, lutes, and
all kinds of instruments except the organ"—all the
more remarkable as being "the first solemn Mass celebrated, in Dublin, for the last forty years." *

The reader can form a good idea of the "full orchestra" of the year 1598, in Ireland, from the constitution
of Queen Elizabeth's Band of Musick, in 1588 :—16
trumpets, 9 minstrels, 8 viols, 6 sackbuts, lutes, harps,
3 players on the virginals, 2 rebecks, and a bagpipe. It
is specially worthy of notice that nearly all the great
composers and musicians of this period adhered to the
the old faith, e.g., Tallis, Byrd, Bevan, Bolt, Phillips,
Dering, Johnson, Mundy, Heywood, Morris, Norcome,
White, and others.

From 1559 to 1595 the musical services of Christ
Church Cathedral, and St. Patrick's Cathedral, Dublin,
were utterly neglected, and it was not till 1595 that a
salaried lay organist†—John Fermor—was appointed to
the former church, who was succeeded, in 1609, by
Thomas Bateson, Mus.Bac.

Trinity College was opened in 1593, but no degrees
in music were conferred till 1610. As is well known,
the doors of Dublin University (founded on the site of
All Hallows Monastery) were practically closed against
Roman Catholics ; and the College has ever been a

* Life and Letters of Father H. Fitzsimon, S.J., p. 207.
† Rev Walter Kennedy acted as organist from 1592 to 1595, as
appears from the Calendar of Christ Church Deeds.

stronghold of the ascendancy faction in Ireland. In the library are preserved two valuable musical manuscripts dating from the last decade of the sixteenth century, namely, Thomas Dallis's *Lute Book* (*cir.* 1590), and William Ballet's *Lute Book* (1594). The latter MS. contains many Irish airs, such as :—" Fortune my foe," " Peg a Ramsay," " Callino Casturame," " Well-a-day," " Sellenger's Round," " All flowers in broome," " Queen Mary's Dumpe," Dowland's " Lachrymae," " Rogero," etc.

Between 1590 and 1600 modern musical art began to make itself felt in Ireland, and already madrigals, ballets, catches, as also music for the virginals, were beginning to be heard. A new musical era was at hand,

CHAPTER XVII.

SHAKESPEARE AND IRISH MUSIC.

THE subject of Shakespeare's acquaintance with Irish music will possess for many, at least, the merit of novelty. Even to the ripe Shakespearean scholar the many Irish airs alluded to by the Bard of Avon are comparatively unknown, and, therefore, a separate chapter on such a theme may not be unacceptable.

With this object in view, I purpose to adduce some convincing arguments in favour of Shakespeare's knowledge of Irish minstrelsy. Let it be premised that Irish music was much in vogue in England during the sixteenth century, and had favour at Court during the last years of Queen Elizabeth's reign, as is evident from the oft-quoted extract from the Talbot Papers, under date of September 19th, 1602, written by the Earl of Worcester to the Earl of Shrewsbury :—" We are frolic here in Court; much dancing in the Privy Chamber of Country Dances before the Queen's Majesty, who is exceedingly pleased therewith. *Irish tunes are at this time most pleasing.*" Let me also add that Viscount St. Albans, or Francis Bacon (whom many writers believe to have written Shakespeare's plays), says that "no harp hath the sound so melting as the Irish harp."

There are many Irish words used by the great English bard, such as *feere* (far = a man), *geck* (a fool), *cam* (crooked), *cailleach* (an old woman), *sprag, kerne,* gallowglasses, rug-headed; whilst the parallelisms of Puck and Puca, Mab and Meave, Lear and Lir, Malvolio and Melville, are equally well known. And does not Mr. Alfred Nutt admit that Shakespeare's fairy mythology is taken from Celtic fairy tales? He says that Ireland possesses "a romantic literature which, so far as interest and antiquity of record are concerned, surpasses that of Wales, and which is obviously and undoubtedly more archaic in character"; and he adds that Oberon and Puck "are members of a clan of supernatural beings having the same origin as the Tuatha de Danaan wizard hero or princess of Irish romance." But with these matters I am not concerned, and, therefore, must fain content myself with the definite topic of Irish tunes, Irish musical allusions, and such kindred matter to be found in the works of Shakespeare.

There are eleven Irish tunes mentioned under various aliases by the bard of Avon, of which two have been previously identified by Malone, Dr. Petrie, Dr. Sigerson, and others. For the identity of the remaining nine I alone am responsible. Taking the list in order, on each of which I shall say a few words, the eleven airs are :—

1. Callino casturame.
2. Ducdame.
3. Fortune my foe.
4. Peg a Ramsay.
5. Bonny Sweet Robin.
6. Whoop! do me no harm, good man.
7. Well-a-day, or Essex's Last Good-night.
8. The Fading.
9. Light o' Love.
10. Yellow Stockings.
11. Come o'er the bourn, Bessy, to me.

1. As regards "Callino casturame," we learn from Halliwell that a ballad of this name was entered on the books of the Stationers Company in 1581-2, and it was printed in *A Handful of Pleasant Delites* in 1584. It is also found in William Ballet's Lute Book, the manuscript of which is in Trinity College, Dublin, dating from *cir.* 1590. In the Fitzwilliam Virginal Book (incorrectly called Queen Elizabeth's Virginal Book), which dates from between the years 1602-1622, our Irish air appears as "Callino casturame," arranged by William Byrd (called the English Palestrina), who died, as he lived, a good Catholic, on July 4th, 1623. It was subsequently printed by Playford, in 1673, arranged in four parts, and headed "An Irish Tune." The only difficulty is in equating the correct Irish for Shakespeare's phonetic rendering. Boswell's *Malone* gives the name as equivalent to "little girl of my heart for ever and ever." Dr. Petrie, Dr. William Stokes, and Sir Robert Stewart regard "Callino casturame" as an attempt to spell as pronounced "Colleen oge asthore," which is also the view of Dr. Sigerson, with a slight modification. However, the "me" at the end persists in all the readings, and so I should venture to give the correct Irish as Cailín og a' rtuine mé, an old synthetic ending now obsolete, which is concurred in by my friend, Mr. David Comyn, the editor of the first volume of Keating.

2. In the fifth scene of "As You Like It" there is reference to "Ducdame," an invitation calling fools into a circle, and "a verse to this note." Now "Ducdame" is an anglicised form of the Irish invocation: An o-tiocraidh = "Will you come," which is sung twice in the third verse of "Eileen a roon." "Verse

passages" in the sixteenth century meant passages for
solo voices; and here Jacques sings the song in answer
to the preceding song. An almost equally well-known
seventeenth-century Irish song was *An tiocfadh tu a
bhaile liom.* As very properly pointed out by Dr. Sigerson, the real ballad containing this apparently enigmati-
cal name is Eıblín ᴀ ᴘúın, which was then exceedingly
popular in England. Another phrase which occurs in
the same lovely song is the well-known ceᴀᴅ míle
ᴘáılᴄe, or "a hundred thousand welcomes"—and it is
remarkable that Shakespeare makes Agrippa greet
Coriolanus with "a hundred thousand welcomes," a
purely Irish form of salutation. More remarkable still
is the employment of the invocation, "diuca tu"—
"Will you come," in the form of "Ducket" and
"Tucket," by Shakespeare in "Henry V." (Act IV.,
Scene 2). The ordinary explanation equating *tucket*
with the Italian *toccato* is absurd for many reasons.
Shakespeare gives the word as meaning a signal or
call for the trumpets or drums to sound—"Then let
the trumpets sound the tucket sonance." This explanation is borne out by a stage direction in the "Devil's Law
Case," in 1623, when we read: "Two tuckets by several
trumpets," *i.e.*, two trumpet calls; and in an eighteenth-
century ballad we find a soldier complaining bitterly to
his mistress of the cruelty of the tucket sound with its
reiterated burthen of "Will you come, will you come."
The tune of "Eıblín ᴀ ᴘúın" is too well known to
need illustration, but I shall just mention that it was
sung at the Smock Alley Theatre, Dublin, in the Christmas season of 1728, by Mrs. Sterling, in an opera
epilogue to "The Way of the World," and again by

Mrs. Storer, as an interlude, in Shakespeare's tragedy of "Julius Cæsar," at the same theatre, on December 15, 1743. Within twenty-five years of Shakespeare's death we find Joe Harris, an Irish actor, in London, singing Irish songs. In 1666, when "Henry V." was presented, one of the principal attractions was Harris's singing of a song in the Irish language. From Pepys we learn that the beauty of the Irish air, wedded to its original Irish words, completely captivated the audience. He thus writes: "Among other things, Harris, *a man of fine conversation, sang his Irish song, the strangest in itself, and the prettiest sung by him that ever I heard.*"

3. "Fortune my Foe" is an exquisite sixteenth-century Irish melody, alluded to by Shakespeare, the music of which is to be found in William Ballet's *Lute Book*, in 1593; also, in the Fitzwilliam *Virginal Book*, and in William Forster's *Virginal Book*, dated January 31st, 1624, now the property of King Edward VII. As far back as 1565-6 it was licensed as a ballad, and is mentioned in "The Merry Wives of Windsor" (Act II., Scene 3). Chappell says that "Fortune my Foe" was known as the *Hanging Tune*, "from the metrical lamentations of extraordinary criminals being always chanted to it." In February, 1649-50, we read in a contemporary chronicle that the Irish pipers attached to Lord Inchiquin's army drew off from Naas to the march of "Fortune my Foe"; and in 1676 this Irish tune was used by Thomas Duffet, himself an Irishman, for the well known lyric, "Since Coelia's my Foe." The earliest tune to which Duffet's words were set is in Playford's, dated 1676, whereas another air, claimed as *the* "Irish tune," is "King James's March to

Ireland," to be found in the Leyden MS., about the
year 1692-3, also known as "Lochaber no more."
"Fortune my Foe" is an early sixteenth-century air,
whilst the Irish tune to which "Since Coelia's my
Foe" was adapted in 1730, is "Limerick's Lamentation," dating from 1691, and translated by Dermot
O'Conor in 1720.

4. "Peg a Ramsay" is another old sixteenth-century
Irish tune, included in William Ballet's *Lute Book*. It
is called a "dump tune" by Thomas Nash, in 1596, in
"Have with you to Saffron Walden"; whilst in his
"Shepherds' Holiday," in 1598, he alludes to "Roundelays, Irish Hayes, Cogs and Rongs, and Peg a Ramsay."
Shakespeare makes Sir Toby call Malvolio a "Peg a
Ramsay" in "Twelfth Night" (Act II., Scene 3), proving
the popularity of our Irish "dump tune." Some persons
may naturally wonder what was a "dump tune" or a
"dump.' Shakespeare makes mention of merry dumps
and doleful dumps. Chappell says that a dumpe was a
"slow dance," which is incorrect, whilst Mr. Comyn
equates it with "the Irish *duan* or *dan*, a song or
poetical composition of any sort." Neither of these
explanations is satisfactory. The dump was the music
of the old Irish instrument known as the ᴄιοmpᴀn,
a small stringed instrument, akin to the harp, and
which was very popular in England during the fifteenth
and sixteenth centuries; so much so that the English
language was enriched with the names "dump" and
"thump"—the music produced by plucking or striking
the ᴄιοmpᴀn. Shakespeare, in the fourth act of "Romeo
and Juliet," begs the minstrels to cheer him with a
"merry dump" (which would, of course, be absurd

were a dump synonymous with a slow dance), and later on he alludes to "doleful dumps," whilst in the third act of "The Two Gentlemen of Verona" he again mentions a "deploring dump." He refers to dull and heavy dumps in "Much Ado," whilst in "Titus Andronicus" he uses the phrase "dreary dumps." Thomas Ford, in 1606, refers to "pavans, galiards, almains, toies, *jiggs, thumps,* and such like."

Here, perhaps, it is well to explain Thomas Nash's "Roundelays, Irish Hayes, Cogs and Rongs, and Peggie Ramsay." Rounds and Roundelays are Irish terms, the word *lay* being admittedly Celtic. *Irish Hayes* were Irish round dances as distinguished from other forms of dances, the round being the old Irish *corr* or *reel.* In a printed book of 1588 the Irish Hey de gie is illustrated as danced by four men, with bare arms, in imitation of a combat, and the music for it is printed in Playford's *Musick's Handmaid,* in 1678. Shakespeare, in the fifth act of "Love's Labour Lost," written in 1591, says : "Let them dance the hay," whilst in *England's Helicon,* written in 1600, we read : "Shall we go dance the hay." In Martin's *Month's Mind,* written in 1589, there is reference to "Irish Hayes, Jiggs, and Roundelays," and Shakespeare, in the second act of the "Midsummer-Night's Dream," says : "Come now, a roundel and a fairy song." It is almost unnecessary to explain that a "fairy song" is the exact English equivalent of our Irish Ceól-ṗíḋe ; and the roundel was a reel or dance in a circle.

5. "Bonny Sweet Robin" is another Irish tune quoted by Shakespeare, and has been known in Ireland since the sixteenth century.

6. "Whoop! do me no harm, good man." twice referred to in "A Winter's Tale" (Act IV., Scene 3), is better known in Ireland as "Paddy Whack," and adapted by Tom Moore to "While History's Muse."

7. "Welladay; or Essex's last Good-night," is of Irish origin, dating from the early part of the sixteenth century. New words were set to it in 1576, on the death of the unfortunate Walter Devereux, Earl of Essex, in Dublin; and it was also used as a tune for the Anglo-Irish lamentation-song written for Robert, Earl of Essex, Viceroy of Ireland, who was beheaded on Ash Wednesday, 1601. It has all the well-known characteristics of the Irish *caoine*, and was printed by Margaret Allde in 1603.

8. "The Fading," or "With a fading"—mentioned in the fourth act of "A Winter's Tale"—is, even on the testimony of the late Mr. William Chappell (an uncompromising advocate of English music), undoubtedly an Irish dance tune. It is none other than the once-familiar *Rinnce Fada*, which was danced before King James II., when he landed at Kinsale in 1689; a dance which is to this day called "The Faddy," in Cornwall. Of course, all are agreed that the *Rinnce Fada* means the Long Dance, but it has been more generally called the *Contre Dance*—or dance in which the performers are *opposite* each other—a name which is corrupted as "Country" dance. The English Country Dance is merely the Irish *Rinnce Fada*, as is quite evident from the second name given it in the early editions of Playford's *Dancing Master*, between the years 1651 and 1701—wherein we read, "The Long Dance for as many as will"—the best known survival of which is "Sir Roger de Coverley."

Thomas Dineley, who made a tour of Ireland in 1680, says that "the Irish of this day are much addicted to dance after their country fashion, that is, the Long Dance, one after another, of all conditions, master mistress, servants," etc. Another favourite Irish dance mentioned by Shakespeare in the fourth act of "A Winter's Tale" (1611) is the hornpipe, or Uᴘᴘᴀɴ, that is, the corn-pipe of the mediæval Irish. He says: "There is but one Puritan amongst them, and he sings psalms to *hornpipes*."

9. "Light o' Love" is another English annexation from the Emerald Isle.* Shakespeare, in his "Much Ado About Nothing" (Act III., Scene 4), says, "Clap us into 'Light o' love,' that goes without a *burden*; do you sing it and I'll dance it." *Burden* is the same as a drone or drone-bass, generally being a vocal accompanyment of Fa le la, or Hey troly, loly, lo, as quoted by Piers Plowman in 1362, or else the more usual Shakespearean "Hey, nonny, nonny." Strangely enough, the Irish of the sixth and seventh centuries were acquainted with the musical art-form known as the drone-bass; whilst it is a commonplace of musical history that our own John Scotus Erigena is the first writer to allude to the free organum of the fourth, about the middle of the ninth century.

10. "Yellow Stockings" is an undeniably Irish tune. The very name has a reference to the saffron *truis* of the mediæval Irish. Shakespeare introduces it in "Twelfth Night," and the air dates from the sixteenth

* In the "Two Gentlemen of Verona" (Act I., Sc. 2) allusion is made to "the tune of 'Light o' Love.'"

century, being known by the natives as Cuma Liom
"It is indifferent to me," or "I don't care." Playford
printed it as early as 1680, and in 1705, Dean Swift
adapted a nursery song, "Hey my kitten, my kitten,"
to it. Other verses for our Irish tune are "Mad Moll"
(1698) and "The Virgin Queen" (1703); and, finally,
Tom Moore set it to his lyric, "Fairest put on awhile."

11. Shakespeare, in "King Lear" (Act III., Scene 6),
makes Edgar say, "Wantest thou eyes at trial,
madam? Come o'er the bourn, Bessie, to me." This
quaint Irish melody dates from the second half of the
sixteenth century, and was very popular in England.
As regards the play itself, Mr. Sidney Lee says
that it was mainly founded on Holinshed's *Chronicles*,
from our Irish Stanihurst. The air is intensely characteristic.

That Shakespeare was a tolerable musician is almost
self-evident, and, in addition, he had good taste—in
fact he may well be described as a cultured amateur.
We know from his writings that he was acquainted
with the works of Orlando di Lasso. His plays are
invariably heralded by three flourishes on a trumpet by
way of overture, and the orchestra was represented by
a band of fiddlers in an upper balcony, at the ex-
treme back of the stage, and who played music
between the acts. We can have a tolerable idea of the
orchestra of his day from the constitution of Queen
Elizabeth's Band of Music in 1587, as previously
alluded to.

But of all who enjoyed the intimate acquaintance of
Shakespeare, his "very intimate friend "(a man admittedly the greatest lutenist in Europe and a really charming

composer) was an Irishman, John Dowland. In 1599, Richard Barnfield's sonnet, reprinted in Shakespeare's "Passionate Pilgrim," has the following couplet :—

> "Dowland to thee is dear, whose heavenly touch
> Upon the lute doth ravish human sense."

Even Davey, the most recent and most eulogistic historian of English music, is forced to admit that "the grace, tenderness, and frankness of the best Irish character are all present in Dowland's works." Whether as the composer of "Awake, sweet love," "Now, ah now, I need must part," the translator of the *Micrologus* of Ornithoparcus (probably an Irishman also), the author of excellent lessons for the lute and bass viol, Dowland's Lachrimae, the Frog Galliard (which was danced by Queen Elizabeth in her sixty-ninth year), or as an incomparable performer on the lute, Dowland was a marvellous musician. In 1598, he became lutenist to Christian, King of Denmark, at the then unprecedented salary of 500 thalers a year (getting an extra 600 as a douceur in 1600), but returned to England in 1605. Luca Marenzio, the great madrigal composer, wrote to Dowland from Rome on July 13th, 1595. It is not at all unlikely that Shakespeare was indebted for many details of his "Hamlet" to his friend Dowland, whose residence as Court lutenist in that country gave him peculiar advantages, more than could be derived from books. Mr. Sidney Lee says that Shakespeare owed all his information with regard to the Continent and Ireland to the verbal reports of travelled friends or to books, the contents of which he had a rare power of assimilating. It is only to my present purpose to add that Dowland died January 27th, 1626, surviving his "intrinsic friend," Shakespeare, by ten years.

There are some other Irish musical allusions in Shakespeare, like "Jig off a tune," in "Love's Labour's Lost," and "All my merry jigs are quite forgot," in the "Passionate Pilgrim,"—jig, however, in this instance, meaning any metrical composition, generally applied to second-rate drama, whence Shakespeare adverts to "garlic jigs,"—which Mr. Sidney Lee explains as "indifferent entertainments interspersed with dances in the smaller play-houses." To jig off a tune is a common phrase to this day—meaning to lilt or "la la" it, as is still done in some country places. From this fact we are able to draw the conclusion that jig and lilt were originally forms of the geige and the lilt-pipe— whence we read in Chaucer of a lilt-pipe and a corn-pipe, the name of the instrument being transferred to the dance tune, even as the name *choir*, meaning persons who sang in the choir portion of a church, was evolved from the *place* where the singers were. This question naturally brings into notice another Shakespearean allusion to the music of the people, or the old folk tunes. The great Bard of Avon has one famous passage describing the effect of old songs of occupation, those sung by spinners, weavers, knitters, etc.

I have stated that Shakespeare was indebted for most of his information regarding Ireland to Stanihurst and Blessed Edmund Campion, S.J., in Holinshed's *Chronicles*; also, to Captain Barnaby Rich, who spent forty years in Ireland, and to Sir John Harrington, John Dowland, and Edmund Spenser. Indeed, as regards Irish music, Dowland and Spenser would appear to

be Shakespeare's chief sources of information.   It is
a singular circumstance that in the fiant of Elizabeth
apportioning Kilcolman Castle and lands to Spenser,
on October 26th, 1590, he was to hold it for ever in
fee farm by the name of "Hap-Hazard." More singular
still, notwithstanding the harsh things which the author
of the *Faerie Queen* has left on record regarding Ireland,
he himself succumbed to the charms of a fair daughter
of Erin named Elizabeth Boyle, of Youghal, whom he
wedded, in June, 1594.

Shakespeare, in "Richard III.," alludes to Irish
bards, one of whom, he says, had told him "that
he would not live long after seeing Richmond."
Again, Rosalind in "As You Like It" (Act III., Scene
2), says: "I was never so be-rhimed that I can
remember since Pythagoras's time, when I was an Irish
rat"—alluding to the doctrine of the transmigration of
souls.   Many writers of Shakespeare's day allude to the
power of Irish bards of being able to rhyme men as well
as rats to death.   Senchan Torpest, chief poet of Ireland
in the seventh century, is said to have uttered a *aer*
(satire) on rats which killed ten of them on the spot.

Thus, Shakespeare's acquaintance with Irish music is
much greater than has been previously pointed out by
any of his commentators.

CHAPTER XVIII.

IRISH MUSIC IN THE SEVENTEENTH CENTURY.
1601-1650.

POLITICALLY, no more gloomy outlook could be imagined of any country than the state of Ireland during the last years of Queen Elizabeth's rule. The capitulation of Kinsale was signed on January 13th, 1602, and Dunboy Castle was taken on June 18th. A deliberately planned famine ensued. Red Hugh O'Donnell died on September 10th; Rory O'Donnell submitted on November 14th: and the great O'Neill, Earl of Tyrone, agreed to accept the terms offered by Mountjoy on March 24th, 1603.

Numerous pardons to Irish minstrels appear in State documents for the years 1601 and 1602, and their names —though little more is known of most of them—are a distinctly valuable addition to our musical history, the majority being unknown to Walker, Hardiman, Bunting or Petrie.

On March 18th, 1601, pardon was given to John O'Lynch, *harper*, and to Murtagh MacCoyne, of Kilmallock, *piper*; on March 28th, to Art MacGillegrome MacDonnell and Geoffrey M'Glade, *harpers*; also, to Tadhg O'Dermody, *harp-maker*, County Kilkenny, whose son Donal made the famous Fitzgerald (Dalway) harp in 1621—remarkable as being the oldest dated Irish harp now in existence. Two days later a piper called Owen MacHugh *na bralie* was pardoned.

On April 11th, 1601, there is chronicled a pardon to

Nicholas *dall*, of Ratoo, County Kerry, *harper*. This is none other than the famous Nicholas *dall* Pierce, the blind harper of Ratoo, in whose praise there were three different odes written, as O'Curry mentions. O'Curry however, merely conjectured that he lived about the year 1625, but the State pardon of April, 1601, is a convincing proof that Nicholas *dall* must have exercised his art at the very commencement of the seventeenth century.

John *intlea*, a wandering piper from County Cork, was pardoned on April 25th. On May 5th, Cosney MacClancy, of Cloonanna, County Limerick, *piper*, was received into favour. Two days later a similar clemency was extended to Dermot O'Sgingin, of Donore, County Westmeath, *harper*, and to Donogh O'Phelan, of same, *rhymer*.

Pardon was granted to David MacDonal O'Rahilly, of Schull, Co. Cork, *rhymer*, on May 14th—the ancestor of the famous Egan O'Rahilly, who flourished a century later. On May 15th, four pipers from County Wexford were received into favour, namely, Bryan MacGillachrist, Fergus O'Farrell, Donal MacFergus O'Farrell, and Patrick *oge* O'Farrell—the last mentioned surviving till the period of the Confederation.

On May 28th, 1601, Donal MacConmee, of County Westmeath, *harper*, was taken into favour on giving due security, and on the following day pardons were granted to Daniel O'Cullinane, and Conor O'Cullinane, of Burren, County Cork, *pipers*. On May 30th, Richard Forstall, of Cloughnageragh (Wilton), County Wexford, *harper*, was pardoned, as was also Richard *buidhe* MacJames, of County Wexford, *piper*. Two days later,

Turlogh Piper, of Tubberdower, *piper*, was pardoned, and, on June 10th, two other pipers, Owen and Dermot O'Delaney, of the Park, Queen's County, were received into favour, as was also James O'Nolan, of Donore, County Westmeath, *harper*.

A distinguished harper called Tadhg MacDonal MacRory, of Townagh, County Clare, received pardon, on July 21st, whose name is imperishably associated with the lively air known as "Teague's Rambles," printed by Playford in 1651.* He is also credited with the composition of "Fort Mountjoy," called in honour of the new fort built by his patron, Lord Mountjoy.

On August 3rd, 1601, five of the family of Halpin (MacAlpin, or Halfpenny) were outlawed, and, as was customary by the Irish bards, a lament was composed for one of the ladies of this family, ever since known as "Molly MacAlpin." The air is known in Scotland as "Gilderoy," in consequence of the Irish air being adapted to new verses, written on the execution of Gilderoy (Gilla-ruadh), who suffered death in July 1636. It was printed as far back as the year 1719 by Tom D'Urfey, who got the air from the Irish actor, Thomas Dogget, about the year 1700. Matthew Concannon, an Irishman, selected it as the ninth air in his version of "The Jovial Crew," in 1731.†

Eneas *ruadh* O'Heffernan, of Shronehill, County

* The English title of this tune, as printed by Playford in 1651, is "The Irish Lady, or Anniseed Water Robin." It will be found in the first edition of the *English Dancing Master*, an exceedingly scarce book.

† It may be necessary to explain that "Molly MacAlpin" is now best known as "Remember the Glories of Brian the Brave," being Moore's setting, in 1807, from Bunting. Mr. Alfred Moffat, in his *Minstrelsy of Ireland*, seems not to be aware that "MacAlpin" and "Halfpenny" are the same names.

Tipperary, a famous bard, was pardoned on August 6th, and on the following day pardon was extended to John O'Treacy, of Liscarrol, County Cork, *piper*, and, Melaghlin O'Duane, of Clogh Kelly, *harper*. On August 30th, Donagh O'Cullinane, of Mara, County Cork, *piper*, was received into favour.

On September 24th, 1601, pardon was granted to Cathal O'Kelly, Donogh *buidhe* O'Byrne, and Donal the Piper—all three County Wicklow pipers—at the special instance of the Lord Deputy, Lord Mountjoy. From this date until May, 1602, no pardon was granted to Irish musicians, indicating clearly that the minstrels had thrown in their lot with those who had flocked to the standard of O'Neill and O'Donnell. In fact, the date of the last-mentioned pardon (September 24th) almost coincides with the landing of the Spanish troops at Kinsale.*

Donal O'Killeen, of Cloghan, County Westmeath, *piper*, and Owen O'Killeen, of Ratra, Co. Roscommon, *piper*, were pardoned on May 6th 1602 ; and on the same day two harpers, Gillaglass and Owen O'Shalvey, both of Annaghmore, received a pardon, on a warrant by the Lord Deputy. On June 12th, John O'Moloney, of Pallas, County Longford, *harper*, was taken into favour, and on July 2nd Rory *albanach*, of Castleroe, County Westmeath, *harper*, was pardoned. This Rory *albanach* (the Scot) was the eldest brother of two celebrated harpers, John and Harry Scott—*albanach* signifying " a Scot"—of whom Bunting makes mention.

* On May 4th, 1602, O'Daly, the rhymer, was brought before Sir George Carew, charged with bringing messages from the Irish (to induce Owen O'Sullivan, a neighbouring Milesian chief, to join them), and was committed for trial.

John Scott composed the "Lament for the Baron of Loughmoe" (1599), whilst Harry composed a "Lament for the Baron of Galtrim" (1603), "Kitty Scott," etc.

On July 26th, 1602, another distinguished harper was pardoned, namely, Owen MacKiernan, of Kildare; and on the same day a similar favour was extended to Tadhg O'Laffan, of Scablerstown, *harper*, and his wife, Margaret Tyrrell.

During the autumn and winter of the year 1602, Irish music was fashionable at the Court of Queen Elizabeth. Nay, more ; the virgin Queen kept an Irish harper, Donal *buidhe*, in order to sooth her nerves. In the previously quoted letter from the Earl of Worcester to the Earl of Shrewsbury, dated September 19th, 1602, it is distinctly stated :—"Irish tunes are at this time most pleasing." Some of these Irish tunes are in the Fitzwilliam *Virginal Book* (a manuscript dating from the first quarter of the seventeeth century), three of which are arranged by Dr. William Byrd, one of the greatest composers that ever England produced.*

On December 6th, 1602, pardon was granted to Edmund O'Gibney, of Mulrankin, County Wexford; and, on the 4th, to Shane *ballagh* M'Geough, of County Monaghan, *harper*, and to another harper, named Cormack MacGillecosgelie, of a Levitical family in the diocese of Clogher, erenachs of Derrybrusk.†

Now, that the war was over, severe measures were taken against the minstrels. On January 28th, 1603, a proclamation was issued by the Lord President of

---

* For a good account of the Fitzwilliam *Virginal Book*, see Grove's *Dictionary of Music and Musicians*.
† The name "Gillecosgelie" is now written "Cuskelly."

Munster, by the terms of which the Marshal of the Province was strictly charged "to exterminate by marshal law all manner of Bards, Harpers," etc. Within ten days after said proclamation, Queen Elizabeth herself ordered Lord Barrymore "to hang the harpers wherever found, and destroy their instruments."

The last three pardons to Irish musicians under Elizabeth were to Owen MacDermot *reagh*, of Mallow, *harper*, on February 28th, and to Donal MacDonagh *gankagh*, of County Cork, *piper*, and to Dermod O'Dugan, of Garryduff, *harper*, on March 30th.

Queen Elizabeth died on March 24th, 1603, and on the same day the great Earl of Tyrone agreed to accept the terms offered by Lord Mountjoy, being present at the proclamation in Dublin, on April 6th, of King James I., to whom he formally submitted in London on June 7th.

During the year 1604, eleven bards and five harpers were pardoned. All the bards were of one clan, namely, MacConmidhe (MacNamee or Conmee). However, before the close of that year, Sir John Harrington (whose brother was killed at the battle of the Blackwater), Seneschal of County Wicklow, was ordered "to banish bards and rhymers out of his limits, and *whip* them if they did not quit after proclamation duly made." (2 James I.) Any bard who failed to leave the country of the O'Byrnes within twenty days was to be tried by court-martial and executed.*

The one great harper and composer under King

---

* Sir John Harrington is best remembered as the translator of Ariosto into English. He presented copies of his English versification to the children of the Earl of Tyrone.

James's rule was Rory *dall* O'Cahan, who spent most of his life in Scotland between the years 1601 and 1650. He was a close relative of Donal O'Cahan, chief of O'Cahan's country (of which Coleraine was the principal stronghold), and, in 1602, he attended the Scottish Court of King James. In 1603, in proof of his reconciliation with Lady Eglinton, he composed "Ⅽᴀʙᴀɪ𝔯 ᴠᴀᴍ ᴠᴏ Ⅼᴀ́ᴍ" ("Oh, give me your hand"), which is also known by its Latinised title of "*Da mihi manum.*" It has been printed by Wright (1727) and Bunting.

Rory *dall* is best known as the composer of numerous *puirts*, or Ports, like "Port Gordon," "Port Athol," "Port Lennox," generally called after the persons in whose honour they were written, somewhat akin to the Planxties of O'Carolan. In fact O'Carolan retouched some of the melodies or *puirts* of the old minstrel, which have, in consequence, been included among his own works, just as Samuel Lover dressed out anew some dozens of old Irish airs, now regarded as composed by himself.

In the Straloch musical manuscript, dated 1627-1629, appears "Rory dall's Port," and it was printed in Walshe's *Country Dances*, in 1750, being subsequently used by Robert Burns for his song commencing "Ae fond kiss, and then we sever." To many concert-goers his "Port Gordon" is best known, as re-touched by O'Carolan, adapted to the Irish song, "ᴍᴀ́ɪ𝔯ᴇ ʙᴇ́ɪⱡ ᴀ́ᴄᴀ ʜ-ᴀᴍɴᴀɪ𝔯." Another air of his is known among the Gaels of Scotland as "Lady Catherine Ogle" and "Bonny Katherine Oggy," printed in 1686.[*]

---

[*] Perhaps the most beautiful of all his compositions is "ᴀɴ ʙᴀᴄᴀᴄ̇ ʙᴜɪ𝔯ᴅᴇ" (the lame yellow beggar)—printed in 1729.

Rory O'Cahan died at the house of Lord Macdonald, leaving to that nobleman his harp and exquisite tuning key. The late William Elliot Hudson was strongly of opinion that the so-called " Lude " Harp (whose history cannot be traced further back than 1650) was really the favourite harp of Rory *dall*. Gunn, in 1807, describes it as 38 inches high, furnished with 30 strings, and it has all the characteristics of an Irish harp. Moreover, Dr. Johnson, in his *Tour in the Hebrides*, tells that in 1773 a valuable harp key, finely ornamented with gold and silver, and with a precious stone, worth eighty to a hundred guineas, was then in possession of Lord Macdonald, who presented it to Echlin O'Cahan. But the matter seems placed beyond doubt by the manuscript autobiography of Arthur O'Neill, wherein it is stated that Rory's harp and tuning-key had been left by the great Irish minstrel at the house of a Scotch nobleman, whose descendant, in 1773, presented the key to Echlin O'Cahan (incorrectly called " Ackland Kane "), who sold it in Edinburgh. Sir Walter Scott introduces Rory *dall* as the musical preceptor of Annot Lyle in his *Legend of Montrose*. Bunting prints three of his tunes, including " The Hawk of Ballyshannon," also known as " Port Athol," and retouched by O'Carolan as " O'Moore's Daughter."*

From várious " Relations " sent by the Irish Jesuits to Rome between the years 1608 and 1640, it appears that Irish was universally spoken throughout Ireland, and

* On March 8th, 1607, Sir John Egerton, son of the Lord Chancellor of England, wrote to Sir John Davies, Attorney-General for Ireland, reminding him of his *Irish Harp*. (*Cal. S. P.*, Ireland, March 8th, 1606-7.)

that even in Leinster it was more generally used than English.

Dr. Geoffrey Keating, the author of the "ꝼopar ꝼeara aꞃ Éꞃꞇꞇꞃ," or *History of Ireland* (finished in 1634), kept a harper named Tadhg O'Coffey, whom he thus addresses in a beautiful Irish poem of nine stanzas, about the year 1615 :—

" Who is the artist by whom the harp is played,
  By whom the anguish of the envenom'd spear's wound is healed,
  Through the sweet-voiced sound of the sounding-board,
  Like the sweet-strained peal of the organ."

During the first decade of the seventeenth century, or probably earlier, was composed the exquisite air, " Ceann ꝺuꞃ Ꝺíꞁꞇꞃ," or " Black-headed Dearie," printed by Playford in 1713. It was known in Scotland as " The Auld Jew," and in England as " The Irish Round, or Kennington Wells." *   Burke Thumoth (1740) styles it " Currie koun dilich."

About the same period was composed the plaintive " Uꞁꞁeacán Ꝺuꞃ Ó," to which, in 1746, Donogh MacConmara (Macnamara), or Ꝺonncaꝺ Ꞃuaꝺ, adapted the well-known song, " ꞃán cnuꞇc Éꞃꞃeann Óg"— " The Fair Hills of dear Eire." The air was printed by Walker in 1786.

Captain Barnaby Rich (who fought for forty years in the Irish wars, and was a voluminous pamphleteer from 1574 to 1624), in his *New Description of Ireland*, in 1610, says : " The Irish have harpers, and those are so reverenced among them that in the time of rebellion they will forbear to hurt either their persons or their

---

* Moffat, in his *Minstrelsy of Ireland*, says that the air is printed in Playford's *Dancing Master*, vol. ii., 1728, but I find it in the 1713 edition, at page 146.

goods, but are rather inclined to give to them; and they are very bountiful either to rhymers or fools." Moreover, he adds, that " every great man in the country hath his rhymer, his harper, and his known messenger to run about the country with letters."

In 1615 William FitzRobert FitzEdmond Barry, a famous blind harper, was a retainer of Lord Barrymore, and in 1620 we find Daniel MacCormac *dubh* O'Cahill as harper to Viscount Buttevant. Even the "great" Earl of Cork, one of the most unscrupulous adventurers that ever came to Ireland, kept an Irish narper in his service.

In 1616 Father Nicholas Nugent, an Irish Jesuit, was taken prisoner at the house of his relative, Lord Inchiquin, and was imprisoned in Dublin Castle for four years. During his imprisonment he solaced himself by composing Irish hymns, set to old tunes, which, as his biographers tell us, " became very popular, and were sung throughout Ireland."

Between the years 1618 and 1625 Father Robert Nugent, S.J. (who spoke Irish equally well with English), laboured in County Westmeath, a very musical county. The better to win over the native population, he cultivated the Irish harp so assiduously that he became a most proficient performer. Not content with excelling as a harper, he invented a new form of harp, minutely described by Archdeacon Lynch, author of *Cambrensis Eversus.*

Walker, writing in 1786, says: "The Irish harp received considerable improvements from the ingenuity of Robert Nugent, a Jesuit, in the fifteenth century, who resided for some time in this kingdom." Passing over the absurdity of making Jesuits exist in Ireland in the fifteenth century, it is merely necessary to mention that Father Robert Nugent laboured for forty years in Ireland, his native country. He was a cousin of Elizabeth, Countess of Kildare, who, in 1634, gave him Kilkea Castle, County Kildare, for a novitiate of the Order, of which he became Superior in 1640. His improvements mainly consisted in having a double row of strings extended along the framework of the harp, giving two strings to each sound (after the manner of a bi-chord pianoforte), which, when vibrating in unison, "produced a rich and sonorous quality of tone, also affording increased facilities for the uninterrupted progression of the passages with either hand." *

Nor are we left to mere descriptions of the harp as used in Ireland in 1620. We have still preserved a splendid instrument, dated 1621, made for Sir John FitzEdmond Fitzgerald, of Cloyne. Bunting gives a long account of it in his second volume (1809), but he fails to identify the maker, whose name appears as "Donatus filius Thadei." This harp maker is none other than Donal MacTadhg O'Dermody, whose father received pardon on March 28th, 1601, as previously mentioned. The inscription proudly proclaims—" Ego sum Regina Cithararum," and, in truth, it is a queenly instrument. The name "Dalway" harp is incorrectly applied, the explanation being that the instrument was for a century in the family of Noah Dalway, of Bellahill, near Carrickfergus.

King James died March 27th, 1625, and was suc-

---

* Conran's *National Music of Ireland*, p. 187. The full Latin description will be found in *Cambrensis Eversus*.

ceeded by Charles I., under whom there was a lull in
the persecution against Irish minstrels, owing to the
expectancy of the "graces," in consideration of the
sum of £120,000 to be paid to the King. The Irish
harp was even fashionable in England from 1626 to
1676, and there was a book of instructions published
for it in London in 1630, arranged by Martin Pierson,
Mus. Bac., Master of the Children of St. Paul's
Cathedral—remarkable as being the first printed work
in which tunes were arranged for the Irish harp.

There is a quaint letter from the Earl of Cork, Lord
Justice of Ireland, dated October 14th, 1632, to his
friend, Captain Price, in London, which I quote from
the State Papers * as follows :—

"Noble Captain Price,
    "Thank you for kindness to my son. The bearer
is to give the Lord Keeper an *Irish Harp*, and Lady
Coventry a runlet of mild Irish uskebath sent unto her
ladyship by my youngest daughter Peggie, who was so
much bound to her ladyship for her great goodness and
care of her. . . . I pray help Mr. Hunt to deliver
them, and let me add that if it please his lordship next
his hart (?) in the morning to drink a little of this
Irish uskuebagh, as it is prepared and qualified, it will
help to digest all raw humours, expel wind, and keep
his inward parts warm all the day after, without any
offence to his stomach."

A popular air of the period 1615-1630 was " An
Cnotaḃ ḃán," or " The White Cockade," the song of
which was written by Muiris mac Daibhi mac Gerailt
(Maurice FitzDavid FitzGerald), in reference to a then
prevalent fashion of white-ribboned plumes worn by

* *Calendar of State Papers relating to Ireland*—Charles I. (1625-
1632), p. 674.

the ladies of Munster on festive occasions. It was one of the two airs played by the war pipers of the Irish Brigade at Fontenoy on May 11th, 1745. The Scotch subsequently appropriated it, but it was not printed as a Scotch air till 1778. About the year 1730 Seaghan *Claragh* MacDonnell adapted a rousing lyric to the air of "Δn Cnocaύ ƀάn," which will be found as the very first song in Father Dinneen's excellent edition of that great Irish poet.

Some years later was composed a jig-tune, "Δn Cocα ƀuιὸe," or "The Yellow Jacket," which was printed by Playford in 1652 as "Buff-coat; or, Excuse Me," and was afterwards altered by the Scotch as "The Deuks gang o'er my daddie" in 1740. Our Irish air appeared as one of the tunes in the ballad opera of "Polly," in 1729, and Moore tells us that it was also adapted to a popular song commencing: "My husband's a journey to Portugal gone."

About the year 1635 was composed a variant of the lively Irish tune, "1ς Cumα Lιom," that is "It is indifferent to me," or "I don't care," which was printed in London in 1680. It was variously known as "The Nurses' Song," "Mad Moll," and "Yellow Stockings." Dean Swift was much enamoured of the melody, and set it to a nursery song, entitled "Hey my Kitten, my Kitten," in 1705.

Although Dr. Geoffrey Keating—"clarum et venerabile nomen"—finished his *History of Ireland* in 1634, he did not write the Όίonƀιοllαċ (preface or vindication) till 1635, when he was parish priest of Cappoquin and Affane, County Waterford.   From this learned preface, so carefully edited by Mr. David Comyn, I quote the following passage :—

"Stanihurst finds fault with the people who play the harp in Ireland, and says they have no music in them. It is probable that he was not a judge of any music, especially of this Gaelic music of Ireland, he being unacquainted with the rules which appertain to it. . . . And I am surprised that he did not read Cambrensis. . . . Likewise, it is not true for Stanihurst to assert that the greater number of Irish instrumen-talists and vocalists are blind, for it is certain that when he wrote his History (1584) there was a greater number of persons with eyesight engaged in the arts of playing and singing in Ireland than of blind people, which is equally true of the present time (1635), as can be attested by all our own contemporaries."

At the period of the Confederation of Kilkenny, from 1642 to 1648, Irish minstrely was much in evidence. One of the "laments" of that epoch was composed for Maelmuire O'Reilly, popularly known as "Myles the Slasher," who was slain on the bridge of Fenagh, near Granard, in 1642, by the Scotch Covenanters, and was buried in the Franciscan Friary, Cavan. Another glorious "lament" was composed on the death of Owen Roe O'Neill, in 1649, whose body was interred in the grave of "Myles the Slasher." No monument marks the graves of these two heroes in the now dis-mantled Friary of Cavan, but the "laments" are still well known to students of Irish folk music.*

M. Boullay le Gouz, writing in 1644, says :—" The Irish march to battle with the bagpipes, instead of

---

* In February, 1653, Primate O'Reilly died at Trinity Island, and was buried in the tomb of Myles the Slasher and Owen Roe O'Neill, in Cavan Friary.

fifes, but they have few drums." He adds:—"They are very fond of the harp, on which nearly all play, as the English do on the fiddle."

A splendid Irish war-march of this epoch is "Mac Alisdrum's March," the date of which is readily known from the fact that the gallant Alaster Mac Donnell, also known as Mac Alisdrum, or Colkitto, was slain at the battle of Knocknanoss (Shrub Hill), near Mallow, on November 13th, 1647. The ill-fated warrior, after having performed prodigies of valour, was basely assassinated whilst parleying with an officer. His remains were placed in the ancestral tomb of the O'Callaghans at Clonmeen, County Cork, and the Irish war-pipers who accompanied the funeral played a specially-composed death-march over all that re-mained of the brave soldier, described by the Papal Nuncio Rinuccini as "militem praestantissimum."*

In 1648 was composed the lovely air known as "Ọ̆ṗuimṛ́ionn ḃonn ọ̆iḃiṛ," or "The white-backed brown Cow," a version which was Englished by the Irish actor, Thomas Dogget, and sung by him, in 1690, as "Colly, my Cow."

We are also safe in dating the ever-popular "Grama-chree" as from the period of the Confederation, as it is alluded to in a pamphlet printed in 1649. Mr. Alfred Moffat could discover no earlier edition of the melody than that issued in 1746, but it was printed in Dublin in 1737, and was purloined by James Oswald in 1742,

---

* Dr. Charles Smith, writing in 1750, says:—"There is a very odd kind of Irish music, well known in Munster, by the name of 'MacAlistrum's March,' being a wild rhapsody made in honour of this commander, which to this day is much esteemed by the Irish, and played at all their feasts."—(*History of Cork.*)

whose rendering has the Scotch title of " Will ye go to Flanders, my Molly, O?" In 1759 George Ogle wrote English words to the Irish air, namely, "As down by Banna's banks I strayed," and it was subsequently utilised by Sheridan in "The Duenna." It is almost unnecessary to add that the melody is now best known as "The Harp that once thro' Tara's Halls."

Five other airs of the same period are " Old Langolee," "'Twas down in a Meadow," or "Contented I am " ; "Oonagh," or "While gazing on the Moon's light"; "Paisthin Fionn," and *An Maidhrin Ruadh*, printed in 1670.

Bishop Dease of Meath (1622-1650) was alike famous as a timpanist and an Irish song-writer. He made his will in 1648, and bequeathed, as a valuable heirloom, his tiompan, which solaced him during his last years. His death occurred at the Jesuits' residence in Galway, in 1651.

CHAPTER XIX.

IRISH MUSIC IN THE SEVENTEENTH CENTURY (*continued*).
1650-1700.

ONE of the most renowned harpers in 1650 was Pierce Ferriter, of Ferriter's Castle, County Kerry,* whose fame is not confined to tradition. We read that he was presented with a beautiful harp by Edmond Mac an Daill (son of Donnell Mac an Daill), of Moylurg, County Roscommon, on which occasion he wrote an Irish poem of twenty-six stanzas. The "gentleman harper" (as he was called in County Kerry), headed a band of troops to defend his property, but surrendered on condition of quarter for his men and himself. Notwithstanding this he was thrown into a filthy prison, where, however, he had the happiness of being consoled by the ministrations of Father Maurice O'Connell, a Jesuit, who, in the guise of a labourer, gave him the last sacraments. Pierce Ferriter was led out to execution in the year 1652, at Killarney, on Cnocán na ζCaopac, now Fair Hill, and was hanged. The Rinuccini MS. adds that though famous as a Confederate leader, he was still more famed as an orator and bard—"et praesertim Hibernica lingua insignem"—especially for his genius as an Irish poet. Ferriter composed many fine airs, but I have failed to recover any of them save the *caoine* on the death of

* Ferriter's Castle was dismantled by a gale in May, 1845.

the Knight of Kerry in 1642—published by Crofton Croker.* The Puritans, not content with hanging the Kerry bard, also hanged his brother-in-law, Father Thady Moriarty, Prior of the Dominican Convent, Tralee, whose martyrdom is chronicled on October 15th, 1653.

In 1649, the Irish regiments, who still were faithful to the faithless Stewarts, kept Irish pipers on their staff. Among the companies who thus returned one piper each, as recorded in the State Papers, are those of Captain Donogh O'Kennedy, Major Conor O'Callaghan, Captain Laurence O'Byrne, Captain John FitzMaurice FitzGerald, Captain Sorley MacDonnell (with seventeen soldiers belonging to Colkitto, the hero of Knocknanoss), Captain Tadhg O'Connor, Captain Phelim O'Connor, Captain Mooney, and Colonel Conway. Their pay was 28s. a month—equivalent to almost £20 of our present money. In 1650, Sir James Dillon's regiment was conspicuous for its many pipers, whose names are a sufficient proof of their nationality. One of the best known bagpipe tunes of this period is "Cold and Rough," which the great English composer, Henry Purcell, utilised as a bass part for a Royal Birth-day Ode in 1692—and which was annexed by our "brither Scots" as "Cold and Raw."

As early as September 25th, 1650, there was a Pro-

* The definitive edition of Pierce Ferriter's Irish poems has recently been published by the Gaelic League, Dublin, edited by Rev. P. Dinneen. The poem on the harp is particularly interesting, as giving the Irish names for the coṗṗ (harmonic curve or crosstree), the Láṁċṗann (front pillar), and the com, or soundboard, of the harp given to Ferriter by Mac an Daill. It was designed by MacSithduill, made by Cathal, bound and emblazoned by Bennglan, and decorated with gold by Parthalon *mor* MacCathail.

clamation issued by Ormonde against Tories and Wolves. The proclamation describes the Tories as Idle Boys who were masterless and out of protection, and consequently traitors. On December 20th, 1652, a public hunt was ordered by the State to destroy the numerous wolves in County Dublin. As is well known, priests, schoolmasters, and minstrels were put in the same category as wolves, and were outlawed. In 1654, all harpers, pipers, and wandering musicians had to obtain letters from the magistrate of the district where they hailed from before being allowed to travel through the country, and this passport contained full particulars as to the age, stature, beard, colour of hair, condition of life, etc., of the recipient.

A melodious tune of this epoch has been fortunately preserved in John Gamble's MS., dated 1659, and which was picked up by some of the Puritan troops in Ireland. It appears under various names, and is called " I'll never Love thee more," by Gamble, but the Irish tune was previously adapted to other words by James Graham, Marquis of Montrose, who was executed in 1650. The Irish character of the melody is very marked.

Another pretty melody, which dates certainly prior to the year 1660, is " Cailín veaṛ," to which variations were added by Lyons, the Harper, in 1698. Bunting calls it " A lovely lass to a Friar came," but he was apparently unaware that the tune had been printed under this name in Gay's " Beggars' Opera" in 1728, and by Thomas Odell in 1729, after which it became very popular in England.

No words can adequately describe the horrors of the

Cromwellian rule from 1650 to 1660. The pages of Prendergast, Gilbert, and Moran supply sickening details of that dreadful period. As regards music, it is a commonplace of history that the Puritans destroyed all the organs in the churches—Protestant as well as Catholic —regarding them as savouring of Popery. They also broke all the harps they could find, as a contemporary writer, Archdeacon Lynch, states. In fact, to such an extent was the harp-breaking mania carried that Lynch was of opinion that within a short time scarce a single instrument would be left in Ireland.

Apropos of the harp, Evelyn, the diarist, under date of 1654, waxes most enthusiastically, and thus records his opinion :—" Such music before or since did I never hear, the Irish harp being neglected for its extraordinary difficulty ; but, in my judgment, *far superior to the lute itself, or whatever speaks with strings.*"

Yet in spite of the Cromwellian atrocities, the harp still was heard in tuneful lays, accompanying the dear old tongue of the Gael, in strains that appealed even to the Puritans themselves. Who will deny that the harp was a potent factor in softening the hearts of the grim Ironsides? Anyhow, within thirty years from the pious Oliver's landing in Ireland, many of the children of the planters were completely absorbed by the native Irish, and had adopted not only the Roman Catholic faith, but were found to speak nothing but Irish. A rare pamphlet, written in 1697, bewails the degeneracy of the Williamite settlers as follows :—

" We cannot so much wonder at the degeneracy of the present English when we consider how many there are of the children of Oliver's soldiers in Ireland who cannot speak one word of English; and what is strange, the same may be said of some of the children of King William's soldiers, who came but t'other day into the country. This misfortune is owing to the marrying Irish women. *'Tis sure that no Englishman in Ireland knows what his children may be, as things are now ; they cannot well live in the country without growing Irish.*"

The story of the Act of Settlement is trite, and it were an ungracious task to touch on it, except to mention that the dispossession of the ancient proprietors, confirmed by that abominable Act, drew forth some exquisitely-plaintive caoines and laments. In an old manuscript, the date, 1664, is assigned to that quaint tune "ᴌom bó ᴀᵹuᵼ um bó," to which new Irish words were set by Geoffrey O'Donoghue, of Glenflesk, a few years later, as may be seen in Father Dinneen's excellent little volume of that popular Kerry poet, who died in 1690.

Another very characteristic melody of the pre-Restoration epoch is the well-known "Aᴄáim ım' ċoᴅᴌᴀᴅ 'ᵼ ná ᴅúıᵼıᵹ mé," or " I'm asleep, and don't waken Me." Although Mr. Moffat failed to trace it farther back than the year 1726, we have ample evidence of its existence in 1645, and it was printed by John Playford in 1652. It appeared in Scotland fifty years later, and was printed in Allan Ramsay's *Tea Table Miscellany* in 1726, under its Irish name. Charley Coffey, of Dublin adapted the air to a song in the " Beggar's Wedding " in 1728, commencing :—

" Past one o'clock on a cold, frosty morning."

We read in an old manuscript that this air was generally used by the " hedge schoolmasters " of the last years of the seventeenth century, set to the first Ode of Horace.

Not only did the Scotch purloin the air itself in its original state, but they evolved a new melody out of it by a simple change of rhythm, calling it "Peggy, I must Love Thee." In 1687 this transformed version was printed as "a Scotch tune in fashion," arranged by the celebrated Henry Purcell, England's greatest composer of that period.*

Tom Moore, in 1810, utilised this lovely air for his lyric "When Cold in the Earth," keeping fairly close to the original. In *Moore's Melodies Restored*, by Sir Charles Villiers Stanford, there is a note that "Moore's version is wholly different from Bunting's and Carolan's, and is probably his own," a statement that is absurd, suggesting, indeed, that the restorer never examined the old versions.

Amongst the harpers of the period 1660-1670, the most celebrated were Myles O'Reilly and the two Connellans. Of O'Reilly no particulars have come down, save the imaginings of Bunting. However, the brothers Connellan (Thomas and Laurence) were famed not only in Ireland, but also in Scotland. Thomas O'Connellan was born at Cloonymahon, County Sligo about the year 1625, and spent twenty years in Scotland —famous alike as a bard and a harper. He returned to Ireland at the close of the year 1689, and died in 1698, at Bourchier's Castle, near Lough Gur, County Limerick, being at the time an honoured guest at the house of Mr. Bayley, agent to the Earl of Bath. His remains were reverently interred in the adjoining church-yard of Temple Nuadh, and over his grave a

* Robert Burns wrote a song, " 'Twas past one o'clock," to this beautiful old Irish air.

few pipers appropriately played, by way of funeral dirge, the introductory and concluding phrases which Connellan had added to "The Irish Tune," the version being known as "The Breach of Aughrim."

From this period must be dated the once popular air "Maggie Láıvoıp," to which new words were adapted by John O'Neachtan about the year 1676. Hardiman writes :—

"The air, as well as the words, of 'Maggie Laidir,' though long naturalised in North Britain, is Irish. When our Scottish kinsmen were detected appropriating the ancient saints of Ireland, they took a fancy to its music. Not satisfied with borrowing the art, they despoiled us of some of our sweetest airs, and amongst others, that of 'Maggie Laidir.' This name signifies in the original, strong or powerful Maggy, and by it was meant Ireland.'

One thing is certain, that John O'Neachtan, about the year 1676, wrote the original Irish song of "Maggie Laidir," of which Hardiman, in 1831, published a version from a transcript made in 1706. However, Hardiman merely relied on tradition for the Irish origin of the air to which the song was set, and could give no proof. Fortunately I have succeeded in tracing the tune as far back as the year 1696, when it was sung by the Anglo-Irish actor, Thomas Dogget, in his comedy of "A Country Wake," and again by him, in the variant of the same play, under the title of "Hob, or the Country Wake," at Drury-lane, in 1711.

It was utilised in the "Quakers' Opera," in 1728, and again by Charles Coffey, in 1729, in his "Beggar's Wedding," under the title "Moggy Lawther." The Scotch version was first printed in 1729 in *Craig's*

Collection, the melody being set to words in celebration of Maggie Lauder, a reigning courtesan of Crail.

The English diarist Evelyn writes under date of November 17th, 1668 :—

"I heard Sir Edward Sutton play excellently on the Irish harp; he performs genteely, but not approaching my worthy friend, Mr. Clarke, who makes it execute lute, viol, and all the harmony an instrument is capable of. *Pity it is that it is not more in use;* but, indeed, to play well takes up the whole man, as Mr. Clarke has assured me, who, though a gentleman of quality and parts, was yet brought up to that instrument from five years old, as I remember he told me."

Apropos of Irish harps, there is still preserved a fine specimen known as the "Fitzgerald Harp," or the "Kildare Harp," inscribed "R. F. G., 1672"—having been the property of Robert FitzGerald (second son of George, sixteenth Earl of Kildare), who died in January, 1698. Another beautiful harp is the "Fogarty Harp," dating from 1680, formerly belonging to Cornelius O'Fogarty, of Castle Fogarty, County Tipperary a captain in the army of King James II. An excellent drawing of the latter appeared in the *Dublin Penny Journal* in 1838, and it was stated as being then in the possession of James 'Lanigan, Esq., Castle Fogarty. Amongst those killed at Aughrim on July 12th, 1691, was Edward FitzGerald, the last Baron of Cluain (County Kilkenny), generally known as "Edward the Harper," from his skill on the harp. He was a member of the Confederates from 1644 to 1649, and was attainted in person and property under Cromwell, but got back a small portion of his ancestral lands in 1661.

As an illustration of a splendid air, dating from about the year 1690, "Ⲧⲓⲅⲉⲁⲣⲛⲁ Ⲙⲁⲓⲅⲉⲟ" may here be quoted. It has frequently been attributed to Turlogh O'Carolan, but the real composer was Thady Keenan, the harper, to words by David O'Murray. This statement is quoted by Hardiman from Walker, on the authority of the venerable Charles O'Conor, of Belanagare.

Of course, the advent to Ireland of King James II. in 1689 filled the Irish minstrels with high hopes, which, alas! were dashed to earth in 1691. Three of the best airs of this period are " Lilliburlero,"* "The Battle of Killiecrankie," and "The Boyne Water." The second was composed by Thomas O'Connellan on the occasion of the battle of Killiecrankie, fought on July 27th, 1689, and is also known as "Planxty Davis." Its Irish origin is sufficiently clear from the fact that in a Northumbrian MS. of the year 1694 this tune appears as "The Irish Gillicranky," and the music of it may also be found in the Leyden MS. in 1692, to which Burns subsequently adapted verses. As for "The Boyne Water," the composer is unknown, but the air certainly dates from *circa* 1645, long before the battle. "Ⲣⲓⲅ Ⲥeumuⲣ" (printed in the *Dublin Citizen* in 1842) also dates from this period, but is better known as "Rodney's Glory," the English words of which were by the famous Irish poet Owen Roe O'Sullivan in 1782.

The flight of the Wild Geese in 1691 and 1692

---

* "Lilliburlero," as a tune, goes back to the early years of the 17th century, and was known at the Confederation period. New words were set to it in 1688, and in 1689 it was published in *Music's Handmaid* as " a new Irish tune."

afforded a theme for a really exquisite song, known
as " Na Séaóna Fiaóaine," which Tom Moore amus-
ingly equates as "Gage Fane," and to which he set
"The Origin of the Harp," commencing, "'Tis believed
that this harp which I wake now for thee." Both
Glover and Mr. Alfred Moffat persist in calling it
"Gage Fane," oblivious of the real Irish name, for
which Holden, in 1806, was primarily responsible. This
exquisite song, printed in 1745, became popular in 1772
when republished in *M'Lean's Collection* as "Old Ireland,
Rejoice," and was a favourite with Tom Moore. Dr.
Madden tells us that Moore's lyric was suggested by
a visit which the modern bard of Erin paid to Edward
Hudson, one of the State prisoners in Kilmainham
Jail, in March, 1799, and it was printed in the third
number of the *Melodies* in 1810. Not even Sir Charles
Villiers Stanford, in his "restored" edition of *Moore's
Melodies*, has any comment on the absurd title—"Gage
Fane." However, the correct title is "Na Séaóna
Fiaóaine," or "The Wild Geese," commemorative of
the thousands of Irish who fled to France and Spain
after the Treaty of Limerick. Variant forms of the air
appear as "Armstrong's Farewell," "The Old Head
of Denis," "The Meeting of the Waters," "Todlin'
Hame," "My name is Dick Kelly," "An bacaċ buióe,"
and "An Cána Opaigeann éille." Bunting's setting
was not published till 1840, and it is very corrupt,
though he says that it is the version played by Patrick
Quin in 1803.* The antiquity of the melody may be
guessed from the fact that as far back as the year

The oldest *printed* version of the air is as " An bacaċ buióe "
(composed by O'Cahan), in Coffey's ballad opera, 1729.

1670, John Fitzgerald, son of the Knight of Glin, wrote a song to this air.

We may date "Once I had a Sweetheart" as composed about the year 1695. It is a most characteristic specimen of an Irish air, and yet it is included in Moffat's *Minstrelsy of England*. Mr. Kidson describes it as "an old and pretty folk-melody taken from Daniel Wright's *Complete Tutor for ye Flute, circa* 1735, and he adds that no earlier copy is now accessible. Fortunately, the air may be found in the Anglo-Irish ballad opera of the "Beggar's Wedding," produced in Dublin in 1728 by Charles Coffey, and printed, with the music, in 1729.

However, incomparably the finest Irish ballad of the period, 1698-1704, is "Éamonn an chuic," or "Ned of the Hill," written in memory of Edmond Ryan, who was an outlaw under King William. Poor Ned Ryan, the scion of an old family, the O'Ryans of Kilnelongurty, County Tipperary, was forced to become a Rapparee, and to do a man's part in spoiling the spoiler. After many vicissitudes he died in 1724, and was buried near Faill an Chluig, in the parish of Toem, in the upper half barony of Kilnemanagh, County Tipperary Perhaps in the whole range of Irish minstrelsy no melody has been so transformed as "Éamonn an chuic." Though the air dates from the close of the sixteenth century,* it underwent various modifications between the years 1600 and 1760, and it may be found under a score of different titles, *e.g.,* "The Young Man's

---

* The earliest *printed* version was in 1729. A Scotch variant appeared in Johnson's *Museum*, in 1788, as "I dreamed I lay," with words by Robert Burns.

Dream," "The Green Woods of Truagh," "Colonel
O'Gara," "The Groves of Blarney," "Castle Hyde,"
"Lady Jefferie's Delight," etc.   Beethoven adapted
this beautiful melody to words commencing, "Sad and
luckless was the season," but from a corrupt version,
and it was worked into a fantasia by Mendelssohn in
1829, as Op. 15, from Moore's setting "'Tis the last
Rose of Summer," published in December, 1813. Flotow
introduced it into his opera of "Martha," and was much
enamoured of it.*

The subjoined version is the earliest yet discovered,
taken from a manuscript of the year 1726, of which a
variant was printed by Bartlett Cooke in 1794 :—

"éamonn an cnuic" (NED OF THE HILL).

* Berlioz, whilst condemning the opera of "Martha," highly
praises our old folk tune as follows: "The delicious Irish air was
so simply and poetically sung by Patti that its fragrance alone was
sufficient to disinfect the rest of the work.

CHAPTER XX.

ANGLO-IRISH MUSIC IN THE SEVENTEENTH CENTURY.

ALTHOUGH Mystery or Morality Plays had disappeared in England in the opening decade of the seventeenth century, they still lingered on in Ireland, especially in Dublin, Wexford, and Kilkenny. On July 2nd, 1610, the Corporation of Kilkenny voted a salary of twenty shillings for keeping " the apparel used on Corpus Christi Day station, and the dresses of the Morris dancers," as also " the apparel of the players of the Resurrection." As before stated, music entered largely into these mumming performances. However, the " legitimate" drama was being gradually introduced, and in 1634 John Ogilby (dancing master and translator) was appointed " Master of the Revels."

An old record has frequently been quoted regarding the performance of " Gorboduc " at Dublin Castle in September, 1601, on Queen Elizabeth's birthday, but apparently this was a private performance, and it was not till 1635 that John Ogilby opened a public theatre, at a cost of £2,000, in Werburgh-street, Dublin. The only other notice of a play before the year 1634 is an entry in the Black Book of the King's Inns, from which it appears that, in the Hilary Term of the year 1630, a sum of two pounds was given to " the players for the grand day." *

* Lewy Barry, an Irish Lawyer, wrote *Ram Alley* in 1611 ; reprinted in 1636.

Thomas Bateson, Organist and Vicar-Choral of Christ Church Cathedral, Dublin, from 1609 to 1630, was the first who received the degree of Mus. Bac. from Trinity College in 1615. In 1618 he published his *Second Set of Madrigals*, printed by Thomas Snodham, of London, the successor of Thomas Este. Nothing now is known of Bateson's subsequent career, save that he provided handsomely for his family in Ireland. He was succeeded as organist of both cathedrals by Randal Jewitt (1631-1639), who also received the degree of Mus. Bac. of Dublin University.

In 1626 there was printed at Dublin a ballad entitled "Mount Taragh's Triumph," to the tune of "The Careere" ("Maister Basse, his Careere, or The Hunting of the Hare"), principally remarkable as being the earliest English ballad printed in Ireland. Four years later Father James Myles—called Milesius by Wadding—a native of Drogheda, wrote an admirable work on theory and vocal music. This work, *Ars nova Cantandi, sive Brevis Methodus Musicae addiscendæ*, was printed at Naples in 1630, and, as Ware adds, "is still held in esteem among the adepts in Musick." Father Myles (Moelisu) was a Franciscan, and lived for some years at the Irish College, Rome, whence he removed to Naples. He also wrote an English Catechism, one of the earliest of its class. His death took place at Naples in 1639. According to contemporaries he was not only a good theorist, but a practical musician as well.

The opening of a public theatre in Werburgh-street, Dublin, under the patronage of the Viceregal Court, in 1635, was a memorable event. In order to secure the monopoly, an Act of Parliament was passed to punish all wandering minstrels, players of Interludes, etc., and to confine them in houses of correction in the same category as "rogues, vagabonds, sturdy beggars, and other lewd and idle persons." A stock company was formed for the season 1636-7, and among the members were the best of the itinerant players "who had formerly been necessitated to stroll from booth to booth in the principal towns and cities, and to wander from hall to hall amongst the rural mansions of the gentry and nobility." *

James Shirley's plays of *The Royal Master* (dedicated to George, Earl of Kildare), *The Doubtful Heir* (first styled *Rosania, or Love's Victory*), *St. Patrick for Ireland,* and *The Constant Maid,* were specially written for, and first performed at, the Dublin theatre in Werburgh-street. Nay, more, there were Dublin editions of these plays printed by T. Cotes, and sold by "Thomas Allot and Edmond Crook, near the Castle in Dublin." Strafford was a great patron of the play-house, and hence the Anglicising process went on, *St. Patrick for Ireland* being one of the first attempts at the "stage Irishman." During Shirley's stay several of Ben Jonson's plays were produced by Ogilby, as also plays by Beaumont and Fletcher, and Middleton. Shirley returned to England at the close of the year 1639, or early in 1640.

Between the years 1615 and 1635 there are evidences of organs being procured for the Protestant cathedrals of Cork, Waterford, Kilkenny, and Limerick, though it was not till 1634 that a salaried organist—Richard

* Walker's *Essay on the Irish Stage.* (Trans. R.I.A., 1788.)

Galway—was appointed to Armagh. Bernard Adams, Protestant Bishop of Limerick from 1604 to 1630, describes, in the *Black Book of Limerick*, that "two organs had grown old in his cathedral before the wars of Elizabeth," and that he had procured "a very beautiful new organ," and had also reorganised the choir, "providing scientific choirmen and four boy choristers." Under date of November 4th, 1633, the Dean and Chapter of Cork Cathedral approved of the sum of £10 in payment for "the completion of a musical instrument, called in English *organs*, as is the custom to have in cathedral churches." In the same year was ratified the choir foundation of Armagh Cathedral out of the lands of the Culdees for the support of "eight singing men, four choristers, and an organist," to be called "the College of King Charles in the church of St. Patrick, Armagh," and one year's endowment was to be reserved "to provide a pair of organs for the church." On September 5th, 1637, the "reformed" Chapter of Armagh was incorporated, with Peter Wentworth as Dean.

Although editions of the Psalms of David were printed in Dublin in 1637 and 1644, yet no music was printed till late in the seventeenth century. A version of the Psalms in Metre, with music, by William Barton, M.A., was published in London in 1644, of which a Dublin edition appeared in 1697, but without the music. Sternhold and Hopkins—which Mr. J. E. Matthew pronounces a "a sorry production"—held the field till supplanted by Tate and Brady. It is remarkable that Ravenscroft's Psalter found no favour in Ireland.

The "Great Rebellion" of 1641, followed by the Cromwellian *régime*, militated against the development of music, and Ireland suffered much from the Puritan destruction of organs, and the opposition to minstrelsy generally. The last play acted in Werburgh-street Theatre, in 1640, was *Landgartha* by Henry Burnell—described as a Tragi-Comedy in Five Acts, printed in Dublin in 1641. After this date, by order of the Lords Justices, no theatrical performances were allowed, and Werburgh-street theatre closed for ever.

Sunday, January 27th, 1661, was the first time that the organ again pealed forth in St. Patrick's Cathedral, Dublin, on which occasion an anthem was sung, composed by Rev. Dr. William Fuller, Dean of St. Patrick's, subsequently Bishop of Limerick, Ardfert, and Aghadoe, whence he was translated to Lincoln in 1667. Although a copy of this anthem is in the British Museum, yet the music was not printed, and was sung from a manuscript score.

On May 9th, 1644, organs were ordered to be removed from all churches and colleges, and the mandate was carried out with ruthless barbarity. In 1647 the beautiful organ of Cashel Cathedral was broken to pieces. Regarding the Parish Church of St. Mary's, New Ross, County Wexford, it is recorded in the Corporation books that "Lieut.-Colonel John Puckle, Govenor of New Ross in 1652, *took away the fayre payre of organs* and a ring of five bells from St. Mary's Church." Again, the Governor of Waterford, Colonel Sadleir, pulled down the "great paire of organs" in the Cathedral of

Waterford, and the pipes were sold by Town Major Rickards in 1651.*

Those interested in early cathedral music for Protestant worship will be glad to learn that in the library of Trinity College, Dublin, there is a unique printed *Book of Anthems* for the use of Christ Church Cathedral, Dublin, dated 1662. However, it only contains the words, and the music must have been in manuscript, probably arranged by John Hawkshaw, who was organist of both cathedrals from 1661 to 1686.

One of the most distinguished Anglo-Irish musicians of this period was John Birkenshaw, " [Birckensha]," of Dublin, son of Sir Ralph Birkenshaw, Comptroller of the Musters and Cheques. He fled to London in 1640, and settled down as a teacher of singing, composition, and the viol. Not only was he a skilled performer, but he was also a good theorist and a classical scholar, praised especially by Playford in 1652 as a " Master for the Voice or Viol." In 1664 he published an English translation of *Templum Musicum*, by Alstedius. This work was printed by William Godbid, London, with an engraved frontispiece. He is best known as the music master of Samuel Pepys, who makes several references to him in his *Diary*. Evelyn also praises Birkenshaw, who brought out *Syntagma Musicæ* in 1672,† and was buried in Westminster Abbey, May 14th, 1681.

It has been asserted that the Psalm Books issued by John Crook, of Dublin, in 1661 and 1664, were set to music, but this is not so. I have examined both

* *Journal of the Royal Society of Antiquaries of Ireland*, vol. ii., 1852.
† For interesting details of Birkenshaw see Sir Frederick Bridge's *Sa uel Pepys' Lover of Musique* a charming volume, issued in October, 1903.

editions, and they merely contain the words. Another interesting liturgical work was printed by Crook in 1666, namely, the French Protestant Prayer-book, for the use of the refugees who had been given the Lady Chapel of St. Patrick's Cathedral, in 1663. A copy of this scarce duodecimo of 140 pages is in possession of Professor Mahaffy.

In 1661 John Ogilby had his patent renewed for a theatre, and fixed on Smock-alley as a suitable site, acquired from Sir Francis Brewster. Accordingly, a new play-house was erected, and opened to the public in 1662. One of the first plays performed was *Pompey*, being a translation from the French of Corneille, by Mrs. Katherine Phillips, the famed Orinda, with a prologue by the Earl of Roscommon, and an epilogue by Sir Edward Dering. It must have been popular, as an edition was printed by John Crook, of Dublin, in 1663, a copy of which is in the Bodleian Library.* Ogilby (the translator of *Virgil* in 1666, and of *Homer* in 1669, both printed in Dublin) met with a sad reverse in 1671, when during the performance of Ben Jonson's *Bartholomew Fair*, on December 26th (Boxing Night), the upper gallery of his theatre fell, by which three persons were killed and several wounded.

Although it is generally known that King Charles II., after the Restoration, introduced a band of twenty-four Instrumentalists into the Chapel Royal (whose services were first heard on Sunday, September 14th, 1662), few are aware that the frivolous monarch was indebted to

* John Dancer's *Agrippa* was played by Viceregal command in 1664, and Sir Robert Howard (who lived for a year in Ireland) gave a performance of *The Committee*, in Dublin, in 1665.

an Irishman, Rev. Peter Talbot, S.J., for many of his musical ideas. When residing at Madrid in 1659, Father Peter Talbot was commissioned by King Charles to procure for him some Spanish music, which commission was duly fulfilled in January, 1660. The Irish priest also supplied the English monarch with French and Portuguese airs.* Readers of Irish history need scarcely be told that this distinguished ecclesiastic was afterwards Archbishop of Dublin, and was arrested in October, 1678, for supposed complicity in the " Popish Plot "—dying a confessor in Dublin Castle two years later.

In 1665 Archbishop Talbot writes thus of Father Peter Walshe, who lived in Kennedy's-court, Dublin :—

" The Remonstrants treated Walsh and his Commissary, Father Redmond Caron, very splendidly at the sign of the *Harp and Crown*, in Dublin, almost every night, with good cheer, dancing and danes [ᴠᴀɴᴀ], or *Irish cronans*, especially the famous *Ballinamone*, which was styled in a letter to Rome, ' cantio barbara et agrestis,' and called by the soldiers of the guard in Dublin (hearing it every night at midnight) Friar Walsh and Friar N. singing of psalms ! Call you suffering to see your grave Remonstrants *dance jigs and country dances*, to recreate yourself and the Commissary ? " †

The song alluded to was the famous " Ballinamona Oro," which was subsequently introduced by Henry Brooke into his *Jack, the Giant Queller*, in 1748, and by O'Keeffe, into his *Poor Soldier*, in 1783. Mr. Alfred Moffat says that the air, as " Balin a mone,"

* *Spicilegium Ossoriense*, by Cardinal Moran.
† Gilbert's *History of Dublin*.

is included in Burke Thumoth's *Collection* in 1745, but he was apparently unacquainted with the above reference to it by Dr. Peter Talbot.

There are not wanting evidences of the cultivation of the virginal, or spinet, and the viol in Ireland between the years 1660 and 1665, and an examination of old wills and deeds of that time prove the point. Only to quote one instance at random.* In an inventory of of goods belonging to Edmund Ronayne, deceased, Blarney, County Cork, taken on August 12th, 1665, we come across the two following items : " A payre of Virginalls, vallued ten shillings, and an old violl."

Perhaps it is as well to explain that the name " virginal" gradually got out of use after the year 1663, and was replaced by that of " spinet " or "espinette," the French designation. The vogue of spinets continued till about the year 1780, though harpsichords were more popular after the year 1730, and both instruments were superseded by the pianoforte in 1765.

From a description of Ireland, printed in London in 1673, the following extract is interesting :—" The Irish gentry are musically disposed, and therefore many of them play singular well upon the Irish harp ; they affect also to play at tables. The common sort are much given to dancing after their country way, and the men to play upon the Jews-harp."

Thomas Dineley, in his *Tour of Ireland*, in 1681, seems to have the above volume before him. His description of " Old Irish Feasts " is as follows :— " They [the Irish] are at this day much addicted (on holidays, after the bagpipe, Irish harp, or Jews' harp)

---

* *Journal of the Royal Society of Antiquaries of Ireland*, 1856.

to dance after their country's fashion, that is, the Long Dance."

The Smock-alley Theatre was rebuilt in 1672, and John Ogilby retired in favour of Thomas Stanley, who gave up his post as Master of the Revels in 1683, which was then conferred on William Morgan. Meantime, Joseph Ashbury was Deputy Master of the Revels, who continued in office until 1720. Ashbury, like his predecessor, was a classical scholar and a cultured man. Unfortunately, details are wanting of his managership of Smock-alley, from 1674 to 1688, but all the London successes were brought over to Dublin, including the *Indian Queen* and *The Committee.* The original Teague—the anglicised form of the Irish Ⲧⲁⲟⲅ—in the latter play was an Irishman, John Lacy, originally a dancing master, and then a lieutenant in the army. He was styled " Roscius " by Evelyn, and was notable for his impersonation of Falstaff. Till his death, in 1681, he continued the favourite comedian of King Charles II.

A remarkable volume of songs, was published by an Irishman, Thomas Duffet, in 1676, entitled : *New Poems, Songs, Prologues, and Epilogues.* In this volume are many Irish tunes, including the lovely melody to which Duffet wrote " Since Coelia's my Foe," previously known as " Fortune my Foe." I subjoin the version of this air, as printed by Playford, in 1676 :—

" SINCE COELIA'S MY FOE "—1676.

(Playford's *Choice Ayres and Songs.*") 1676.

Since the publication of Birkenshaw's translation of Alstedius, in 1664, other treatises had appeared treating music from a mathematical and philosophic aspect. In 1676, Dr. Narcisus Marsh, whilst at Oxford, wrote a tract on the " Sympathy of Viol or Lute Strings," which was printed in Plot's *Oxfordshire* (1677). Marsh played the viol and the harp, and held in his rooms " a weekly consort of instrumental and vocal music," on each Thursday afternoon. He was made Provost of Trinity College, Dublin, in 1678, and continued his musical studies. In 1680 he revived the *Irish* lectures, and in 1683 helped to found the Dublin Philosophical Society, before which he read a valuable paper on Acoustics, suggesting, *inter alia*, the term Microphone.* Another musical member of this Society was Sir William Petty, M.D. (formerly Gresham Lecturer in Music), the author of the *Down Survey*, who died in 1687.

And now we come to a noteworthy landmark, the founding of the Hibernian Catch Club in 1679-80. Its origin is due to the social gatherings which had been customary among the lay vicars-choral of the two

* Stokes's *Worthies of the Irish Church*, by Lawlor, pp. 82 and 138.

Dublin Cathedrals. It appears that at the inaugural
performance of *Pompey*, in 1663, the choral interludes were sung by the stock company, assisted by
the "gentlemen of the choirs of both Cathedrals."
This singing in play-houses was objected to by the
ecclesiastical authorities, and there is a significant
entry in the Chapter Book of Christ Church Cathedral, under date of February 22nd, 1662-3—"Mr. Lee,
one of the stipendiarii of this church, having sung
amongst the stage players in the play-houses, is ad-
monished that he do so no more." A few years later
musical dinners took place and, at length, in the winter
of 1679-80, the Hibernian Catch Club was inaugurated.
There are no details of its first years, but we have a
reference to the meetings of the Club in 1698, the place
of meeting being in Francis-street. Among existing
European musical societies, the Hibernian Catch Club
is easily the first, as the Leipzig Gewandhaus Concerts
were only started in 1733.

In 1676 an Organ was bought for St. Werburgh's
at a cost of £50. It is described as an "old organ," and
had been purchased from John Hawkshaw, organist and
vicar-choral of Christ Church. Five years later, in 1681,
the records of St. Audeon's Church contain an entry
relative to a new organ, built by Mr. Pease at a cost of
£110.*

In 1680, Luke Wadding, Bishop, of Ferns, published a
small volume entitled *A Pious Garland of Godly Songs
for the Solace of his Friends and Neighbours in their
Afflictions*. It is of special interest as supplying the
names of many now-forgotten tunes to which the verses

* Gilbert's *History of Dublin*.

were adapted, *e.g.*, " Patrick Fleming," " Ochone,"
" Bonny Broom," "The Dumpe," " Since Coelia's my
Foe," " Farewell, Fair Armelia," " The Knell," " The
Skilful Doctor," " Fortune my Foe," " How Cold and
Temperate am I Grown," " Alas ! I cannot keep my
Sheep," " That time the Groves were clad in Green,"
" Norah oge nee Yeorane " (Norah oge O'Ryan),
" Neen Major Neal " (1nᵹeᴀn=the daughter of Major
Neale), and "Shea veer me geh hegnough turshogh "
(Se ṁıṗ mé ᵹo h-eᴀᵹneᴀċ=It is lonely you have left me).

Bishop Wadding wrote hymns and Christmas Carols
to the above tunes, and it is remarkable that these lyrics
of two hundred and twenty years ago are still sung in
the Parish Church of Kilmore, Barony of Forth, County
Wexford. The little volume was several times printed,
the fourth edition being published in London in 1731,
but it is now very scarce, and it was only after a long
search I was able to get a loan of the third edition,
printed in London in 1728.

Dr. Petrie in 1855, was indebted to the late Mr. Wm.
Chappell for a knowledge of Thomas Duffet, previously
mentioned, whose song of "Since Coelia's my Foe "
(printed in 1676), was utilised by Bishop Wadding for
carols. Chappell acknowledges that Duffet (Duhbthach,
or Duffy) was certainly an Irishman, and that the tune
quoted was Irish. In fact, many of the tunes used by
D'Urfey were taken from Duffet.

Bishop Wadding was a fair musician, and lived at
New Ross, where Father Stephen Gelosse, S.J., had a
famous school. On March 22, 1686, King James II.
ordered him a pension of £150 a year, and he died a
martyr in October, 1691.

Perhaps the most convincing proof of a growing musical taste in Ireland in the first year of the reign of James II.——that is in the year 1685, is the introduction of music-printing into Dublin. The first Dublin music publisher was Robert Thornton, who on March 21st, 1685, had issued a newspaper, printed by Joseph Ray, in College-green. Only one specimen of his work has remained, but Mr. E. R. M'Clintoch Dix discovered in Marsh's Library one of his advertisements, which proves that half-sheet songs, engraved on copper, were printed in Dublin in 1686.* In a list of " Books printed for and sold by Robert Thornton, at the sign of the Leather Bottle, in Skinner Row," there is included the following advertisement :—

" The Choicest New Songs, with Musical Notes, either for voice or instrument, fairly engraven on copper plates, will be constantly printed, and sold at Twopence a Song by the said Robert Thornton."

In 1688 Thomas Godfrey (who had been organist of St. Patrick's Cathedral since 1686) became a convert to the Roman Catholic faith, and was appointed organist of Christ Church Cathedral, of which the Dean was Dr. Alexius Stafford, a priest of the Diocese of Ferns. The ancient Catholic ceremonial was observed in Christ Church from 1689 to 1690, and St. Patrick's was converted into a temporary barracks for King James's troops. The Protestant Archbishop of Dublin, Francis Marsh, fled to England in February, 1689, after which Archbishop Russell was given jurisdiction.

* The only example of Thornton's printing is a reprint, in 1686, of " A New Irish Song," as sung in the Masque of " The Triumphs of London," by Thomas Jordan, as performed in London on October 29th, 1682. The musical setting was by John Playford.

Meantime English opera had been making head-way. Henry Purcell's *Abdelazar* was written in 1675, followed, in 1688, by *Dido and Aeneas*, the libretto of which was written by an Anglo-Irishman, Naham Tate, better known for his partnership with another Anglo-Irishman, Nicholas Brady, in the once popular version of the Psalms. It is interesting to add that the epilogue to this opera was spoken by an Irish gentlewoman, Lady Dorothy Burke. The complete score of Purcell's *Dioclesian*, dedicated to the Duke of Somerset, was published in 1691, and it is an excellent example of that master's style, whose *chef d'œuvre*, *King Arthur*, was produced the following year.

As may be well imagined, the usurpation of Prince William of Orange, and the troubled period of 1688-1692, retarded the development of music, but the last years of the seventeenth century more than compensated for the comparative barrenness of the previous fifty years.

The first indication of a revival of music, after four years turmoil, was the formation of a scratch orchestra for the interludes during the inaugural performance of Shakespeare's *Othello*, at Smock-alley Theatre, on March 23rd, 1692. As is well known, singing and dancing were *de rigeur* in all performances, whether tragic or comic, and almost every great actor or actress introduced his or her favourite song. Between the years 1692 and 1700 nearly all the most eminent performers played in Dublin under Joe Ashbury. An Anglo-Irishman, Thomas Doggett (born in Castle-street, Dublin, in 1669) was one of the best commedians in London from 1691 till his retirement in

1713, but his claim to notice, from a musical point of view, is that he made known many Irish tunes set to English words.

At this date the old-time May-pole festivities were revived at Finglas, County Dublin, and continued for a century and a-half in unabated popularity. Indeed, as a matter of fact, the May-pole remained in the village as late as the year 1844. Among the many Anglo-Irish ballads commemorative of these festivities, usually attended by a piper, the writer picked up one some thirty years ago, which was sung to the air of " Nancy Dawson," the second half of the first verse concluding as follows :—

> " Ye lads and lasses all to-day
>   To Finglas let us haste away,
>   With hearts quite light and dresses gay,
>   To dance around the May-pole."

There was a May-pole in New-street, Dublin, long before the " Great Rebellion," to which allusion is made in the Fourteenth Report of the Hist. MSS. Commission.

On August 12th, 1695, an agreement was made between the Dean and Chapter of St. Patrick's Cathedral, Dublin, and Renatus Harris, of London, for £505, to build a new organ for said Cathedral, he allowing £65 for the old pipes. The new instrument was duly erected on March 11th, 1697, and on May 10th following the Dean and Chapter further agreed to give Harris £350 for additional stops. It is satisfactory to note that an Irishman, Thomas Fennell (who had been appointed Organist and Vicar-Choral of Christ Church Cathedral in the year 1689) was organist of St. Patrick's from the close of the year 1693 to 1698, and opened the new organ. He was apparently of a contentious disposition, and was superseded three times by Peter Isaac, William Isaac, and Robert Hodge, but managed to retain his post till June, 1698, when Daniel Roseingrave, an Englishman, was appointed.

Harris built an organ for Christ Church Cathedral in 1697, being portion of the instrument discarded in the famous contest at the Temple Church. It was erected at the north side of the choir, and on November 11th, 1698, Roseingrave was appointed organist of both cathedrals. This historic instrument, originally built in December, 1687, was exchanged for a new one in 1751, and it is now in St. John's Church, Wolverhampton.

At Dublin, on January 9th, 1694, the centenary of the founding of Trinity College was celebrated with much *éclat*. Henry Purcell composed an ode specially for the occasion, entitled "Great Parent, Hail!" words by Nahum Tate. Although Joseph Ray, of College-green, Dublin, printed the words, the music was left in manuscript, and perhaps it is just as well, as it was composed in a hurry and shows evidence of being merely a *piece d'occasion*. The words, as Professor Mahaffy truly says, were "a fulsome eulogy on King William and Queen Mary." Dr. Blow's anthem, "I Beheld, and lo!" was also sung.

Thomas Lindsay, Dean of St. Patrick's from 1693 to 1695 (when he was made Bishop of Killaloe), made a strenuous effort to improve the choral services in St. Patrick's Cathedral, and presented a new bell to the church, cast by Henry Paris, who had cast the treble and tenor bells for St. Audeon's Church in the previous year.

Tate and Brady's *Psalter* was published in 1695, and a Dublin-printed issue of Barton's *Psalms* was issued by Eliphel Dobson in 1697, but without music. Three years later Henry Dodwell, the great Anglo-Irish writer, who had refused to take the oath of allegiance to King William, wrote *A Treatise on the Lawfulness of Instrumental Music in Holy Offices,* which went through two editions in the year 1700.

A new era was now at hand, when opera, oratorio, and orchestra were to revolutionise the existing style of music in the opening years of the eighteenth century. From this date forward Ireland was destined to figure conspicuously in the musical world.

CHAPTER XXI.

O'Carolan and his Contemporaries.

ALTHOUGH many distinguished harpers flourished during the first quarter of the eighteenth century, yet Turlogh O'Carolan stands pre-eminently as the representative Irish musician of that period. O'Carolan has been styled "the last of the bards," but, in truth, he scarcely deserves the appellation. He certainly combined in himself the three offices of poet, harper, and composer, but cannot be rightly named a bard.*

Numerous memoirs of O'Carolan have been written, and, therefore, I shall merely give a short biography of him. Walker and Hardiman furnish ample details, whilst Goldsmith's account is a classic.

Trulogh O'Carolan was born at Newtown, near Nobber, County Meath, in the year 1670, and in 1675-6 his parents changed their residence to Carrick-on-Shannon, on the invitation of Lady St. George. In his twenty-second year he became blind, and having displaying much proficiency on the harp, determined to pursue the avocation of harper. Accordingly, in 1693 we find him travelling " on a good horse, with a servant, well mounted also, to carry his harp and wait on him "—all provided for him through the generosity of Madame MacDermot, of Alderford House, County Roscommon.

O'Carolan's first success as a professional minstrel

* Dr. Douglas Hyde's *Literary History of Ireland*, p. 598.

was at Letterfyan, the seat of George Reynolds, in 1693, where he composed the words and music of the "Fairy Queens," founded on a supposed battle between the fairies of *Sidhe Beag* and *Sidhe Mor*. The words are poor enough, but the music shows evidence of a high order, "so tender, so fairy-like," writes Kohl, "and at the same time so wild and sweetly playful that it could represent nothing but the dancing and singing of the elves and fairies by moonlight."[*]

Two of his early compositions are " Down beside me " (*Sios agus sios liom*) and " Planxty Reynolds ; " followed by a song for Grace Nugent, first cousin of Mr. Reynolds —which was actually printed in London some years later as " Grace Nugent, by Carrallan "—to which air Robert Burns adapted " Louis, what reck I by Thee ? "

The number of these Planxties composed by O'Carolan from 1694 to 1737 is very considerable, most of which were in honour of his patrons. Thus, for the families of Dillon, Peyton, Kelly, Sudley, Wilkinson, Wynne, Bellew, Jones, Wrixon, Drew, O'Flynn, O'Hara, Cruise, Bermingham, Judge, Irwin, Maguire, O'Kelly, Stafford, Power, etc., he wrote effusions wedded to incomparable airs. Many of these airs were utilised by Tom Moore, *e.g.*, " Planxty Peyton " (The Young May Moon), " Planxty Kelly " (Fly not Yet), " Planxty Irwin " (Oh ! Banquet not), " Planxty Tyrrell " (Oh ! Blame not the Bard), " Planxty Sudley " (Oh ! the Sight Entrancing), and " Planxty O'Reilly " (The Wandering Bard), better known, in Lover's setting, as " Molly Carew."

In 1696 Carolan composed " Young Terence Mac-Donogh," in honour of the son of Terence MacDonogh,

* Kohl's *Ireland in* 1843, p. 188.

the only Catholic barrister who was permitted to practice from 1692 to 1718, in which latter year he died.*

Of a later date is "Donnchadh MacCathal *og*,'
composed for Donogh (Denis) O'Conor, at whose house
O'Carolan was always a welcome guest. Charles
O'Conor of Belanagare tells us that O'Carolan was
present at Midnight Mass on Christmas Eve of the year
1726, and led a band of harpers who played "a solemn
concert" in the oratory at Belanagare, when Bishop
O'Rourke, O.F.M., sang the Mass.†

Between the years 1693 and 1710 O'Carolan had several
love affairs, notably an unrequited attachment for Miss
Bridget Cruise, of Cruisetown, County Longford, and
also for Miss Margaret Brown. The song, "Bridget
Cruise"‡ has been highly praised by critics, whilst
"Peggy Brown" is still popular. The latter lady mar-
ried Theobald, sixth Viscount Mayo, on July 8th, 1702.
This "Lord Mayo" was a great patron of O'Carolan,
though the song of that name was composed by Thady
Keenan the harper, according to the testimony of Charles
O'Conor. But the bard was not inconsolable, and he

---

* The MacDonaghs were relations of the MacDermots.

† Bishop O'Rourke ruled the see of Killala from 1707 to 1735. In
1734 he came on his last visit to the O'Conors of Belanagare, and
died there in 1735.

‡ Twenty years afterwards O'Carolan made a pilgrimage to Lough
Derg, or St. Patrick's Purgatory. Whilst assisting some pilgrims
on board the boat he chanced to take a lady's hand, and instantly
exclaimed : "By the word of my gossip, this is the hand of Bridget
Cruise!" And so, indeed, it proved to be. This fact is attested by
Charles O'Conor, who also tells us that the original song written by
O'Carolan for Bridget Cruise was often sung by the bard for his
patron (O'Conor). It is well known in Furlong's translation, whilst
Dr. Sigerson has versified another song under the title of "Gentle
Brideen." The episode regarding O'Carolan's meeting with Bridget
Cruise after twenty years has been utilised by Lover in his "True
Love will ne'er Forget."

married Miss Mary Maguire, a lady of good family in
County Fermanagh, in 1720. A short time previously
(1719), he composed a splendid air for Miss Fetherstone,
of Ardagh, County Longford, chiefly remarkable as being
the only melody set by O'Carolan to English words. It
is entitled "Carolan's Devotion," and was very popular,
although the compass of the tune is almost two octaves.

For the only existing portrait of O'Carolan the musical
world is indebted to Charles Massey, Dean of Limerick,
to whom the minstrel paid a visit at Doonass, County
Clare, in 1720, on the invitation of Mrs. Massey, *née*
Miss Grace Dillon, the daughter of Sir Charles Dillon,
of Lismullen, County Meath. On the occasion of this
visit O'Carolan composed " Dean Massey " and " Mrs.
Massey," and his portrait was drawn by a Dutch artist
who was then in the neighbourhood. Petrie says that
the portrait is by " Van der Hagan, a distinguished
Dutch artist," but this is scarcely probable, inasmuch
as Van der Hagan did not come to Ireland till 1730 or
1731. However, the portrait dates from 1720-1, and on
the death of General Massey, at Paris, in 1780, it was
brought to Ireland, and was sold to Watty Cox in 1809,
who presented it to Thomas Finn, of Carlow. Mr.
Finn had it engraved by Martyn, of Dublin, in 1822.*

As early as 1726 a collection was printed in Dublin
containing six or seven airs by O'Carolan. In the following year (1727-8) many others by him were printed
in Daniel Wright's *Aria di Camera* — the settings of

* An excellent copy, by Rogers, of this picture is prefaced to
Hardiman's *Irish Minsterlsy* in 1831. The original was painted on
copper, and measures 8 inches by 6. It was in possession of Sir
Henry Marsh, Bart., M.D., in 1845. A copy of Martyn's line
engraving (1822) is now in the Dublin National Gallery.

which are very corrupt indeed—noted by Dermot O'Conor, the translator of Keating's *History of Ireland* into English, in 1723.

Who has not heard of "Pleraca na Ruarcach," or "O'Rourke's Noble Feast," the words of which were translated from the original Irish (by MacGauran, of Leitrim) by Dean Swift, in 1721, the music by O'Carolan. But a better known convivial air is "Bumpers, Squire Jones," by O'Carolan, the English paraphrase of which was written by Arthur Dawson, Baron of the Exchequer in 1730.*

We are safe in dating the lovely air "Fanny Power" as composed before the year 1728, by O'Carolan, in praise of the daughter and heiress of David Power, County Galway. Lady Morgan tells us that O'Carolan called her "the Swan of the Shore," from the fact of her father's residence being situated on the edge of Lough Riadh. Miss Power changed her name to Mrs. Trench on March 13th, 1732, on her marriage to Richard Trench, and was the mother of Lady Clancarty, surviving to the year 1793.† Hence the melody was published in 1745 and 1779 as "Mrs. Trench," which satisfactorily explains Mr. Alfred Moffat's difficulty over the two names for the same tune.‡ Twentieth-century concert-goers will recognise O'Carolan's beautiful melody as set by Thomas Davis

* The "Squire Jones" commemorated in Baron Dawson's song was Thomas Morris Jones, of Moneyglass, County Antrim, not Mr. Jones, of Moneyglass, *County Antrim*, as asserted by Bunting. Squire Jones died in 1743.

† Richard Trench died in 1768. His third son, William Power Keating Trench, was born in 1741, and was created Baron Kilconnel on Nov. 25, 1797; Viscount Dunlo on Jan. 3, 1801; and Earl of Clancarty on Feb. 11, 1803. He had 18 children, and died April 27, 1805.

‡ Moffat's *Minstresly of Ireland*, pp. 26, 27.

in 1843, to his well-known song, "Bright Fairies by Glengarriff's Bay."

Other well-known airs by O'Carolan, composed in honour of lady patrons, are "Madame Judge," "Madame Bermingham," "Lady Dillon," "Fanny Dillon," "Fanny Betagh," "Madame Costello," "Bridget O'Malley," "Rose Dillon," "Mild Mabel Kelly," etc But, to English persons, the tune known as "The Princess Royal" has been popularised in the setting called "The Arethusa." In fact, the English have annexed the melody and included it in their collections as an "old English" air. It is absolutely certain that O'Carolan composed it in honour of Mary Mac-Dermot (the daughter of the Princess of Coolavin), who was the Princess Royal of the MacDermot family, and for whom O'Carolan composed another song, "Maire an Cuilfhin" (Fair-haired Mary).*

"The Princess Royal" was composed in 1725, and was printed in 1730 in Walsh's *Complete Dancing Master*, and in 1731 by Daniel Wright, being several times reprinted between the years 1735 and 1745. From the fact of having been introduced into Shield's "Lock and Key" to a song called "The Arethusa"—words by Prince Hoare—it has been claimed as the composition of Shield, and been included in English collections.

Perhaps the greatest tribute to O'Carolan's powers as a composer may be cited in the fact that dozens of his airs were printed during his lifetime, many of them being introduced into the various ballad operas that were fashionable from 1728 to 1738.

---

* Miss Mary MacDermot became the wife of Owen O'Rourke, who lived on the Banks of Lough Allen, County Leitrim.

For the MacDermot family, in addition to "The Princess Royal," O'Carolan composed "MacDermot Roe," "Madame M'Dermot Roe," "Anna MacDermot Roe," and "Edmond MacDermot Roe." His lovely lyric, "The Hawk of Ballyshannon," was written for Charles O'Donnell, the brother of Nanny, daughter of Manus *roe* O'Donnell, of Westport. This Nanny was married to Henry, the only son of MacDermot Roe, and their daughter, Eliza, married Robert Maguire, of Tempo, for whom O'Carolan composed "Planxty Maguire." It was whilst on a visit to Colonel Maguire, of Tempo, that O'Carolan became acquainted with James Courtney, or Seumas MacCuarta, (sometimes called *dall* MacCuairt), also a poet and harper, who composed a famous "Welcome" in honour of O'Carolan. Another visitor at Tempo to meet our bard was Patrick Linden, of the Fews, County Armagh.

In 1730, among the printed airs of O'Carolan are the following :—" Molly St. George," " Thomas Burke," " Ulick Burke," " Festus Burke," " Carolan's Cap," " Letitia Burke," " Carolan's Dream," " Carolan's Nightcap," " Colonel Irwin," " Madame Crofton," " James Plunket," " Johnny Reynolds," " Johnny Cox," " Madame Cole," " Grace Nugent," " Down beside me," etc.

An interesting episode is told of O'Carolan :—" At the house of an Irish nobleman, where Geminiani was present, Carolan challenged that eminent composer to a trial of skill. The musician played over on his violin the fifth concerto of Vivaldi. It was instantly repeated by Carolan on his harp, although he had never heard it before. The surprise of the company was increased when he asserted that he would compose a concerto himself at the moment, and the more so when he actually played that admirable piece known ever since as 'Carolan's Concerto.' " *

It seems rather a pity to spoil this story, but it appears from O'Conor, who knew O'Carolan, that Geminiani never had the pleasure of meeting the Irish minstrel. Thus writes O'Conor:—" In the variety of his musical numbers he knew how to make a selection, and seldom was contented with mediocrity. So happy was he in some of his compositions, that he excited the wonder, and obtained the approbation, of *a great master who never saw him—I mean Geminiani*." †

The following seems to be the true version of the incident :—" Geminiani, who resided for some years in Dublin, heard of the fame of O'Carolan, and determined to test his abilities. He selected a difficult Italian concerto and made certain changes in it, 'so that no one but an acute judge could detect them,' and forwarded the mutilated version to Elphin. O'Carolan listened attentively to the violinist who performed the concerto, and at once pronounced the composition beautiful, but, to the astonishment of all present, added humorously in Irish : ' Here and there it limps and stumbles.' He was then desired to rectify the errors in musical grammar, which he immediately did, and his corrections were sent to Dublin to Geminiani. No sooner did the Italian composer see the changes than he pronounced O'Carolan to be endowed with *il genio vero della musica*."

* The *Monthly Review*.   Old series.   Vol. lxxvii.   The story is substantially the same as that told by Goldsmith.

† The venerable Charles O'Conor, of Belanagare, died July 1st, 1790, aged 82.

O'Conor adds :—" O'Carolan outstripped his predecessors in the three species of composition used amongst the Irish, but he never omitted giving due praise to several of his countrymen who excelled before him in his art. The Italian compositions he preferred to all others, and was enraptured with Corelli's music."

In 1733 O'Carolan's wife died, leaving him seven children. On her death he composed a fine lament, or monody, in Irish, of which Walker published a free translation in his *Irish Bards.*

Dr. Hyde says :—" He composed over 200 airs, many of them very lively, and usually addressed to his patrons, chiefly to those of the old Irish families. He composed his own words to suit his music, and these have given him the reputation of a poet. They are full of curious turns and twists of metre to suit his airs, to which they are admirably wed, and very few are in regular stanzas. They are mostly of a Pindaric nature, addressed to patrons or to fair ladies ; there are some exceptions, however, such as his celebrated ' Ode to Whiskey,' one of the finest bacchanalian songs in any language, and his much more famed but immeasurably inferior ' Receipt for Drinking.' Very many of his airs and nearly all his poetry, with the exception of about thirty pieces, are lost." *

O'Carolan's " Receipt for Drinking " was composed at the house of Mr. Stafford, of Portobello, near Elphin, and it is also known as " Planxty Stafford." † Most

* Dr. Douglas Hyde's *Literary History of Ireland*, pp. 598-9.
† In regard to " Planxty Stafford," or " Carolan's Receipt," the minstrel only furnished the first verse, the second being added, at O'Carolan's request, by Charles MacCabe.

writers tell of the dissolute habits of our bard, and of his over-indulgence in drink, but this is an exaggeration. O'Conor, whose testimony is at first hand, tells us that O'Carolan did indulge rather freely in the use of spirituous liquors, "a habit which he imagined added strength to the flights of his genius," but he adds: "In justice, it must be observed that he was seldom surprised by intoxication." And he continues: "Constitutionally pious, he never omitted daily prayers, and fondly imagined himself inspired when he composed some pieces of Church music. Gay by nature, and cheerful from habit, he was a pleasing member of society, whilst his talents and his morality procured for him esteem and friends wherever he visited."

It seemed like a design of Providence that in the year 1738 O'Carolan, stricken with illness, found himself at the hospitable mansion of his old patroness, Madame MacDermot, at Alderford, near Boyle. His illness was of short duration, and he died after a last performance on the harp—"crowning a life of song with a wild and touching 'Farewell to Music'"—on Saturday, March 25th, 1738. Charles O'Conor briefly, and yet expressively, wrote as follows in Irish, which may be translated:—"Turlogh O'Carolan, the talented and principal musician of Ireland, died. May the Lord have mercy on his soul, for he was a moral and religious man."

Hardiman writes:—"The woman who attended Carolan in his last illness, and who lived till about the year 1787, used to say that the bard merely tasted a little whiskey to stimulate decaying nature . . . On the fifth day after his death upwards of sixty clergymen of different denominations, a number of gentlemen from the surrounding counties, and a vast concourse of country people, assembled to pay the last mark of respect to their favourite bard. All the houses in Bally-farnon (on the border of County Sligo) were occupied by the former, and the people erected tents in the fields around Alderford House. The harp was heard in every direction. . . . Old Mrs. MacDermot herself joined the female mourners who attended ' to weep,' as she expressed herself, ' over her poor gentleman, the head of all Irish music.' The funeral was one of the greatest that for many years had taken place in Connacht."

O'Carolan was buried in the east end of the old church of Kilronan, adjoining the vault of the MacDermots. From a letter written by Charles O'Connor the following extract is of interest :—" In my pensive mood, at Kilronan, I stood over poor Carolan's grave, covered with a heap of stones ; and I found his skull in a niche near the spot, perforated a little in the forehead, that it might be known by that mark." * The then parish

---

* In regard to O'Carolan's skull, Sir Robert Stewart, Mus.Doc., thus wrote in Grove's *Dictionary of Music and Musicians*:—" Early in the present (nineteenth) century it occurred to a Ribbonman named Reynolds to steal the skull of O'Carolan, and dispose of it to Sir John Caldwell, for his museum. The museum, however, has long ceased to exist, and the skull and letter describing it are both gone." Hardiman tells us that in 1750, on opening O'Carolan's grave to receive the remains of a Catholic clergyman, " whose dying request was to be interred with the bard," the Hon. Thomas Dillon, brother of the Earl of Roscommon, " caused the skull to be perforated a little in the forehead, and a small piece of ribbon to be inserted, in order to distinguish it from other similar disinterred remnants of mortality." The skull was then placed in a niche over the grave, where it remained till 1796. Sir Robert Stewart is in error regarding the Ribbonman legend. It was George Nugent Reynolds, the song writer, who presented the skull to Sir John Caldwell for his museum, and it remained at Castlecaldwell from 1796 till 1852, when it was exhibited in the Belfast Museum. In 1874, on the dispersion of the

priest of Kilronan was Dr. Thomas MacDermot Roe, afterwards (1747) Bishop of Ardagh and Clonmacnoise, who died in 1750, and was buried in a splendid tomb in Kilronan, overlooking Lough Meelagh.

Although no monument marks the grave of O'Carolan, yet the late Lady Louisa Tenison got the cemetery enclosed, and had an Irish-designed gate surmounted by a central cross. Over the arch of the gateway is the inscription: "Within this churchyard lie the remains of Carolan, the last of the Irish bards, who departed this life March 25th, 1738. R.I.P."

Lady Morgan, who was ever an admirer of old Irish music, got a splendid bas-relief of O'Carolan placed in the north aisle of St. Patrick's Cathedral, Dublin. This monument was executed by Hogan, a son of the great Irish sculptor, at Rome.

O'Carolan left seven children, namely, six daughters and one son. His son, who might have easily got together the best of his father's airs (as he was a talented musician), published an indifferent volume in 1747, under the patronage of Dean Delaney, and others. This volume was reprinted in 1750 and 1760, and the fourth edition appeared on January 1st, 1779, with the imprint of John Lee, No. 70 Dame Street. Walker adds: "His son went to London, where he taught the Irish harp. On inquiry, I find that he brought his father's harp with him to London, and, also—another man's wife."

If it is true, as alleged by Walker, that O'Carolan's

museum by Mr. Bloomfield, it was acquired by Mr. James Glenny, of Belfast, and in 1884 was in the collection formed by that gentleman's cousin, Mr. John Glenny, at Glenfield, near Newry.

son brought his father's harp to London, it must have been an instrument used by the great minstrel in middle life. However, "O'Carolan's harp" was bequeathed to Madame MacDermot, and is now in possession of The O'Conor Don, P.C., at Clonalis, Castlerea.

A good edition of the best compositions of O'Carolan is much to be desired, and the marvel is that such a work has not long since been undertaken. Let us now take a cursory glance at some of his contemporaries.

Reference has previously been made to MacCabe* and MacCuarta (Courtney), the friends and contemporaries of O'Carolan. Another friend was Cornelius Lyons, harper to Randal, fourth Earl of Antrim, famous not only as a composer, but as an arranger of Irish airs. Arthur O'Neill relates the following story of Lyons:—

Our harper and his patron being in London on one occasion, went to the house of Heffernan, a famous Irish harper, whose hotel was much frequented by the gentry, and it was previously agreed that his lordship was to call the bard "Cousin Burke," while the latter was to call his noble friend either "Cousin Randal" or "my lord" as he pleased. Having regaled themselves, they sent for Heffernan, who by this time was aware of the dignity of his guest from the conversation and livery of his lordship's servants. Heffernan complied with the wish of his noble guest, and played many of his best pieces in good style, after which his lordship

* MacCabe outlived O'Carolan by ten years. Hardiman writes "He was a frequent companion of Carolan, and had a good knowledge of the Irish language, as also of Greek, Latin, and English. Having obtained a licence to teach as a 'Popish schoolmaster,' he earned a scanty subsistence in his old age, and, finally, died in want."

requested " Cousin Burke " to try an air on the harp.
The supposed cousin, after some apologies, took the
instrument, and performed some melodies with such
effect that Heffernan, on hearing him, exclaimed : " My
lord, you may call him ' Cousin Burke,' or what cousin
you please, but *dar dich* [ᴅᴀʀ ᴅɪᴀ] he plays upon Lyons's
fingers." To accentuate this story, O'Neill says that
Heffernan had never met Lyons before.*

Heffernan was a celebrated Irish harper, who resided
in London from 1695 to 1725, and there is a reference
to him in Drake's *Memoirs* in connection with the year
1708. "From March 25th to June 5th, 1708, while the
captured Irish officers of the ship ' Salisbury,' fifteen
in number, under Colonel Francis Wauchop, who came
over to England with the Old Pretender, were awaiting
trial in Newgate, London, they seldom missed a day
without having a visit from one *Mr. Heffernan, famous
for the harp*, which he never failed to bring with him, to
divert the gentlemen, and would sometimes leave it there
for three weeks to avoid the trouble of fetching it." It
is of interest to add that the fifteen officers, after the
trial at the Old Bailey, in June, 1708, were exchanged
for Hugenots who had been captured by the French.

Another great Irish harper who settled in London in
the first years of the eighteenth century was Maguire,
from County Fermanagh. He, too, like his contemporary, Heffernan, kept a tavern near Charing Cross, and

* Lyons is best remembered as the composer of " Miss Hamilton,"
and for the variations which he added to " Eibhlin a ruin." His
patron, Randal, fourth Earl of Antrim, married Rachel, sister of
Clotworthy, 2nd Viscount Massareene, and died October 19th 1721.
Probably, on account of his mother being one of the Burkes
(Helen, daughter of Sir John Burke), he gave the cognomen of
" Cousin Burke" to Lyons.

lived for a time in affluence. Walker tells us that his
house was patronised by the Duke of Newcastle and
several of the Ministry, from 1753 to 1756, and he died
a year later of a broken heart, consequent on neglect
by his former patrons. Walker adds :—" An Irish
harper who was a contemporary of Maguire, and, like
him, felt for the sufferings of his country, had this
distich engraven on his harp :—

> ' Cur Lyra funestas edit percussa sonores?
> Sicut amissum sors Diadema gemit.!' "

Perhaps the most popular of O'Carolan's contemporaries, after Cornelius Lyons, was John Murphy, of
County Wexford. He is described by Arthur O'Neill
as an excellent harper. " Having travelled into France
he performed before, and met with the approbation of
Louis le Grand," about the year 1710. In one of the
Dublin papers of the year 1737-8 I find a notice that
on February 4th, 1738, John Murphy, the Irish harper,
was one of the attractions at Smock-alley Theatre,
when a double bill was presented in aid of the poor
prisoners in the city Marshalsea. It is satisfactory to
learn that the receipts on this occasion totalled almost
£130. The last I find of Murphy is his appearance
at the various " assemblies " held at Mallow between
the years 1746 and 1753, when Mallow was a fashionable health resort.

In regard to Irish harps at this period, there are
some dated specimens still preserved. Walker gives
an illustration of a harp, drawn by William Ousley, of
Limerick, the original of which was then (1786) in the
possession of Jonathan Hehir of that city. This harp

was made by John Kelly, and was dated 1726. It had thirty-three strings, and was made of red sally, and is said to have been five feet high. The Kellys, or O'Kellys, were famous harp-makers of Ballynascreen (Draperstown), County Derry, and one of them (Cormac O'Kelly) made Hampson's harp in 1702. This Cormac also made the "Castle Otway" harp, dated 1707, which afterwards passed to Patrick Quin, the harper, who played on it at the Belfast meeting in 1792. It is now at Castle Otway, County Tipperary. Another harp, made by John Kelly, dated 1734, belonged to Rev. Charles Bunworth, and subsequently came into possession of Crofton Croker, after whose death it was sold in London in 1854, being now the property of Rev. F. W. Galpin.

Hugh O'Neill deserves notice as being a yeoman-harper and an ardent admirer of O'Carolan, and as the teacher of Arthur O'Neill. He was born at Foxford, County Mayo, his mother being a cousin to Count Taaffe. Having lost his sight at the age of seven, he took to the harp, and was subsequently given a large farm in County Roscommon, at a nominal rent, by Mr. Tenison, of Castle Tenison. Owing to his family connections and his own excellence of character, we read that "he was received more as a friend and associate than as a professional visitor, among the gentry of Connacht." He died of fever whilst still in the prime of life, and was buried in the tomb of O'Carolan.

CHAPTER XXII.

THE JACOBITE PERIOD—1705-1775.

IT has been well said that the lyrics of the Jacobite period are among the finest in the whole range of Irish poetry. Dr. Douglas Hyde writes :—" So popular did Jacobite poetry become that it gave rise to a conventional form of its own, which became almost stereotyped, and which seems to have been adopted as a test subject in bardic contests, and by all new aspirants to the title of poet. This form introduces the poet as wandering in a wood or by the banks of a river, where he is astonished to perceive a beautiful lady approaching him. He addresses her, and she answers. The charms of her voice, mien, and bearing are portrayed by the poet. He inquires who and whence she is, and how comes she to be thus wandering. She replies that she is Erin, who is flying from the insults of foreign suitors, and in search of her real mate. Upon this theme the changes are rung in every conceivable metre, and with every conceivable variation, by the poets of the eighteenth century. Some of the best of these allegorical pieces are distinctly poetic, but they soon degenerated into conventionalism, so much so, that I verily believe they continued to be written even after the death of the last Stuart."

I have previously alluded to " Maggie Láıoıɲ," or Maggie Lauder, to which John O'Neachtan, of County

Meath, set immortal words. About the year 1707 was written the still popular "Blackbird," in praise of the Old Pretender. Mr. Sparling, in his *Irish Minstrelsy*, surmised that the song dated from "before 1715, when the Blackbird made his Scotch attempt," but I have found allusion to the song in 1709. It is chiefly remarkable as one of the earliest Irish lyrics written in English, and a copy of the verses was given to Allan Ramsay in 1724, who printed the song to his *Tea Table Miscellany*. So well understood was the name "Blackbird," as applied to King James III., that the Earl of Thomond, in 1709, had a horse of that name. The tune has been reprinted dozens of times, and is a splendid specimen of Irish airs of that period.

From the songs of Egan O'Rahilly and John ċláṗaċ MacDonnell one can form an idea of the airs that were popular in the first quarter of the eighteenth century. O'Rahilly, whose poems have been admirably edited by Father Dinneen, died in 1728, but MacDonnell lived until 1754.

One of the most beautiful airs in 1703 was, "The Day we Beat the Germans at Cremona," commemorative of the great victory gained by the Irish Brigade at Cremona on February 1st, 1702. This air was a particular favourite with the great Irish piper, James Gandsey, to whom reference will be made in the next chapter. However, Irish Jacobite minstrelsy really dates from 1707-8, when King James III. (the Pretender) determined on the invasion of England. A few years later was composed the exquisite "Caoine Ċill Ċaiṡ," or "The Lament for Kilcash," the venerable mansion of the Butler family, where resided the heroine of the song, Lady Iveagh. The song now sung was set to the air, about the year 1745, by a Father Lane, who had been educated for the priesthood through the liberality of Lady Iveagh, whose death occurred on July 19th, 1744. Lady Iveagh's second daughter, Honor, married Lord Kenmare in 1720, and on the occasion of the marriage, Egan O'Rahilly wrote the beautiful Irish song, " ᚱeᴀℓⱦᴀn Ċiℓℓ Ċᴀinnic," or " The Star of Kilkenny."

In the spring and summer of the year 1714 recruiting went on in various parts of Ireland for the cause of James III. In May of that year, one hundred and fifty Jacobites were arrested at Howth, and three of them were executed in Stephen's-green. Numerous songs were sung ridiculing the House of Hanover and the Whigs. One of the favourite lyrics in 1715 commenced :—

> " Let our great James come over
> And baffle Prince Hanover.
> With hearts and hands, in loyal bands,
> We'll welcome him at Dover."

All readers of history are familiar with the attachment of the Duke of Ormonde to King James III. in 1715. The Lords Justices of Ireland, in that year, offered £10,000 as a reward for apprehending the Duke, which offer was repeated in 1719. On this occasion a very fine lament, known as " Ormonde's Lament," was composed, and the tune was subsequently used for the still popular " Billy Byrne's Lament." The song certainly dates from the year 1715, or the spring of the year 1716.

There is still preserved a beautiful *caoine*, or lament,

on the death of Queen Mary, widow of King James II., in May, 1718. But, again, as illustrating the " tear and the smile" character of Eire, there are some rousing tunes in honour of King James III., hoping fondly that he would enjoy his own again.

The " bardic sessions " held at Charleville, Whitechurch, and other places, at intervals, between the years 1725-1775, resulted in much native poetry and songs. In order to rouse the feelings of the masses in favour of the Stuarts, the poets sang of " Moirin ni Chuillenain," " Roisin dubh," " Graine Maol," " Sighile ni Ghadharadh " (Sheela O'Gara), " Caitilin ni h-Uallachain," " An Londubh," " Druimfhionn Donn dilis," etc., all allegorical names for Ireland.

The Rev. Charles Bunworth, Rector of Buttevant, County Cork, was chosen five times to act as adjudicator at the bardic sessions held at Bruree, County Limerick, every three years from 1730 to 1750. He was not only a patron, but a skilled performer, of Irish music. His house was ever open for the wandering harper or bard, and his favourite harp was expressly made for him by John Kelly in 1734. This lovely instrument came into the possession of Crofton Croker (Bunworth's maternal grandson), and was sold in London in 1854.* A drawing of it was made by Maclise, and will be found in Hall's *Ireland* (vol. ii.). This distinguished amateur musician died about the year 1770, and he left behind him fifteen Irish harps, the gifts of wandering minstrels whom he had be-

---

* It was acquired by Rev. F. W. Galpin, who had it on view at the Music Loan Exhibition at Fishmongers' Hall, London, in July, 1904. This enthusiastic ·musical amateur also exhibited an Irish harp, dated 1750.

friended. These fifteen Irish harps were subsequently *burned as firewood* by a careless servant.

A pretty tune, "Seaghan Buidhe" (Yellow John), a name applied to the followers of King William, was composed early in this century, to which John Cunningham, in 1740, adapted a fine song, entitled "Teacht na n-geana fiadhaine," or "The Return of the Wild Geese." This tune was annexed by the Scotch Jacobites in 1744, and appears in Johnson's *Two Hundred Country Dances*, in 1748, and as "Shan-buie" in Oswald's *Collection*, in 1752. About the year 1736 the air was published in Dublin as "Shaun bwee," and in 1742 it appeared with the title, "The Irish Pot Stick." The Scotch adaptation of this fine Irish melody is "Over the water to Charlie," under which name it was printed in 1752.

From about the same epoch date "All the way to Galway" (Yankee Doodle), and "An Sean duine," or "The Old Man," also known as "Hob or Nob," published in 1745. The latter was annexed by the Scotch and set to the song of "The Campbells are coming," first printed in 1751.

As can well be imagined, the great victory of Fontenoy, on May 11th, 1745, gave heart to the Jacobites, but the defeat at Culloden was a considerable damper.* For all that, we have still some hundreds of fine Jacobite songs that certainly date from 1744 to 1750. In addition, the songs of Andrew Magrath, John O'Tuomy, Father English, William

---

* It is well known that of the "seven men of Moidart" who accompanied Prince Charlie to Scotland in July, 1745, four of the seven were Irish. Moreover, it may be added that two of the four— Rev. George Kelly and Sir Thomas Sheridan—were Protestants.

Heffernan, Edward Nagle, etc., have preserved for us
old tunes of a date even prior to the eighteenth century. Numerous Irish lyrics too, denouncing the
Whigs, are wedded to charming melodies, some of
which have survived to our own day. One of the
best known of the Anti-Whig songs is "ᾱⲉⲓᴘ-ᴘⲩⲁⳁⲁᴘ
Whiggiona," by the Merry Pedlar (Andrew Magrath),
set to the tune of "ⲡⳑⲁⲛⲥⲁⲙ ⲡⲉⲓᴘᵬⲓⳍ," or "Leather
the Wig"—that is, to thresh the "wig," as symbolis-
ing the Whig. A fairly good version of this air was
published by Playford in 1713, and by B. Cooke, of
Dublin, in 1795, under the absurd title of "Will you
come plank, come plank." *

Thurot's expedition, in 1759, also furnished many
ballads during the year 1760. It is a mistake to
suppose that the Jacobites in Ireland gave no evidence of their sympathies after the year 1746; and the
fact is that enlisting for the "French service"—meaning, of course, the service of Prince Charlie—went on as
late as 1790. It was only in 1765, when King James III.
died at Rome, that the Stuart cause was regarded as
hopeless, and the end came in January, 1788, with the
death of King Charles III., generally known as Prince
Charlie.

Of the many distinguished harpers who flourished in
the second half of the eighteenth century Donnchadh
a Haimpsuigh (Denis O'Hampsey or Hampson) was the
most remarkable. Born at Craigmore, near Garvagh,
County Derry, in 1697, he lost his sight at the age of
three, and at twelve was placed under the tuition, for

* This fine Irish melody was popular in England as "The
Bunter's Delight."

the harp, of Bridget O'Cahan. In 1711, he studied with John C. Garragher, a blind, itinerant harper (whom he accompanied to Buncrana), and he finished his musical course with Loughlin Fanning and Patrick O'Connor, both Connacht harpers of repute.

During ten years, commencing with the year 1715, when he was presented with a valuable harp (made by Cormac O'Kelly in 1702), Hampson travelled through Ireland and Scotland. In 1745 he made a second journey to Scotland, and was presented to the Young Pretender, Prince Charlie, at Edinburgh, " by Colonel Kelly, of Roscommon, and Sir Thomas Sheridan." *
As may be supposed, our Irish harper brought over to Scotland many beautiful airs, which in course of time were more or less naturalised, and claimed as " Scottish." In particular, he familiarised the Scotch with the lovely melody, " Eiblín ᴀ Ruin," or " Robin Adair," the Irish origin of which is beyond any question.†

At a meeting of the Belfast harpers in July, 1792, Hampson played : "The Dawning of the Day," "The County of Leitrim," and " Uileacan dubh O !" and, though then aged ninety-five, he confided to Mr. Sampson, with the honest feeling of self-appreciation :— " When I played the old tunes, not another of the harpers would play after me." His style of performing

---

* These are the names as given by Hampson himself, in 1805, to the Rev. G. V. Sampson, but the two persons really meant were Rev. George Kelly (a non-juring parson, who was an ardent Jacobite from 1715-1750) and Sir Thomas Sheridan, the Prince's Secretary, who died at Rome, November 25th, 1746.

† For an account of this melody see an article by the present writer in the new edition of Grove's *Dictionary of Music and Musicians*. (1904.)

was marvellous, and the rapidity of his execution was unapproached. He plucked the strings in the old style, with long nails, and had the traditional method of harp-playing.

General Hart sent an artist to take a drawing of Hampson in 1804, and this was reproduced by Bunting in his second *Collection of Irish Airs*. The old harper died at Magilligan on November 5th, 1807, aged 110, and he left his harp to his patron, Rev. Sir W. Hervey Bruce, of Downhill.* This harp is described as follows by Rev. Mr. Sampson, in 1805 :—" The sides and front are made of white sally ; the back of fir, patched with copper and iron plates. Sculptured on the harp are the lines :—

> ' In the days of Noah I was green ;
> After his flood I've not been seen
> Until seventeen hundred and two I was found
> By Cormac Kelly under ground ;
> He raised me up to that degree,
> Queen of Music they call me.' "

A pathetic story is told of O'Hampson's last days. Twenty-four hours before his death he was visited by his patron, Rev. Sir W. Hervey Bruce (made a baronet of the United Kingdom on June 23rd, 1804), and the aged harper insisted on being allowed to play a favourite tune as a " Farewell to Music." His harp was brought to him, and he struck a few chords of an old Jacobite air, but the effort was too much. He sank back on the pillow exhausted, and died within a few hours. So passed away the last Jacobite harper.

* O'Hampson's harp was for a time in the Museum of the Belfast Natural History and Philosophical Society, and it was lent for exhibition at the Irish Harp Festival held at Belfast in May, 1903. It is now, as Mr. F. J. Bigger informs me, at Downhill.

CHAPTER XXIII.

Irish Pipers in the Eighteenth Century.

THE old Irish *Piob mor*, frequently called the " War Pipes," was almost the same as the Highland pipes of to-day—slung from the shoulder and blown by the mouth, as described by Stanihurst, in 1584. Mediæval writers give the name *Cetharcoire*, or four-tuned, to the " set " of bagpipes, and the term is to be met with in the " Brudihean da Derga." The *cethar-coire*, as the Irish name implies, has reference to the tuning of the chanter, the long drone, and the two reed-drones. Another name for the " set " of pipes was *tinne*, whilst the pipers are called *cuislennach*. As before stated, Uilleann and Cuisle pipes are synonymous, inasmuch as we have Uille or Uilleann = elbow, whilst *cuisle* is the pipe itself. *Uilleann* was subsequently anglicised as " Union."

Almost coincident with the disappearance of the *Piob mor*, about the middle of the eighteenth century, was the gradual spread of the domestic or Union (Uilleann) pipes, blown by a bellows. The Scotch retained the war pipes (of which the earliest mention is made in 1374) and still use them, though the oldest dated Highland bagpipes is only 1409.

During the first quarter of the eighteenth century flourished Pierce Power, of Glynn, County Waterford, whose best known song is " ꝓléꝑꜫꜩ ꜫn ᵹleꜫnnꜫ," or " The Humours of Glynn," which was an especial favourite with Robert Burns, the Scotch poet. Burns was so enamoured of this lovely air (composed by

O'Carolan) that he wrote his well-known song, "Their groves of sweet myrtle let foreign lands reckon " to it. Previously O'Keeffe had set the air to a song, " Though Leixlip is proud."

Even a more famous performer was Laurence Grogan, of Johnstown Castle, County Wexford. He was what was known as a "gentleman piper," and was also a composer. Most people have heard of one of his tunes, "Ally Croker," written and composed by him in 1725, on the vagaries of a disappointed suitor of Miss Alicia Croker, the sister of Edward Croker, High Sheriff of County Limerick. It was quickly taken up by all the ballad singers and introduced into the play of *Love in a Riddle* in 1729, being afterward popularized by Foote in his comedy, *The Englishman in Paris*, in 1753, and by our own Kane O'Hara in *Midas* in 1760. The charming heroine of the ballad was a reigning toast for years, and she married Mr. Charles Langley, of County Kilkenny, dying at an advanced age in 1770. Perhaps it may be necessary to state that the tune is now only known by Moore's song of "The Shamrock," to which it is adapted.

Sir Charles Villiers Stanford omits "The Shamrock " from his edition of Moore, giving as a reason that it is not an Irish air.* This he does, relying on the authority of the late Mr. Chappell, who claimed the tune for England on the ground that it first appeared in *Love in a Riddle*, in 1729. However, Larry Grogan wrote the words and music in 1725 (or 1726 at latest), as is

---

* He also omits " Eveleen's Bower" for the same reason. though it certainly is an Irish air, and was printed as such in 1791 by Brysson.

amply proved by Crofton Croker.   His name is immortalized in the opening lines of "The County of Limerick Buck Hunt," written in 1730 by Pierce Creagh, of Dangan, near Quin, County Clare :

> " By your leave, Larry Grogan,
>   Enough has been spoken ;
> 'Tis time to give over your sonnet, your sonnet."

The tune to which Pierce Creagh's verses were set is the well-known Irish melody, "*Nach mBaineann sin Do*" (" What's that to anyone "). There are six verses, all of a topical character, alluding to noted belles, the Misses Cherry, Singleton, Curry, Bligh, Prittie, and Persse, all of whom reigned in 1725-30. Crofton Croker was unable to identify either Miss Curry or Miss Singleton, but they were both well known beauties, the latter being the daughter of Henry Singleton, who was Prime Sergeant in 1726.

Grogan and Creagh were fast friends, and an evidence of this may be had in an announcement in *Faulkner's Journal* : "On Wednesday, August 31, 1743, the £10 prize at Loughrea Races was won by Pierce Creagh's horse, *Larry Grogan*." This gentleman-piper composed numerous jigs, reels, and hornpipes, including a jig known as " The Girl I Love."

Grogan will be best remembered by " Ally Croker," the tune of which was set to " Unfortunate Miss Bailey," in 1803, by George Colman.

In *Walker's Hibernian Magazine* for August, 1807, there is a capital Latin version of Grogan's song by D. Hickey, of Clonmel. I can find no trace of this distinguished piper after the year 1750, and probably he died soon afterwards. His nephew, Mr. Cornelius

Grogan, Johnstown Castle, who had been a member of Parliament for Enniscorthy in 1782, was hanged on June 27th, 1798, for having joined the Wexford insurgents.

Going back to the year 1720, we find that the football matches of that period were provided with a piper, who headed the contending teams as they entered the field. Matthew Concannen, who published a mock-heroic poem called "A Match at Football," in 1721, describes the enlivening strains of the piper as the rival clubs, six aside, in County Dublin, lined out for play.

A favourite pipe tune in 1726 was "Moll Roe," or "Sweet Molly Roe," written in praise of Miss Molly Roe, the daughter of Mr. Andrew Roe, of Tipperary. The song consisted of ten verses, each of which was written impromptu by ten bucks one night at the County Tipperary Clubhouse, in 1725. I have a long manuscript account of the circumstances under which this once very popular ballad was written, and communicated to a long since defunct magazine, in July, 1773, by Thomas Amory, the last of the assembled guests on the occasion. The concluding verse was as follows :—

> " Come, fill up in bumpers your glasses,
>   And let the brown bowl overflow,
> Here's health to the brightest of lasses,
>   The queen of all toasts—Molly Roe."

The old Irish tune to which this song was set was introduced under the name "Moll Roe" in Henry Brooke's *Jack the Giant Queller*, in 1748, and it was also called "Moll Roe in the Morning." O'Keeffe included it in his *Poor Soldier*, in 1783, and O'Farrell printed it in his now scarce work, *A Pocket Companion for the Irish Pipes*, in 1810.

During the period of the iniquitous Penal Laws—from 1703 to 1746—Catholic priests occasionally went about in the guise of pipers, and even bishops are recorded to have passed as performers on the pipes. Cardinal Moran writes as follows :—

"Some few years ago [1885] an English gentleman paid a passing visit to the house of the venerable Bishop of Kilmore [Dr. James Brown]. He was very much struck by the portraits of the Bishop's predecessors which adorned the sitting-room, but could not conceal his surprise that the place of honour between two of these portraits was allotted to a Highland piper in full costume. Still greater, however, was his surprise when he learned from the lips of the Bishop that that was the portrait of [Dr. Richardson] one of the most illustrious of his predecessors, who, being a skilled musician, availed himself of such a disguise in order to visit and console his scattered flock."

Apparently, Irish pipers were not infrequent performers in England in 1730, as, from the London *Evening Post*, under date of June 17th, 1732, there is mention of "a noted Irish bagpiper" who was concerned in a quarrel in a brandy-shop "by Mermaid Court, near Charing Cross."

It will probably be of more than passing interest to mention that Handel, during his nine months' stay in Ireland, was much struck with the sound of the bagpipes. We all know the story of his marked preference for "Eileen Aroon," but apparently he must have been even more impressed with an old pipe melody called "The Poor Irish Boy," as we find it copied out in musical setting in his MS. sketch book, now in the Fitzwilliam Museum.

In 1744 was written "The Kilruddery Hunt"—the joint production of Thomas Mozeen and Owen Bray, of Loughlinstown, County Dublin, set to the old Irish tune of "Sighile ni Ghadharadh," or Celia O'Gara. It soon became enormously popular, and is called by Ritson "The Irish Hunt," who, however, incorrectly ascribed its authorship to Mr. St. Leger. It was published in a volume called *The Lyric Pacquet* by Mozeen, in 1764, and is quoted with eulogy by John O'Keeffe, who tells us that the tune was utilized by Kane O'Hara, in *Midas*, in 1760. "The Kilruddery Hunt" was a prime favourite with Theobald Wolfe Tone, as we find him, under date of April 25th, 1797, quoting a line of it : "Set out from Cologne 'at five in the morning by most of the clocks,' on my way," etc. Moore's adaption of the old melody to his song, "Oh, had We some Bright Little Isle of our Own," is well known, and was published in 1813.

The Jacobite period—1715-1776—was productive of hundreds of beautiful lyrics, mostly wedded to older tunes, but there are many pipe melodies of this epoch, specially inspired by the feeling in favour of the King over the water, James III., or Prince Charlie. In Henry Brooke's now forgotten musical comedy of *Jack the Giant Queller*, produced at Smock-alley Theatre, Dublin, in 1748, a piper played some Irish airs.

A few of the songs were regarded as Jacobite, and the play was prohibited after the first night's performance.

O'Keeffe gives the following description of the Uilleann bagpipes about the year 1760 :—

"The Irish pipes have a small bellows under the left arm, and a bag covered with crimson silk under the right arm. From these passes a small leather tube of communication for the wind to reach, first, from the bellows to the bag, as both are pressed by the elbow ; and from this tube another small one conveys the wind to the several pipes. That on which the fingers move is called the chanter or treble. There are three other pipes which hang over the wrist. The longest of them is called the drone or bass."

During the first half of the eighteenth century the pipes were much availed of for the country festive dances, and especially for the " cake " dances. From 1664 onward there are references to the cake dance, for which the services of the piper were always secured, who was paid by the various dancers.

About the year 1680 Sir Henry Piers, treating of the social customs in County Westmeath, writes :—" Here, to be sure, the piper fails not of diligent attendance. The cake to be danced for is provided at the charge of the ale wife, and is advanced on a board on the top of a pike ten foot high."

Some time ago, in looking through a file of old Dublin newspapers, I came across the following advertisement from the *Dublin Evening Post* of October 1st, 1734:—"On Thursday next, Mary Kelly, at the Queen's Head, in Glasnevin, near this city, will have a fine plum cake, to be danced for by the young men and maidens of the country, who are generously invited by her, not doubting but they will be pleased with her ale as well as cake." The last inuendo is deliciously naïve, quite

suggestive of the subscriptions generously given by
some country publicans of our own day for Gaelic
gatherings.

It was also the custom in the first half of the
eighteenth century to have bonfires on St. John's Eve
and St. Peter's Eve, with dancing and music.   From an
advertisement in *Faulkner's Journal* I find that on June
19th, 1742, the Lord Mayor of Dublin, William Aldrich,
issued a proclamation, forbidding the customary social
gatherings on the eve of St. John and on that of
SS. Peter and Paul.   This was owing to the growing
movement in favour of the Young Pretender.

For centuries Irish harpers and minstrels had accompanied the Irish troops,   Irish pipers, too, went with
the Irish brigade, and took part in the memorable
battle of Fontenoy on May 11th, 1745.   It is on record
that the two tunes played at Fontenoy were "St.
Patrick's Day in the Morning" and "The White
Cockade."   This is probably the last appearance in
battle of the Irish *Piob mor* (war pipes) of which there
is any mention.

One of the most distinguished pipe players about the
year 1760 was Piper Jackson (a brother of "Hero"
Jackson), regarding whom John O'Keeffe has a couple
of references.   Jackson lived at Ballingarry, County
Limerick, and was not only a good violinist and
bagpipe player, but was also a remarkable composer.
A volume of his airs was published by Sam Lee, of
Dublin, in 1774, entitled *Jackson's Celebrated Irish
Tunes*, a reprint of which was issued in 1790 by
Edmund Lee, 2, Dame-street, price *2s. 2d.*   O'Keeffe
writes:—"Hero Jackson had a brother, a fine gentle-

man of great landed property, and a complete musician on the pipes; they named him 'Piper' Jackson; he composed 'Jackson's Morning Brush.' I wrote a trio to it for my 'Wicklow Mountains,' which was sung by Richardson, Johnson and Fawcett." Many of Jackson's best airs are called after himself, such as "Jackson's Maggot," "Jackson's Strinkin," "Jackson's Coggie," "Jackson's Cup," etc. Among the printed airs, many of which were composed long before Jackson's day, are a few that appeared for the first time, like "*Cuma Liom*," (It is indifferent to me, or I don't care).

To O'Keeffe we are also indebted for a notice of Piper MacDonnell. Writing of the period, 1770, he says:—

"MacDonnell, the famous Irish piper, lived in great style—two houses, servants, hunters, &c. His pipes were small and of ivory, tipped with silver and gold. You scarcely saw his fingers move, and all his attitudes, while playing, were steady and quiet, and his face composed. On a day that I was one of a very large party who dined with Mr. Thomas Grant, of Cork, MacDonnell was sent for to play for the company during dinner; a chair and table were placed for him on a landing outside the room, a bottle of claret and a glass on the table, and a servant waiting behind the chair designed for him; the door left wide open. He made his appearance, took a rapid survey of the preparation for him, filled his glass, stepped to the diningroom door, looked full into the room, saying—'Mr. Grant, your health and company,' drank it off, and threw a half-crown on the table, saying to the servant, 'There, my lad, is two shillings for my bottle of wine, and keep the sixpence for yourself.' He ran out of the house, mounted his hunter, and galloped off, followed by his groom.

"About the same season I prevailed on MacDonnell to play one night on the stage at Cork, and had it announced in the bills that Mr. MacDonnell would play some of Carolan's fine airs upon the ' Irish organ.' The curtain went up, and discovered him sitting alone in his own dress ; he played and charmed everybody."

The reference to the bagpipe as the " Irish organ " was anticipated by Roger North in 1680, as he writes :—" The equipment of the town barge was very very stately, for ahead there sat four or five drone bagpipe —the *North Country organ*—and a trumpeter astern."

Another famed piper of this period was Parson Sterling —not to be confounded with Orange Sterling, who was also a musician. Rev. James Sterling was a Rector, of Lurgan, Co. Cavan, and was not only an excellent performer on the pipes, but also shone as a composer, highly commended by Edmund Burke, in 1754.

From 1740 to 1770 numerous "Laments" com- memorative of Rapparees and Highwaymen were popular. In particular, "Crotty's Lament" (1742) and " Freney's Lament " (1760), were well known in the counties of Waterford, Kilkenny, and Wexford. Freney, was subsequently pardoned ; was appointed to a minor post in the Customs at New Ross ; and died full of years in 1790, being buried at Inistioge.

One of the most celebrated bagpipe tunes in 1770 was " Brennan on the Moor," a setting of a song written in praise of a noted Irish Tory or Rapparee, William Brennan. The melody, with its rousing refrain, is now almost forgotten, and the ballad has not been heard in recent years. In 1775, Rev. Dr. Campbell was delighted with the Irish bagpipes, as also with Irish dances. He was Rector of Galoon and Chancellor of Clogher, and was a friend of Edmund Burke, Johnson, Boswell, and Goldsmith. He died

June 20th, 1795. One tune in particular pleased him vastly (as Pepys would say), namely, "The Rock of Cashel," which he saw danced at Cashel. Whilst a guest at the house of Mr. MacCarthy, of Spring Hill, County Tipperary, he noted some of the native social customs as follows :—

" Here we are at meals, even on Sunday, *regaled with the bagpipe*, which, to my uncultivated ear, is not an instrument so unpleasant as the players of Italian music represent it. After supper I, for the first time, drank whiskey punch, the taste of which is harsh and austere, and the smell worse than the taste. The drinkers of it say it becomes so palatable that they can relish no other. The spirit was very fierce and wild, requiring not less than seven times its own quantity of water to tame and subdue it."

In 1779, Beranger, whilst on a visit to Connacht, found the bagpipe much in evidence at local amusements, and he saw " a rustic dance for a cake "—that is, the cake dance, as it is called. His diary is of especial interest as giving us the names of six dance tunes then popular. Those dance tunes he names as follows :—" Miss M'Leod's Reel," " Batha Buidhe," " The Geese in the Bog," " Madhadh na bplandie," " The Roscommon Hunt," and " The Hare in the Corn." We can, therefore, date these six dance tunes as prior to the year 1779—just one hundred and twenty-five years ago. Another tourist of this period alludes to a favourite air he heard played on the bagpipes, viz., " The Shamrock Shore." A few years later another tourist alludes to a popular Donegal pipe-melody, " Maggie Pickins," which went back to the seventeenth century. It was cribbed by the Scotch between the years 1715 and 1740, and adapted to a song called " Whistle o'er the lave o't "—so indelicate that it had to be rewritten by Robert Burns in 1790. Neither Bunting nor Petrie noticed the interesting fact that this fine pipe-melody was utilized by the Volunteers as a marching-tune.

In the musical instrument room of the National Museum in Dublin, there are six fine specimens of Irish pipes in a case, the oldest of which is dated 1768. There are two others dated 1770 and 1789, made by the elder Kenna of Dublin.   The gem of the collection is the set of " Union " pipes, said to have belonged to Lord Edward Fitzgerald, but I have grave doubts, from a recent examination, of their authenticity.*   Another beautiful set is that which was made for Mr. Matthias Phelan, of Cappoquin, in 1790.

It may not be generally known that the first printed book of bagpipe tunes did not appear till 1784. This was "A Collection of Highland Vocal Airs, never hitherto published . . . and some specimens of Bagpipe Music, by Rev. Patrick M'Donald," followed, a year later, by Daniel Dow's collection.† However, the first distinctly Irish collection for the "Union " pipes was that by O'Farrell in 1799-1801. In addition to a variety of " slow and sprightly Irish tunes," there was added "a treatise with the most perfect instruc-

* The date "1768" is engraved on the silver band of the Ivory Drones with the maker's name, Egan. Lord Edward was then in his fifth year.

† Rev. Patrick M'Donald and his brother had been collecting Highland airs from 1760 to 1780. The former was minister of Kilmore and Kilbride in Argyllshire, and his death took place in 1824, he being then in his ninety-seventh year.   Joseph, his brother, died in 1782, whose *Treatise on the Theory of the Scots Highland Bagpipe* was published in 1803.

tions ever yet published for the pipes—with a vignette of O'Farrell playing on the Union pipes in the pantomime of 'Oscar and Malvina.' "*

In the last years of the eighteenth century, from 1790 to 1800, flourished John Crump, described by Petrie as "the greatest of the Munster pipers." His pipes were acquired by James Hardiman, who generously gave them to Paddy Coneely. Edward Keating Hyland, another Munster piper, composed the "Fox Chase" in 1799. He was an accomplished musician as well as piper, and got lessons in theory and harmony from Sir John Stevenson. When George IV. visited Dublin in 1821, he ordered a new set of pipes for Hyland, at a cost of fifty guineas, as a mark of recognition of his performance. Hyland, who was blind from the age of fifteen, died at Dublin in 1845. Other pipers of fame were Gaynor and Talbot, of whom Carleton writes eulogistically. James Gansey was of a later period.†

Irish pipers, even at the close of the eighteenth century and to this day, made no use of printed music, and taught orally, just as they had been instructed themselves. As late as 1773 Dr. Johnson, in his *Tour in the Hebrides*, alludes to the college of pipers in the Isle of Skye, which had been there "beyond all memory," and he tells of a similar college of pipers at Mull which had closed its doors sixteen years previously. It was only in 1828 that Captain Neill Macleod published "A Collection of Piobaireachd or Pipe Tunes, as verbally taught by

---

* The pantomime of *Oscar and Malvina* was produced in 1791.
† Gansey "the prince of Kerry pipers," died at Killarney in February, 1857, aged 90.

the M'Crummin Pipers in the Isle of Skye, to their Apprentices "—a work distinguished by the use of an extraordinary notation of quasi-cryptic syllables.

But the most celebrated amateur piper of this period was the Rev. Charles Macklin, who is described by Lady Morgan as " a marvellous performer on the Irish bag-pipes—that most ancient and perfect of instruments." Macklin, who was a nephew of the great actor of that name, was dismissed from his curacy for having played out his congregation with a solo on the bagpipes.

According to Dr. Kitto, William Talbot was cer-tainly a talented musician as well as piper. Talbot was born near Roscrea, County Tipperary, in 1780, and lost his sight from small-pox in 1785, at which date his family removed to "the seaside, near Waterford." In 1793, being then but thirteen, he was already a piper of local repute, and was in request for all festive gather-ings. From 1797 to 1801 he became a sailor and voyaged to various parts of the world, but again reverted to his first love, and became a profes-sional piper in 1802. " At Limerick he made his first attempt to build an organ, in which he succeeded admirably without instruction from any person." Re-moving to Cork, he purchased an organ so as to become acquainted with the mechanism, and he soon constructed a fine-toned organ. From the experience thus acquired in the matter of reeds, etc., Talbot improved the " Uilleann " pipes considerably ; and his improvements have been generally adopted by suc-ceeding makers. In April, 1813, he opened a tavern at No. 12 Little Mary Street, Dublin.

CHAPTER XXIV.

ANGLO-IRISH MUSIC FROM 1701 TO 1741.

IN the first years of the eighteenth century it would seem that the " city music," or the Dublin Corporation city band, achieved no small share of admiration for their performances.* On several occasions between the years 1701 (when the statue of King William was formally inaugurated on July 1st) and 1740, the " city music " discoursed most pleasantly. However, the "State Music" or the Viceregal band was also much in evidence, and in 1710 John Sigismund Cousser was appointed master of the King's band in Dublin, being also made master of the choristers in Christ Church Cathedral. From 1710 till his death, in the winter of 1727, Cousser did much for modern music both in the Cathedral and in the State band. He composed several operas, and also various birthday odes, one of which, in 1724, was much above the ephemeral compositions of this kind.

The success of the Hibernian Catch Club led to the formation of other musical societies, and in 1705 the "Bull's Head Society "—so called because the meetings were held at the " Bull's Head " Tavern on the western

---

* In 1692 the " city music " petitioned against persons who under their names "presumed to go about publicly and play for money." New Instruments were provided for them in 1713, and Lewis Layfield was appointed musical director. The uniform consisted of "blue coats and laced hats." In 1714 the salary of the members was increased from £2 to £4 each annually.

side of Fishamble-street—was started. The members met every Friday evening, the subscription being an English crown. A regular programme was gone through, and the entertainment concluded with " catch singing, mutual friendship, and harmony," the series of musical performances for each year being regulated by a committee. Each year a dinner was given in December, and the society ended the season in May. Another society was formed about the year 1710 by Gregory Byrne, and the members were wont to assemble at the " Cross Keys" in Christ Church yard under the presidency of Patrick Beaghan. A few years later, this society removed to the " George " Tavern in Fishamble-street.

Gilbert writes as follows :—

" On Beaghan's death, in 1723, John Neale was chosen President of the ' Bull's Head Club,' which was then removed to the *Bear* Tavern in Christ Church Yard, where the members organised a plan for discharging the liabilities of confined debtors, and assumed the name of the *Charitable and Musical Society*. The number of members of the club rapidly increased after this period; and many noblemen and commoners of high rank having joined it, the *Bear* was found too incommodious for the meetings, which were thence transferred to the *Bull's Head* in 1725."

The fame of Italian opera having spread to Dublin, Joseph Ashbury, Deputy Master of the Revels, invited over Nicolo Grimaldi Nicolini and his Italian opera company from the Haymarket, in March, 1711. Nicolini was the then greatest soprano in the world, and had achieved much popularity in London. Accordingly, he came over to Smock-alley Theatre at the end of March, and produced several plays, including

Rinaldo, Camilla, and *Pyrrhus and Demetrius*—Nicolini singing in *Italian,* whilst all the other performers sang in *English.* The Italian singers captured the Dubliners from April to July of the year 1711, and a further impetus was given to musical art.

In connection with Italian opera it is gratifying to chronicle that the adaptation of Scarlatti's operas of *Camilla* and *Pyrrhus and Demetrius* was due to the Irish theatrical manager, Owen MacSweeny, who produced these works in London. He was manager of the Haymarket Theatre from 1706 to 1708, and died on October 2nd, 1754, leaving his large fortune to Peg Woffington.

At both cathedrals Daniel Roseingrave, a pupil of Henry Purcell and Dr. Blow, was Organist and Vicar Choral, and he did much to improve the musical services both at Christ Church and St. Patrick's. His son Ralph was appointed Organist of Trinity College Chapel in 1705, and was given a Vicar Choralship in St. Patrick's Cathedral in 1719, becoming assistant to his father in 1726. On his father's death, in 1727, he succeeded to both positions, which he held till 1747. His younger brother, Thomas, born in Dublin, showed such musical precocity that the Dean and Chapter of St. Patrick's, in 1710, sent him to Italy to study, where he was placed under Scarlatti, at Venice. Subsequently he settled in London, and was appointed the first organist of St. George's, Hanover-square, in 1725.

Following the fashion of London, a Dublin Academy of Music was founded in 1729, and in the following year the members built the Crow-street Music Hall "for the practice of Italian musick." In the list of subscribers to Handel's twelve grand concertos, published in 1739, is: "The Academy of Music at Dublin, two setts."

The Charitable Musical Society, also known as the Bull's Head Society, Fishamble-street, devoted their funds to the release of debtors in the Marshalsea. In the *Dublin Evening Post*, under date of December 16th, 1735, we read:—"Last week 55 poor prisoners were discharged out of the several gaols in the City and Liberties of Dublin by the *Charitable Musical Society* held at the Bull's Head in Fishamble-street, the year ending the 10th day of December, 1735."

In matters theatrical Dublin could give a lead to London, but it is not within the scope of this work to chronicle the fame of Irish dramatists and actors. At Smock-alley, Elrington produced all the London successes, whilst the first performances of many afterwards celebrated plays were given in Dublin. For instance, Charles Coffey's ballad opera, *The Beggar's Wedding* (dedicated to the Provost and Fellows of Trinity College, Dublin), produced at Smock-alley in September, 1728, was enormously successful the following years in London. It abounded in old Irish tunes, and, when published, ran through four editions in a short time. Though now forgotten, many of the airs are still popular. Coffey was a Dublin man, and his after successes included: *The Female Parson* (1731), and *The Devil to Pay* (1731).*

Perhaps the strongest evidence of the musical tendencies of Dublin in the years 1701-1741 is the number of music shops and music publishers. For long it was

* Charles Coffey died in London, May 13th, 1745.

believed that the Neales were the earliest music publishers in Dublin (in 1726), but it is absolutely certain
that many musical works were printed by Brocas,
Dobson, Hoey, Crampton, Risk, Powell, Rhames, and
Wilson, during that period. For instance, in 1706,
John Brocas, of Ram-lane (Schoolhouse-lane), printed
a good edition of Barton's Psalms, edited by Thomas
Smith, all adapted to the church tunes to be found in
the current editions of Sternhold and Hopkins. This
scarce work—a copy of which is in the British Museum
—has the musical setting in two parts, Treble and
Bass, "with brief instructions for the understanding of
the same." Other Psalm-books were printed by Powell,
including the Huguenot Psalters, in 1731 and 1735.
Neale, of Christ Church Yard, published the *Beggar's
Opera* in 1728, and *Polly* in 1729, previous to which he
had issued collections of Irish airs, dance music, etc.
An edition of Allan Ramsay's songs, with music, was
printed by Risk in 1729, and a pirated edition of
Daniel Wright's "Aria di Camera" in 1731. A collection entitled *The Vocal Miscellany* was printed in
1738, and numerous sheet songs date from the years
1735-1741.

Shakespearean plays were much in vogue in the first
quarter of the eighteenth century, and in 1721 George
Grierson, "at the sign of the *Two Bibles* in Essex-
street," published *Othello, Hamlet*, and *Julius Cæsar*.
It was the custom at this date to have "entertainments
of singing and dancing" between the acts, and therefore most of the actors and actresses had perforce
to be vocalists. Pantomime, too, became popular in
Dublin; and in December, 1729, Madame Violante

created a furore at Smock-alley, in which Cummins danced the "White Joke," a set off to the then popular "Black Joke." This lady became such a favourite that on November 20th, 1730, she opened a booth at Fownes-court, whence in April, 1731, she removed to George's-lane where, at Christmas, her Lilliputian actors and actresses won instant favour with the *Beggar's Opera.*

The ballad opera *Flora, or Hob in the Well,* was produced at Smock-alley Theatre, on April 27th, 1730; and on December 16th, 1731, *Damon and Phillida* was given for Layfield's benefit. Charles Coffey's *Devil to Pay* was heard on February 24th, 1731-2, and Mrs. Sterling's last appearance was in the *Beggar's Opera,* on May 22nd, 1732. Henry Carey's farcical opera, *The Contrivances,* was given on February 15th, 1732-3, as an afterpiece.

But to return to matters more strictly in the domain of music. In 1726 the annual celebrations in honour of St. Cecilia's Day were inaugurated in St. Patrick's Cathedral, although Dean Swift was not partial to any departure from the ordinary Anglican service. These celebrations received a great fillip in the year 1729, when Dubourg appeared for the first time as leader of the orchestra. The performance on this occasion lasted from ten in the morning to three o'clock, including a sermon.

Concerts were not unfrequent at this period. For instance, on August 27, 1734, there was a "Grand Consort of Musick" given at the Taylors' Hall (Back-lane), Dublin. According to the advertisement in the *Dublin Evening Post,* the programme was to be rendered "by the best Masters," the chief attraction being a Mr. de Reck, who was announced to play "a solo on the hautboy and *curtel*."

Organ building must have been carried on in Dublin at this period, for in the year 1719, Thomas Hollister built an organ for St. Werburgh's (of which he became organist), at a cost of £300. Again, in 1725, we read that "Master Cuvellie, of Dublin, built an organ for the church of St. Michan, after twenty years' labour," and the case of it was carved and decorated by William Wilson, of Dublin. St. Werburgh's organ was burned in an accidental fire on November 9th, 1754, but in 1766, Rev. Sir Philip Hoby left a bequest of £1000 to build a spire and procure a new organ.* This instrument was built by Henry Millar, of College Green, at a cost of £400, and was opened by Thomas Carter, on June 6th, 1767. Two years later, Samuel Lawrence was appointed organist, and new stops were added at an additional cost of £70. Crow-street Music Hall was opened on November 30th, 1731, for high class concerts.†

Gavan Duffy writes:—"Addison‡ and Tickell, during their residence in Ireland, introduced the pastoral and romantic ballad into Anglo-Irish poetry. Some of the

---

* Owen Nicholas Egan, an Irishman, about the year 1740, was given the preference over seven rival competitors to build an organ for Lisbon Cathedral. He was a dwarf, being scarcely four eet high.

† Thomas Amory, writing of the year 1735, refers to "the merry dancings we had at Mother Redcap's, in Back-lane; the hurling matches at Dolphin's Barn; and the cakes and ale we used to have at the Organ House on Arbour-hill."

‡ Lord Wharton (Viceroy) brought over Thomas Clayton to superintend performances at Dublin Castle of Addison's opera, *Rosamund*, in 1709.

old English ballads were then making their way into favour; and imitating them was a favourite amusement among the exiled poets. Tickell's 'Leinster famed for Pretty Maids' was extremely popular in its day."

Matthew Concannen, an Anglo-Irishman, deserves notice as having re-arranged the ballad opera, *The Jovial Crew*, in 1731, but previously he had published a volume of "Miscellaneous Poems" (1724), many of which are to be found set to music in the *Musical Miscellany*.

Dean Swift deserves mention, too, as a versifier, especially for his "O'Rourke's Noble Feast," and for his efforts to support Gay, the writer of the *Beggar's Opera*. Though not musical, he patronised the St. Cecilia celebrations, and befriended several of the vicars choral.

In December, 1736 Rainsford-street Theatre collapsed, yet Dublin was sufficiently catered for in the Theatre Royal (Aungier-street), and Smock-alley. It was on February 12th, 1737, that Peg Woffington first appeared as Ophelia at the Theatre Royal, Aungier-street, *Hamlet* being given for the benefit of Mercer's Hospital. There was dancing between the acts by Mr. William Delamain. On January 26th, 1738, Lampe's *Dragon of Wantley* was given—a most popular opera, which held the boards for a quarter of a century. The libretto was by an Anglo-Irishman, Henry Carey, who is best known for his adaptation of an old Irish folk song to "God Save the King," the English national anthem. So popular was the *Dragon of Wantley* in Dublin that several editions of it, with music, were published by Peter Wilson "at Gay's Head, in Dame-street." On January 25th, 1738-9, at Aungier-street Theatre, Carey's ballad opera, *Margery, or a Worse Plague than the Dragon*, was performed for the first time in Ireland; and, on December 13th of the same year, at Smock-alley, a new single act opera called *Whittington and his Cat*, by Samuel Davey, was produced.

In 1738 Geminiani came to Dublin on the invitation of his pupil, Dubourg, and opened an academy at Spring Gardens, a court at the lower end of Dame-street. He remained in the Irish metropolis for over three years, and left in September, 1741—returning to London. Barsanti was in Dublin in September, 1740, and noted down some Irish airs which he subsequently published.

It can truly be said that in 1741 Dublin was a most musical city. And yet, time and again, the statement has been made that Handel first caused a stir in matters musical. I have mentioned that all the ballad operas were heard in Dublin almost immediately after their production in London, whilst some of them got their first hearing in Dublin. At the Theatre Royal, Aungier-street, on February 21st, 1740, a new ballad opera, *The Sharpers*, by a Dublin man, Matthew Gardiner, was produced for the first time, with much success, Peg Woffington reciting the epilogue.

The Right Hon. Luke Gardiner, P.C., who was Master of the Revels, patronised music, and was himself an amateur of known ability. In 1741 he appointed James Worsdale, the painter-dramatist, as Deputy Master of the Revels—the author of a successful ballad

opera, *A Cure for a Scold* (1735), and a musical interlude, *The Queen of Spain.*

Of the five musical societies * that contributed their
quota to art and social enjoyment in Dublin, in 1739,
the Charitable Musical Society was the most prominent. In 1740 Dean Swift requested the Sub-dean
and Chapter " to punish such Vicars as should appear
at the Club of the Fiddlers in Fishamble-street, *as
songsters, fiddlers, pipers, trumpeters, drum-majors, or in
any social quality*, according to the flagitious aggrava-
tion of their respective disobedience, rebellion, perfidy,
and ingratitude ; " and, in 1741, he issued a further
manifesto as follows :—

" I require my sub-dean to proceed to the extremity
of expulsion, if the said vicars [of St. Patrick's
Cathedral] should be found ungovernable, impenitent,
or self-sufficient, especially Taberner, Phipps, and
Church, who, as I am informed, have, in violation of
my sub-dean's and Chapter's order, in December last,
at the instance of some obscure persons unknown,
presumed to sing and fiddle at the club above
mentioned."

In 1740, as appears from *Faulkner's Journal* (March
14-17, 1741) the Charitable Musical Society "released 188
miserable persons of both sexes " from the Marshalsea.
So flourishing was this musical society that the members resolved to build a hall for their meetings and
performances, and they engaged the services of Mr.
Richard Castell to build a suitable " Musick Hall."
Accordingly, on Friday, October 2nd, 1741, the " New
Musick Hall " in Fishamble-street was opened under

* In 1733 a musical society was established at the " Hoop," on
Cork-hill.

the presidency of Mr. Neale, with great *éclat*. It was named the " New " Music Hall in order to distinguish it from the Crow-street Music Hall, built by the Academy of Music (the Anacreontic Society) ten years previously, also known as Mr. Johnson's Hall.

The principal Dublin performers in 1741 were Messrs. Roseingrave, Clegg, Neale, Lee and the Mainwarings. This year is also memorable for the invention of the Musical Glasses by Richard Pockrich, a native of Co. Monaghan, who settled in Dublin in 1715, and established a brewery and distillery at Island-bridge. He was an excellent musical amateur, and was an unsuccessful candidate for the post of Master of the Choristers of Armagh Cathedral in 1742. But further details of his musical career are res erved for the next chapter.

CHAPTER XXV.

HANDEL AND ARNE IN IRELAND.

IN the late summer of the year 1741 the Duke of Devonshire, Viceroy of Ireland, invited Handel to Dublin, and this invitation was the more readily responded to, inasmuch as Handel's friend, Matthew Dubourg, was Conductor of the State Band. Moreover, the Governors of Mercer's Hospital, and of the Charitable Infirmary, had asked Handel to compose something *special* in aid of the Dublin sick. This special work, the immortal *Messiah*, was finished by Handel on September 14th, 1741, having been written in three weeks—a marvellous *tour de force*.

On November 18th, 1741, Handel arrived in Dublin, accompanied by Mrs. Cibber, Maclean, his organist, and others ; and on the 24th arrived Signora Avoglio. From the minute-book of Mercer's Hospital, under date of November 21st, 1741, it appears that Dean Owen, Subdean Wynne, and Mr. Putland were requested to wait on "Mr. Handel," and ask him "to play on the organ at the musical performances at St. Andrew's Church." Handel complied, and played at the Round Church on Thursday, December 10th. Two days later Mrs. Cibber made her first appearance in Dublin, at the Theatre Royal, Aungier-street, as Indiana in *The Conscious Lovers.*

The files of *Faulkner's Journal* supply interesting details of Handel's stay in Ireland. An advertisement announces that on and after December 14th,

"Mr. Handel will be in attendance at his house in Abbey-street, near Liffey-street, from 9 o'clock in the morning till 2 in the afternoon, to receive subscribers for his six musical entertainments at the New Musick Hall in Fishamble-street." Handel's first concert was on December 23rd, consisting of *L'Allegro*, with two concertos for several instruments, and a concerto on the organ. An instantaneous success is recorded— the performance being described by a reporter as "superior to anything of the kind in this kingdom before." Handel's own verdict was equally satisfactory, and he tells his friend, Charles Jennens (who wrote the libretto of the *Messiah*), that the subscription list of six hundred persons was quite filled. He also added that he was looking up voices for the performance of the oratorio, and that the Irish singers were good, especially "the basses and counter-tenors," praising, too, the acoustic properties of Mr. Neale's "charming room," and the high appreciative faculties of the nobility, clergy, and "persons of distinction of this generous nation." By command of the Viceroy this concert was repeated on January 13th, 1742. The third musical entertainment, on January 20th, consisted of *Acis and Galatea*, Dryden's *Ode for St. Cecilia's Day*, "with several concertos on the organ and other instruments;" and a repeat performance was given on January 27th.

Dean Swift at this date, through his sub-dean, permitted six of his Vicars' Choral and two of his choristers to assist at the weekly performances of the Charitable Musical Society, "upon account of their being chiefly intended for the benefit of Mercer's Hospital."

On Wednesday, February 3rd, Handel gave his fifth concert, when the oratorio of *Esther* was produced; and, on February 10th, it was repeated with success. A new series of performances was given, commencing on February 17th, the attraction being "*Alexander's Feast*, with additions." A repetition performance was announced for February 24th, but it was postponed to March 2nd. The four remaining concerts took place on March 10th, 17th, 24th, and 31st, but the only novelty was "the new Serenata of *Hymen*." Finally, an extra concert was given on April 7th, namely, "*Esther*, with several Concertos."

At last, on Thursday, April 8th, 1742, a public rehearsal of *The Messiah* took place, and the critics agreed that it was "the finest Composition of Musick that ever was heard." So unanimous was the approval of Handel's masterpiece that, on the announcement of the first public performance, the Stewards of the Charitable Musical Society, in view of a crowded attendance, requested the ladies to come "without hoops," and the gentlemen without their swords. The actual first performance of Handel's sublime oratorio took place on Tuesday, April 13th, at 12 noon. Neale's Music Hall was densely packed with a most enthusiastic and discriminating audience, and *The Messiah* "made its impression once and for ever." Handel himself forwarded to Mr. Jennens the critical observations of "the Bishop of Elphin [Dr. Edward Synge], a Nobleman very learned in Musick" on the performance, and also a copy of the printed word-book, issued by George Faulkner, of Dublin, "price, a British six-pence." *

* Although the word-book was issued in June, 1742, for the repeat performance, the vocal score of *The Messiah* was not pub-

Handel gave a repetition performance of *The Messiah* "with concertos on the organ," on June 3rd, when a crowded audience again assembled. In the advertisement is added:—"In order to keep the Room as cool as possible, a Pane of Glass will be removed from the Top of each of the Windows. N.B.—This will be the last Performance of Mr. Handel's during his Stay in this Kingdom."

At this repeat performance the chorus was composed of the boys and men of both the Dublin cathedrals who had sung at the inaugural "entertainment." From the Dublin word-book, discovered by Professor Dowden, we are in a position to name the soloists, though the artists were not the same as at the initial performance. Signora Avoglio, Mrs. Cibber, and Mrs. MacLean (Maclaine), took the female parts, whilst Messrs. Bailey, Mason, Lamb, Hill, and Ward, of the Dublin cathedral, were the male soloists. One of the boys who sang was Samuel Murphy, afterwards Mus. Doc. and Organist of both cathedrals.*

Meantime there is chronicled a benefit concert at Fishamble-street Music Hall on April 5th, 1742, for Signora Avoglio. Another benefit took place at Smock-alley Theatre on May 17th for Messrs. William and Bartholomew Mainwaring. So great was its success that it was repeated on the 19th. One of the attractions was the playing of his *Medley* Overture by

lished for twenty-five years later. The actual date of publication was July 7th, 1767, the plates being printed by Messrs. Randall and Abell, successors to John Walsh, Catherine-street, Strand, London. A copy of the original Dublin word-book was discovered by Professor Dowden and a former owner pencilled the names of the singers. This book is now in the British Museum.

* Samuel Murphy was organist of St. Bride's, Dublin, in 1750, and, in 1752, he published "Twelve English Ballad Songs set to Music."

Bartholomew Mainwaring. The brothers Mainwaring, at this date, kept a music shop "at Corelli's Head, in College Green," and published much music.

On Wednesday, May 12th, Mr. Charles, French Horn Master, gave a grand concert in Fishamble-street, when the clarinet, horn, and shawm were heard for the first time in Ireland. However, the principal attraction was the "Overture and Dead March in *Saul*, never performed here before." On the following evening at the Theatre Royal, Aungier-street, Arne's *Comus* was given for the first time in Ireland.

Handel produced his oratorio of *Saul* at Fishamble-street Music Hall on May 25th, which was well received, especially the famous Dead March. After the repeat performance of *The Messiah*, on June 3rd, the great composer visited Cork, where he had some friends Whilst in Dublin he spent most of his evenings at Mrs. Vernon's, of Clontarf Castle. This lady was a Hanoverian, Dorothy Grahn, who came over to England in company with her brother, Herr Hans Otto Grahn, with King George I.

For this lady he wrote *Forest Music*, which has traces of Irish environment. Charles O'Conor, of Belanagare, has left it on record that Handel said he would rather have been the author of "Eibhlin a ruin" than of all his own compositions, but, be that as it may it is certain that the composer of *The Messiah* was charmed with the Irish folk-songs, one of which, "Der arme Irische Junge" (The Poor Irish Boy) may be seen in Handel's Manuscripts and Sketches in the Fitzwilliam Museum. Most probably he heard the air in Dublin.

* He introduced an Irish jig into *Acis and Galatea*.

As appears from an advertisement in *Faulkner's Journal*, Signora Avoglio announced a benefit concert in Fishamble-street Music Hall—"she being a stranger in this city"—to take place on Wednesday, June 16th, but it had to be postponed owing to the excitement consequent on Garrick's arrival the previous Sunday, with whom came Peg Woffington and Signora Barberini. A subsequent announcement gives the information that "the players have given up the Wednesday following [June 23rd] to Signora Avoglio for her performance."

On June 30th, 1742, Dr. Arne and his wife arrived in Dublin from London, no doubt, influenced by the favourable reception given to Mrs. Cibber, sister of Dr. Arne. Mrs. Arne was accorded a benefit at the Theatre Royal, Aungier-street, on Wednesday, July 21st, on which occasion Mrs. Cibber sang " Chi scherza colla Rose," from Handel's opera *Hymen*. In addition to the " great entertainment of musick " there was given a scene from Arne's opera *Rosamund*, also an Overture by Handel, and a selection from *Alfred*. No wonder that a repetition of this performance was announced, intimating at the same time that tickets could be had at " Mrs. Cibber's House in Aungier-street."

Handel left Ireland on Friday, August 13th, and, ten days later, Dr. Arne and Mrs. Cibber, Garrick, and Delane set off from Dunleary Harbour. In parting with Handel it is only pertinent to add that it was only on March 23rd, 1743, the first performance of *The Messiah* was given in London, and Dubourg went over specially from Dublin as leader of the orchestra.*

* Two organs associated with Handel are still in Ireland. One

Dr. and Mrs. Arne returned to Dublin in October, 1742, for the opening of the musical season, taking a house "over against the Ram in Aungier-street." The Charitable Musical Society of the *Bear*, on College-green, removed to Crow-street Music Hall, indifferently known as "Mr. Johnston's Large Room," and were succeeded at the *Bear* by another musical society. In addition there was a third musical society at Vicars-street, off Thomas-street. All these musical associations devoted their funds to some benevolent purpose. Thus the Charitable Musical Society of Fishamble-street Music Hall, handed over their funds to the release of poor debtors; and, in 1742, there were one hundred and forty-two Marshalsea prisoners liberated, "whose debts amounted to £1,225 17s. 1d., besides £33 given in charity to poor creditors and outgoing prisoners." The Society of the *Bear* applied their funds to "putting out poor orphan apprentices to reputable tradesmen." The Crow-street Society, also known as the Philharmonic Society, or the Academy of Music, founded the Incurable Hospital; and the *Bull's Head* devoted their profits to the Dublin Society.

From *Faulkner's Journal* we learn that on Monday, December 6th, 1742, for the benefit of Miss Plunket, a

of them, brought by Handel from England, became the property of the Marquis of Ely, at whose sale, in 1811, it was purchased by Francis Johnston, who removed it to his house, No. 60, Eccles-street. On his death, in 1845, the house, including the organ, brecame the property of the late William Seale, and subsequently of Isaac Butt. It was a Portatif Organ, "8 feet 1 wide, 7 feet 6 high, and 2 feet 10 deep." The second instrument, an old German Organ, was bought by Lord Mornington, and was afterwards used as the parish organ of old St. Paul's, Dublin. When St. Paul's was taken down, in 1820, the organ was removed to the Blue Coat Hospital, where it now is.—(*Handel's Visit to Dublin*, by Townsend, 1852.)

lady violinist, there was a grand concert in Fishamble-street Music Hall. It is added: "Tickets can be had at Mr. Neale's in Christ Church Yard, or from Miss Plunkett, at Mr. Dubourg's house in Henry-street." Five days later* a child pianist was announced at Mr. Johnston's hall in Crow-street, viz., "Miss Davis, a child of six years old, who will perform a Concerto and some other pieces upon the Harpsichord, particularly she will accompany her mother to a song of Mr. Handel's, composed entirely to shew the Harpsichord, the vocal parts to be performed by Mrs. Davis and her sister, Miss Clegg."

Miss Clegg's brother, John Clegg, of Dublin, was one of the greatest violinists of his time. Born in 1714, he studied under Dubourg, and appeared in London as a prodigy, afterwards studying under Buononcini. From 1730 to 1742 he was unapproached, but he was insane from 1742 to 1746, and died soon afterwards.

Another celebrated Irish musician of this period was Abbé Henry Madden, of the Eyrecourt (County Galway) family. He was successively chapel master of Tours Cathedral (1725), then to the King of France (1737), and finally of the Chapel Royal, Versailles (1744), in succession to Campra. Abbé Madden died at Versailles in 1748, aged fifty.

On Friday, December, 17th, 1742, the Charitable Musical Society gave a performance of *Acis and Galatea* at Fishamble-street, on which occasion Mrs. Arne sang, "accompanied on the violin by Mr. Arne, who will introduce Comic Interludes, intended to give relief to

* This performance was postponed to Saturday, February 5th, and was very successful.

that grave attention necessary to be kept up in serious performances." The Coronation Anthem of "Zadok, the Priest" was also performed, and Mr. Dubourg gave a violin solo.

At this date Mr. Charles, the French Horn Master, took over "Mr. Geminiani's Concerns and Great Musick Room in Dame-street," and announced that he gave lessons to gentlemen *and others* from 8 a.m. to 3 p.m. His terms were: "If to the Room, a guinea entrance, and a guinea for 16 lessons to a month. If he waits on gentlemen, a Moydore entrance, and a Moydore for 16 lessons." *

One of the earliest announcements for the year 1743 is the performance of *Comus* at the Theatre Royal, Aungier-street, on January 10th, when an "extraordinary band of music" performed, conducted by Mr. Arne, "who accompanies on the harpsichord." The favourite song of "Sweet Echo" had an obbligato accompaniment on the hautboy by Mr. John Neale, of London. As an additional attraction, "Master Neale, a child of ten years old," performed a concerto on the violin, and *Eibhlin a ruin* "with all its variations."

On February 8th, 1743, the annual performance for the benefit of Mercer's Hospital took place in St. Andrew's Church, the music consisting of Handel's Utrecht *Te Deum, Jubilate*, and two new Anthems.

On February 10th, 1743, Mrs. Arne had a benefit at the Theatre Royal, Aungier-street, when were produced a grand serenata, *Love and Glory*, by Mr. Arne, and *Lucy in Town*. Two days later Mr. Charles had a

---

* By proclamation of September 10th, 1736, *moidores* were made current coin of Ireland, being equivalent in value to £3 17s. 8d.

benefit at "Mr. Geminiani's Concert Room in Spring Gardens."

About the same date Mr. Layfield announced that he had taken "the Great Bowling Green in Marlboro'-street, and is determined to entertain the Nobility and Gentry in the most polite manner." This Bowling Green was a sort of Vauxhall Gardens, and was well patronised for about twenty years. O'Keeffe gives an account of the Bowling Green, and tells that Layfield eventually died mad.*

Sheridan's benefit at Smock-alley Theatre took place on Monday, February 21st, 1742-3, in *Richard III.* Qn Thursday, March 10th, at William Delamain's benefit, *Henry IV.* was played, prefaced by a concert and followed by a farce, whilst between the acts there was "dancing and singing."

On Wednesday, May 4th, 1743, Handel's oratorio, *Alexander's Feast* was given at Fishamble - street Music Hall, under Arne's direction, for the benefit of the Charitable Infirmary. The announcement adds : "Gentlemen of the choirs of both Cathedrals, the celebrated Mrs. Arne, and several other voices will assist." At the last concert of the season at Fishamble-street, on May 10th, Mr. Arne performed a solo of his own composition.

Arne's opera of *Rosamund* was announced to be performed at the Theatre Royal, Aungier-street, on May 27th, but it had to be postponed to June 11th owing to the illness of Mrs. Arne. In October Mr. Dubourg and Mr. Arne announced that they would perform "six oratorios of Mr. Handel's." Two months

* *Recollections of John O'Keeffe* pp. 66-68.

later Arne published his scheme for four performances of *King Alfred* and *Abel*.*

On December 8th, 1743, by command of the Duke of Devonshire (Viceroy), Arne conducted a performance of the *Beggar's Opera* at the Theatre Royal, Aungier-street, at which house Mademoiselle Chateauneuf had a benefit two days later, one of the attractions being O'Carolan's song "Bumpers Squire Jones," sung by Thomas Lowe, the English tenor.

At Smock-alley Theatre, on December 15th, for the benefit of Mr. Phillips, harlequin and dancer, the tragedy of *Julius Cæsar* was performed, in which Sheridan played the part of Brutus. During the acts the entertainments of singing and dancing included an Irish song, *Eibhlin a ruin*, by Mrs. Storer, and the dance of "The English Magot."

Apparently, the attempt at this time on the part of Mr. John Church to act as conductor of the various concerts at which he assisted, was resented by the other professional singers, as may be guessed by the following advertisement in *Faulkner's Journal*:—"Whereas, Mr. John Church, one of the choir, for some time past assumed an authority at all public performances which he is not entitled unto," etc. . . . Now, we, the undersigned, declare that we will not engage or perform in any Society or Concert where the said John Church is any wise concerned.—Barth, Mainwaring, Wm. Mainwaring, George Wade, George Fitzgerald, Sam Lee, Thomas Johnson John Angel Putti, Jos. Lee, James Walshe."

Apropos of Handel's *Messiah*, which was to have

* Added to this notice is the quaint advertisement : " Mr, Arne has for sale the vocal score of *Comus*, price, seven shillings. He

been performed at Fishamble-street on December 16th, an interesting announcement was published some days previously : " The Charitable Musical Society having obtained from the celebrated Mr. Handell a copy of the score of the Grand Musical Entertainment called *The Messiah*, they intended to have it rehearsed on the 12th, and performed on the 16th December for the benefit and enlargement of prisoners confined for debt, but, to the surprise of the Society, several of the choir members thought fit to decline performing and returned their parts, etc." It is added that the "entertainment" was postponed till Friday, February 3rd.

On December 21st, Dr. and Mrs. Arne assisted at a benefit at Fishamble-street for Signor Barbatielli. This took the shape of a grand concert, and the programme also included the names of Mr. Dubourg, Mrs. Storer, Pasqualino, Mr. Lowe, and Mr. Colgan. A few days later Arne repeated *Miss Lucy in Town*.

At a performance of Lampe's *Dragon of Wantley*, for the benefit of Mr. Sparkes, on January 9th, 1744, Mrs. Arne took a comic part for the first time ; and she had a benefit at the Theatre Royal, Aungier-street, on January 28th, when Mr. Arne appeared as an actor for the first—and last—time in his life, taking the part of Henry, Prince of Wales, in *Henry IV*. A fortnight previously, the eighth night of the *Beggar's Opera*, at the same theatre, conducted by Mr. Arne, was a great success, and a repeat performance on January 23rd was equally well received.

At the Music Hall, Fishamble-street, on Tuesday, February 7th, the Charitable Musical Society "for the will also sell very reasonable (*sic*) a curious harpsichord London, made by Kirchmann, Tabel's foreman."

Relief of Poor Prisoners," gave *The Messiah*, "postponed from the 3rd February * on account of Lord Netterville's trial." On February 27th this performance was repeated by the same Society for the benefit of the Charitable Infirmary.

Miss Davis, the child pianist, gave a recital at the Crow-street Music Hall, on February 9th. She is described as "a genius, born and educated in this town." Six days later, at Aungier-street, was announced Spranger Barry's "first time of appearance on any stage" as Othello, but the performance was postponed to March 2nd.

On Saturday, February 18th, Arne's new oratorio, *The Death of Abel*, was given for the first time at the Theatre Royal, Smock-alley, the principal parts being taken by Mrs. Arne, Mr. Tom Lowe, and Mademoiselle Chateauneuf. This oratorio was performed four times with much success. It was not heard in London till 1755. In his elaborate announcement, Mr. Arne explains his reason for having the four subscription performances on Saturday evenings: "The Mondays and Thursdays are taken up with Benefits for six Weeks. On Tuesdays are Vicar's St. Consort, and the Bear on College Green, which take up all the best Hands. On Wednesday are the Philharmonic Society, and Crow-street, where they are likewise engaged. And on Friday is Fishamble-street Consort, where they are obliged to perform."

Mr. Arne produced the comedy of *The Rehearsal*, at Aungier-street Theatre, on March 1st; and, on the

---

* The rehearsal took place on Wednesday, February 1st. In the advertisement it is added: "The Ladies have resolved to come without hoops as when the same was performed by Mr. Handel."

same evening, at Mr. Hunt's Great Auction Room in
Stafford-street, Mr. Richard Pockrich gave a performance on the musical glasses.*

Pockrich demands a brief notice as the inventor of
the musical glasses, a form of musical instrument
which was all the rage for half a century.   On March
15th, 1744, he gave a most successful recital at the
Taylors' Hall, Back-lane, being a repeat of his performance a fortnight previously.   One of the novelties
was a song, "Tell me, lovely Shepherd," sung by
Miss Young, "who never performed before in Publick."
Mr. Pockrich married a widow, Mrs. Francis White,
on April 23rd, 1745, who subsequently eloped with
Theophilus Cibber.†   After unsuccessfully contesting
Monaghan in 1745, and Dublin in 1749, as M.P., he
gave performances through England and Ireland on
the glasses, having as vocalist John Carteret Pilkington.   The great composer Gluck took up Pockrich's
invention, and gave a display in London on April 23rd
1746, namely, "a concerto on 26 drinking-glasses tuned
with Spring water."   Pockrich's end was very sad:
he was burned in an accidental fire at Hamlin's Coffee
House, Sweeting's-alley, London, 1759.   In 1760 one
of his pupils, Miss Ann Forde, was a distinguished
performer on the musical glasses, for which she pub-

---

* Mr. Pockrich shows a pretty turn of wit in the following
advertisement of his performance :—"When the Glasses were first
introduced in Publick, an accident happened which prevented the
Inventor from shewing that instrument to any advantage ; some
imputed it to his taking a Glass too much ; but the real cause of it
was owing to the hurry in removing them, which untuned and
disconcerted that instrument."

† Theophilus Cibber was drowned at the bottom of the Irish Sea
on board an ill-fated cross-channel boat on November 22nd, 1758.

lished a book of Instructions (1762). Miss Lloyd and
the Misses Davies also delighted English and Con-
tinental audiences on the instrument. In 1761, as
appears from the *Vicar of Wakefield*, the ladies from
London could talk of nothing but "pictures, taste,
Shakespeare, and *the musical glasses.*" Benjamin
Franklin improved the instrument, and called it the
"Armonica"; and for it Mozart, Hasse, Beethoven,
Naumann, Dussek, and other masters wrote.

Mr. Arne gave his Serenata of *Alfred*—being its first
production—at the Theatre Royal, Smock-alley, on
March 10th, 1744. This serenata concludes with "a
favourable Ode in honour of Great Britain," beginning,
" *When Britain first at Heaven's command,*" better known
as " Rule Britannia." Five days later Arne conducted
the *Beggar's Opera.*

Mr. and Mrs. Arne, after a two years stay, left Dublin
in July, 1744, Arne having been appointed director of
the music at Drury-lane Theatre, and subsequently
composer at Vauxhall Gardens.

As an evidence of the music makings in Dublin
during the season 1744-45, the following works were
performed by the Philharmonic Society:—Boyce's *Solomon* (libretto by Edward Moore), Handel's *Esther,
Athalia, Acis and Galatea,* and *Alexander's Feast* ;
Boyce's *Pythian Ode* (libretto by Walter Harte).
Eight years later a novelty by an Irish composer,
viz., a new oratorio entitled *Solomon's Temple*, the
composition of Richard Broadway (son of Edward
Broadway, Organist of Cork Cathedral from 1712 to
1720), was performed "for the benefit of the Sick and
Distressed Freemasons." The oratorio was merely a

succès d'estime, and was not heard of afterwards.* However, Mr. Broadway was a good musician, and was appointed Organist of St. Patrick's Cathedral in 1747, in succession to Ralph Roseingrave, for whom he had acted as deputy since 1744. Another Irishman, James Colgan, a splendid bass singer, was appointed full Vicar Choral of St. Patrick's Cathedral on March 24th, 1744. The mandate for his installation was issued by Dean Swift, but was signed by Jo. Wynne, Handel's friend, as Sub-dean.

On June 1st, 1744, Thomas Walker—the original Macheath—produced *Love and Loyalty* at Smock-alley Theatre. He died four days later in Dublin. His *Quaker's Opera* (1728) contains a number of Irish airs. On November 6th of the same year, at the Music Hall, Crow-street, was produced "a new entertainment called an *Ambigu,* to be prepared by Mr, Johnston." Three months later, on February 14th, 1744-5, Handel's Dettingen *Te Deum,* was performed at St. Michan's Church for the support of Mercer's Hospital.

The principal musical event of the year 1745 was the annual performance of *The Messiah* by the Charitable Musical Society at Fishamble-street, for the benefit of the poor prisoners, on Thursday, December 19th, for which the public rehearsal was given three days previously. Mrs. Delaney writes :—" It was very well performed, and I was much delighted." Garrick's *Hamlet* had been given at the Theatre Royal on December 9th, when Mrs. Storer played Ophelia,

---

* This performance took place at the Philharmonic Room, Fishamble-street, on Tuesday, May 15th, 1753.

singing after the close of the performance, "with dancing by Madame Moreau."

Lord Chesterfield, as Viceroy, was a patron of music and the drama, and he was present at Garrick's benefit at Smock-alley Theatre on December 20th, 1745. Another command night was on January 1st, 1746, when Garrick, Sheridan, and Barry played together. At a repetition performance of this on February 14th, Mrs. Delaney was present, and admired Barry's acting very much. Another command night was April 15th, which derived an added attraction from the fact of being the Duke of Cumberland's birthday. The play was *Orestes*, and the prologue was by Sheridan, whilst the epilogue was by Henry Brooke, author of the *Fool of Quality*, spoken by Garrick. On Tuesday, February 4th, Mr. Daniel Sullivan was given a benefit at Fishamble-street, the principal feature of which was a new "cantata" (dedicated to Her Royal Highness the Princess of Wales)—as sung by him at Ranelagh House —"the entertainment to conclude with the celebrated Anthem *God save the King*." Handel's *Esther* was given at the same place, on February 20th, "for the benefit of the Hospital of Poor Lying-in Women in George's-lane," which Hospital had been erected on the site of Madame Violantes's booth. Like Handel, Garrick was enraptured with Ireland and its people, and though he promised to return the following season, he never visited Dublin more. Handel paid a compliment to an Irish singer, Kitty Clive, *née* Rafter, when he selected her for the part of Dalila at the first production of *Samson*, at Covent Garden Theatre, in March, 1743.

CHAPTER XXVI.

ANGLO-IRISH MUSIC : 1750-1800.

GEORGE WALSH, who had been Organist of St. Anne's, Dublin, from 1743 to 1747, was appointed Organist of Christ Church Cathedral on the death of Roseingrave in October, 1747.   On October 23rd, 1752, the new organ of Christ Church (built by Byfield at a cost of £800), was formally opened by Walsh, on which occasion a *Te Deum* and *Jubilate* of his own composing was performed, in presence of the Lords Justices.   He was given the post of Vicar Choral of St. Patrick's in 1760 and was Organist of both Cathedrals from 1761 till his death in 1765.   Among his many sacred compositions is a Morning Service in D, still sung.

Smock-alley Theatre catered a great deal for the taste of the day in the matter of ballad operas, or musical comedies.   Henry Brooke's *Jack the Giant Queller* (1748) was an enormous success, but, as some of the songs were considered of a Jacobite and satirical tendency "it was prohibited after one night's perfor-mance." *   This opera teems with old Irish airs.   At the close of the year 1748, J. F. Lampe and Pasquali were engaged at Smock-alley ; and the Charitable Musical Society, whose funds amounted to £300, engaged for that sum Lampe and Pasquali for a series of concerts. *Acis and Galatea*, conducted by Lampe, was given for Mrs. Arne's benefit, on February 7th, 1749.   In 1750 this society had released 1,200 prisoners, whose debts and fees exceeded £9,000.

* Blaydon's *Theatrical Dictionary* (1792).

In the year 1747, when the Charitable Musical Society of Crow-street removed from Crow-street Music Hall to Fishamble-street, the Music Hall (Johnson's) ceased to be popular, and hence, in July, 1751, we find it leased to a syndicate (including Stephen Storace, Signor Marella, Daniel Sullivan and Samuel Lee) at an annual rent of £113 15s. Two years later, subscription balls were given there, and finally, in 1754, it was used for the exhibition by Mr. Rackstraw, of the series of anatomical wax works, now in Trinity College.

At this date the Fishamble-street Music Hall (Neale's) was still the home of high-class performances,* and, on February 11th, 1748, by command of the Lord Lieutenant, the Earl of Harrington, Handel's *Judas Maccabæus* was given for the benefit of the Lying-in Hospital. This performance is memorable as being the first given in Ireland of Handel's fine oratorio, and also as being one of a series of music-makings that contributed for half a century to the upkeep of the "Hospital for the Relief of Poor Lying-in Women"— said Hospital being "the first of the kind in His Majesty's Dominions." The concerts for this charity from 1750 were held in Granby-row, conducted by Castrucci (the last pupil of Corelli), who died in Dublin, 29th February, 1752. Walker, writing in 1785, says :—

"Castrucci has often been seen gathering chips to make his fire, dressed in the suit of black velvet which he usually wore when he appeared in public. But his poverty was not known to those who could relieve him till after his decease ; his proud spirit would not permit

---

* On February 3rd, 1752, by command of the Duke of Dorset Handel's *Joshua* was given for the Hospital for Incurables— Dubourg being conductor.

him to solicit pecuniary assistance.* To his memory, indeed, all due honours were paid; his funeral was superb, and graced with some the first Characters in the Nation; and the concourse of people that attended on the occasion was so considerable that the parish beadle was crushed to death in the execution of his office. His remains were interred in the churchyard of St. Mary's, Dublin."

On Monday, February 25th, 1751, at Fishamble-street Music Hall, Pergolesi's *Stabat Mater* was given for the first time in Ireland—" solos by Signor Marella, and vocal parts by Miss Oldmixon, Mr. Sullivan, and others." Tickets were 5s. 5d., and the book of words in Latin and English was to be had gratis. Two days later the Charitable Musical Society performed *Alexander's Feast* for the benefit of Signor Storace.

Between the years 1748 and 1754 the Methodists developed choral music in their meeting houses. In 1749 Charles Wesley published in Dublin a Methodist Hymn Book—*A Collection of Hymns and Sacred Poems* —the music being edited by Lampe, then in Dublin.†

It is of interest to add that O'Carolan and other Irish composers were drawn on for the tunes of the Methodist Hymn Book. In 1750 Pasquali published in Dublin his *Triumph of Hibernia*, introducing some Irish airs, whilst in the same year Lampe published a new collection of songs, ballads, etc., entitled *The Ladies' Amusement*. This volume was printed by " James Hoey, at the sign of the Mercury, in Skinner-

---

* This was Pietro Castrucci. He was in his 85th year.

† Lampe, who married a sister of Mrs. Arne, died at Edinburgh, on July 25th, 1751, and Charles Wesley wrote a hymn on his death; "'Tis done! the Sovereign Will's obeyed!" Pasquali also died at Edinburgh in 1757.

row, Dublin, for the author," and was for sale at " Mr. Mainwaring's musick shop," in College-green. Under date of November 3rd, 1753, Mainwaring advertises " all the new Hymns set to musick, by John F. Lampe."

In 1750, Garret Wesley, only son of Lord Mornington, was a musical prodigy. Mrs. Delaney, in one of her gossipy letters, under date of October 15th, 1748, writes :

"Last Monday we set out for Dangan, Lord Mornington's. . . . My godson, Master Wesley, is a most extraordinary boy ; he was thirteen last month ; he is a very good scholar, and whatever study he undertakes he masters it most surprisingly. He began with the fiddle last year ; he now plays everything at sight."

The future Earl of Mornington was born on July 19th, 1735, and at fourteen years old was an excellent violinist and organist. In 1753 he took some lessons from Thomas Roseingrave and Dubourg, but both masters informed him that he already knew all they could teach him. He graduated B.A. of Dublin University, in 1754, proceeding to M.A. in 1757.

In 1757 he founded the Academy of Music, an aristocratic body whose aim was to relieve distressed families by small loans. In this he was ably seconded by his friend Kane O'Hara. There were three grades of members, all of whom were to be non-professionals, namely, *Academics*, *Probationers*, and *Associates* ; and the meetings were to be held weekly, on Wednesdays, at 7 o'clock, at Fishamble-street Music Hall. Once a month an invitation concert was given by special ticket, and once a year a grand performance was announced for a stated charity. This performing

body consisted of a President (Lord Mornington), four
Vice-Presidents, and a Secretary. The *Academy* was the
first to introduce ladies into the chorus—an innovation
that has incorrectly been claimed for Dr. Arne.   In
1757 the masque of *Acis and Galatea* was performed by
"male and female amateurs of the first rank," for the
benefit of the *Charitable Loan Fund*.   Thus originated
the *Charitable Musical Loan*, which was supported by
music till 1765, and was formally incorporated in 1780.*

From the *Calendar of Ancient Records of Dublin* we
learn that in 1752 the "band of the city music" was
reorganised, and Samuel Lee was appointed Band-
master at a salary of £40, said allowance to be petitioned for yearly, "with a certificate from the Lord
Mayor and Sheriffs that they had employed such band
and were satisfied with their behaviour and attendance."
The band consisted of Messrs. Samuel Lee, William
Jackson, John Clark, James Forster, Rowland Jacob,
Frederick Seaforth, George Fitzgerald, Thomas Kelly,
Callaghan MacCarthy, and George Wade ; and, in
1753, the corporation increased the allowance for the
"city music" to £60 a year.   Samuel Lee, in addition
to being an excellent violinist, kept a music shop at
the Little Green, and published a good many songs.
One of his publications was called Lee's *Masque*, consisting of four songs in each number, "price, a British
sixpence."

Thomas Roseingrave, who returned to his native city

* This society must not be confounded with the Charitable
Society "for the support of decayed musicians" which was founded
in 1752 by Bartlett Cooke and the orchestra of Smock-alley.   In
1794 it was incorporated as the "Irish Musical Fund Society," and
still flourishes.

in February, 1753, conducted a performance of the opera *Phoedra and Hippolitus* at the Fishamble-street Music Hall, on Tuesday, March 6th, 1753,* which was repeated on October 8th of the same year. Mr. and Mrs. Arne, Miss Young, Miss Pollie Young, and Miss Charlotte Brent came to Dublin in November, 1755, and remained until June, 1756, producing many novelties, including *Eliza*, on November 29th, 1755.

Crow-street Music Hall disappeared in 1757, and on its site was built Crow-street Theatre, which opened on October 23rd, 1758, under the control of Spranger Barry and Harry Woodword. The opening play was *She Would and She Would Not*, and Sam Lee was appointed musical director. Crow-street soon proved a formidable rival to Smock-alley Theatre, and, in addition, the Dublin citizens of that period had attractions at Mosse's (the Rotunda) Gardens, Marlborough Bowling Green,† and Ranelagh Gardens.‡ Of course, the Anacreontic and Philharmonic concerts were also well supported, whilst Lord Mornington's Academy of Music was patronised by the élite.

Dubourg still led the State Band at Dublin Castle, and composed numerous birthday odes. Walker gives the following anecdote of Handel's friend :—

" Dubourg often wished to enjoy, unobserved, the sports of an Irish Fair. An opportunity of gratifying

* He died at Salthill (Kingstown) in 1766.

† In August, 1752, George A. Stevensgave his celebrated monologue entertainment at Marlborough Green.

‡ The Ranelagh Gardens (the mansion house of which was previously an episcopal residence) were established by Mr. Hollister a Dublin organ builder, consisting of "a great tavern, gardens, and a theatre for Burlettas," with a good orchestra. This was in 1768. The Discalced Carmelite Nuns acquired Ranelagh in 1806, and opened the mansion house as St. Joseph's Convent, in 1807.

this wish occurred while he was on a visit to a Mr. Lindsey's, in the town of Dunboyne, near Dublin, where one of the greatest Fairs of the Kingdom is annually held. Having disguised himself as a country fiddler, he sallied forth amongst the tents another Crowders. He was soon engaged, and a company of dancers stood up. But though he exerted himself to play in character that is, discordantly, there was still a sweet charm in his playing that fixed his audience with rapture. At length the crowd pressed and gazed so upon him that he thought it but wise to retire."

It was whilst on a visit to Dubourg that the great violinist, Geminiani (who came to Ireland in January, 1759, as violin master to Mr. Charles Coote, at Coote-hill), died September 17th, 1762. Dubourg returned to London early in 1765, where he died, July 3rd, 1767, and was buried in Paddington churchyard.

In 1759-1760 Kane O'Hara, at the request of Lord Mornington, wrote his charming burletta of *Midas*, which was first performed at the private theatre attached to the residence of the Right Hon. William Brownlow, at Lurgan, in April, 1760, and afterwards at Crow-street Theatre.* Private theatres were all the rage from 1752 to 1782, and at one memorable perfor-mance of the *Beggar's Opera*, at Carton, in 1761, the caste was as follows :—Captain Morris (Macheath), Lord Charlemont (Peachum), Rev. Dean Marlay (Lockit), Thomas Conolly (Filch), Miss Martin, Polly), Lady Conolly (Lucy), the Countess of Kil-dare (Mrs. Peachum), Viscount Powerscourt (Mrs.

* *Midas* abounds in Irish airs. The vocal score of it was pub-lished by Walshe, of London, 1764, a copy of which is in my musical library. From O'Keeffe we learn that the original caste in-cluded Mr. Robert Corry, Mr. Vernon, Mr. Robert Mahon, Mr. Oliver, Captain Morris, Miss Elliott, Miss Polly Young, and Miss M'Neill.

Slammeckin), Miss Vesey (Jenny Diver), and Miss
Audley (Coaxer).

In 1762-1764 the Passerini family delighted Dublin
with their serenatas, and gave a fine performance of
Pergolesi's *Stabat Mater* in the Fishamble-street Muics
Hall. This was the year memorable for Arne's
Artaxerxes, produced at Covent Garden, on February
2nd, 1762, the part of Mandane having been specially
written for his pupil, Miss Brent, who married Thomas
Pinto, the violinist, four years later. John O'Keeffe
tells us that Arne and Tenducci were delighted with the
reception accorded *Artaxerxes* in Dublin, on February
18th, and on March 28th, 1765, at Smock-alley.[*]

In 1764 the Professorship of Music was founded in
Trinity College, with the Earl of Mornington as first
Professor, and the degree of Mus. Doc. was conferred
on both Mornington and his friend, the Right Hon.
Charles Gardiner, M.P. Gardiner was a distinguished
musical amateur, and he died on November 15th, 1769,
leaving issue Luke, created Baron Mountjoy in 1789.
Between the years 1764 and 1771 the degree of Mus. Doc.
was conferred on Richard Woodward, Samuel Murphy,
and Sampson Carter. Lord Mornington resigned the
Professorship in 1774, and the chair remained vacant
till 1847, when Dr. John Smith was appointed.

On the death of George Walsh, in 1765, his son
Henry was appointed Organist of St. Patrick's
Cathedral, whilst Richard Woodward was appointed
to Christ Church, being also made Master of the

---

[*] Tenducci's singing in Dublin of "Water Parted" was magnifi-
cent. He introduced Irish airs at some of his performances, and
"at his benefit had 30, 40, and 50 guineas for a single ticket."—
(O'Keeffe's *Recollections*, p. 139.)

Choristers of both cathedrals. Henry Walsh was a good executant, but was delicate in health, and he only survived his father four years, dying in 1769.

From Gilbert's *History of the City of Dublin* we learn that, in 1766, the "Amicable Catch Club" held their meetings at the *Phœnix*, in Werburgh-street, "which appears to have been closed after the death of its proprietor, James Hoey, in 1773." Another musical body, called the *Mecklenburgh Musical Society*, gave concerts in the Fishamble-street Music Hall in 1768, assisted by the choirs of both cathedrals, and were patronised by Lord and Lady Townsend.

Tommaso Giordani and his brother brought an Italian opera company to Dublin in 1762, and played with much success at Smock-alley Theatre. So pleased was Tommaso with the Irish metropolis that he remained in it for some years as Conductor of the State Music. His *Love in Disguise* (libretto by Henry Lucas), was produced on April 24th, 1766 ; and on August 1st, 1769, his Ode (words by Gorges E. Howard) was performed at the Rotunda, "with much applause," in presence of Lord and Lady Townsend.*

It may be well here to give a programme of a fashionable concert in Dublin at this period. The following is a copy of a music-making at Fishamble-street Music Hall, in aid of the Lock Hospital, on Tuesday, January 31st, 1769, and repeated on February 4th :—

"Mr. Pope's *Ode on St. Cecilia's Day*, set by Dr. Murphy. Between the first and second acts of the Ode

---

* On December 15th, 1783, Pilon's *Siege of Gibraltar*, music by Giordani, was produced at Capel-street Theatre ; and on November 28th, 1796, a new opera, *The Cottage Festival* (Libretto by M'Nally), was given at Crow street Theatre.

will be introduced an Interlude of Catches and Glees,
preceded by a Medley Overture, namely,

> "First Catch: 'Jack thou'rt a toper,' for three
>   voices. Set by Mr. H. Purcell.
> "First Glee: 'Gently touch the warbling lyre,' for
>   four voices. Harmonized by Dr. Hayes.
> "Second Catch: 'Good neighbours, be quiet,' for
>   four voices. Set by Dr. Arne.
> "Second Glee: 'Fair and Ugly,' for three voices.
>   Set by Dr. Travers.
> "Third Catch: 'Hark ye, my dear,' for three voices.
>   Set by Dr. Arne.
> "Third Glee: 'Old I am,' for three voices. Set by
>   Dr. Travers.
> "Fourth Catch: 'Here lies Judge Boate,' for four
>   voices. Set by Dr. Hayes.
> 'The Interlude to end with a grand chorus of
>   'God Save Great George Our King.'

" The catches and glees to be accompanied by instrumental parts, composed on purpose by Dr. Murphy, and
performed in a manner quite new, and much approved
of. The principal vocal and instrumental performers
are the first in this Kingdom. The whole to conclude
with a grand ball, where the ladies and gentlemen will
appear in fancied habits [fancy dress] of Irish manufacture, and all the rooms will be illuminated with different
coloured wax lights."

On March 16th (St. Patrick's Eve), 1770, there was
another great fancy ball at Dublin Castle, given by
Lord and Lady Townshend, and all the guests were
commanded to appear in dresses of Irish manufacture.
Michael Arne (son of Dr. Arne) spent the autumn of
the year 1770 in Cork, where several concerts were give
under his direction. He came to Dublin early in 1771,
and produced Cymon * at Capel-street on March 4th.
We find him again in Ireland in 1775, when he had
a few weeks of opera at Smock-alley and Crow-street.

* Arne composed Cymon in 1767. It contains a song by John
O'Keeffe, set to an old Irish tune, namely, "Fatima's Song."

Another eminent musician Thomas Pinto, sought a
friendly home in Dublin in 1773, and was leader of
the band at Smock-alley from 1773 to 1779.* At this
theatre, on November 26th, 1772, a comic opera, *The
Milesian*, composed by an Irishman, John M'Dermott,
was produced.

The veteran Irish violinist, Samuel Lee, who had an
extensive music publishing business at No. 2, Dame-
street, and a coffee house in Essex-street, died " at his
house in Dame-street," on February 21st, 1776, described
in *Walker's Magazine* as " a great Professor in Musick."

Surely, Dublin could boast of its musical celebrity
in 1773. At a typical concert given by amateurs, the
orchestra included:—Violins—Count M'Carthy, Right
Hon. Sackville Hamilton, Very Rev. Dean Bayly, Deans
Burke and Hamilton, Surgeon Neale, E. B. Swan,
Mr. Conner, and Dr. Hutcheson; bassoons—W. Deane,
Colonel Lee Carey; 'cellos—The Earl of Bellamont, Sir
John Dillon; flutes—Lord Lucan, Captain Reid, Rev.
J. Johnson; harpsichord—Right Hon. W. Brownlow,
Lady Freke, Miss Cavendish, Dr. Quin, and Miss
Nicholl. Among the vocalists were Lady Russell, Mrs.
Monck, Miss O'Hara, Miss Stewart, Miss Plunket, etc.

Charles Clagget was a most remarkable Irish
musician of this period, being particularly famed as
an accompanist on the violin, and as an ingenious
inventor. A good memoir of him will be found in
Grove's *Dictionary*, to which the reader is referred.
Sampson Carter, Mus. Doc., and his younger brother,
Thomas Carter (the composer of "O Nancy wilt thou

---

* Mrs. Pinto (Miss Charlotte Brent), sang in Dublin during the
years 1773-1775. On October 1st, 1779, Pinto played a concerto on
the violin at a Rotunda concert, and he died soon afterwards. Mrs.
Pinto returned to London, where she died April 10th, 1802.

go with Me "), are also treated of in Grove.   Richard
Woodward, Mus. Doc., Organist of Christ Church
Cathedral, died November 22nd, 1777, aged thirty-four.
He was the son of Richard Woodward, Vicar Choral
of St. Patrick's Cathedral, and was born in Dublin in
1744.   His well-known canon, "Let the words of my
mouth "—awarded the gold medal of the Glee and Catch
Club, in 1764*—is inscribed on his monument in Christ
Church Cathedral.   He also wrote much sacred music,
including a service in B flat and seven anthems, and
published a folio volume of cathedral music, dedicated
to Archbishop Smyth, which is marked Op. 3, and was
printed by Peter Welcker, of London, in 1771.

Among the theoretical works on music issued in
Dublin, a volume of one hundred and forty pages of
letterpress, with fifty-one pages of musical illustrations, may be cited.   This work is entitled, *Two
Essays on the Theory and Practice of Music. . . .*
by the Rev. John Trydell, and was printed for
the author by Boulter Grierson, King's Printer,
at Dublin, in 1766.   It contains "the rules of harmony, composition, and thorough bass, as also a
new and short method of attaining to sing by note."
Dublin printing and bookbinding was unsurpassed at
this period, as is admitted by Horace Walpole.†   A
rare volume, entitled *The Gentleman's Catch Book*, was
edited and published by Henry Mountain, a distinguished Dublin violinist, in 1778, the dedication being
to "the Hibernian Catch Club."   Mountain published

---

* This was the second Gold Medal awarded by the Hibernian
Catch Club.
† Walpole to Montague, dated "Arlington-street, December
30th, 1761."

a good deal of music from No. 20, Whitefriar-street, after which he removed to 44, Grafton-street.

We find an Irish clergyman, Rev. Michael Sandys, M.A., as Organist of St. Patrick's Cathedral, Dublin, from 1769 to 1773. He was appointed Vicar Choral of St. Patrick's in 1772, and resigned the organ appointment the year following, becoming Minor Canon and Dean's Vicar in 1778. His successor was Dr. Samuel Murphy, who, as a boy, had sung at the original performance of Handel's *Messiah*. Dr. Murphy was a brilliant organist, and also a distinguished composer. In 1777, on the death of Dr. Woodward, he was appointed to Christ Church Cathedral, and was also Master of the Choristers of both cathedrals. He died at Carrickmines, near Dublin, on November 25th, 1780.

On January 27th, 1777, the Fishamble-street Music Hall was opened as a theatre by Vandermere and Waddy, but the venture was short-lived. Thus, Dublin had at this date four theatres—Smock-alley, Crow-street, Capel-street, and Fishamble-street. The glories of the music hall where Handel performed disappeared after the death, in 1769, of Mr. Neale. Neale's son, Surgeon John Neale, of Mary-street, was a marvellous amateur violinist, and was commanded by King George III. to play at a State concert in 1787.

Garret Wesley, first Earl of Mornington, Mus. Doc., died at Kensington on May 22nd, 1781. His most famous son, the Duke of Wellington, was born in Mornington House, Merrion-square, Dublin, on April 29th, 1769.* Two years later Lord Mornington built a

* From the Baptismal Register in St. Peter's, Dublin, it appears that Arthur Wesley was baptized in that church on Sunday, April 30, 1769. The Mornington family lived temporarily in Antrim House, Merrion-square, in 1769.

new house in Merrion-st., which he renamed after himself, and where he resided until 1777. Though he resigned his Professorship of Music at Trinity College in 1774, he published his best works after that date, and gained prizes from the Catch Club in 1776 and 1777. In 1779 the Catch Club awarded him the prize medal for his glee, "Here in cool grot," which was published by Anne Lee, of Dublin, in 1780. He also composed much sacred music, including his well-known Chant in E flat, the charm of which is almost destroyed in the version in general use—differing materially from the form as traditionally sung in the Dublin cathedrals. Lady Mornington surviv till September 10, 1831. A fine edition of Lord Mornington's Glees and Madrigals was edited by Sir Henry Bishop in 1846.

Michael Kelly in his *Reminiscences* tells us of the great taste for music in Dublin during the years 1775-1780. Kelly himself had commenced the pianoforte with Mr. Murland, and finished with Dr. Cogan, a distinguished Cork musician who was Organist of St. Patrick's Cathedral from 1780 to 1806. Murland had a pianoforte factory some years later, and made a square instrument for Tom Moore. It is mahogany inlaid, dated 1808, and is now in the National Museum.* An early upright harpsichord, of about the year 1774, made by Rother, Dublin, is also in the Dublin Museum.

Kelly tells us that Dr. Cogan's execution on the

---

* As early as 1772, Ferdinand Weber, of Marlborough-street commenced making square pianofortes. A beautiful specimen dated 1774, was exhibited at the Cork Exhibition in 1902. It was purchased by John Philpot Curran for his daughter Sarah, the *fiancée* of Robert Emmet. Strangely enough, it was described as "a spinet or harpsichord," though, undoubtedly (as the late Mr. Hipkins informed me), it is an *early square pianoforte.*

pianoforte was astonishing, and that " his compositions possess great merit." *   In 1778, when Michael Arne was in Dublin, he was possessed of a desire to study alchemy, and took a house at Richmond, near Clontarf. The result was disastrous, and when he was confined or a time in the Marshalsea, Kelly's father sent him a loan of a pianoforte, in return for which kindness Arne gave lessons to Michael Kelly.   Towards the close of April, 1779, Ryder, of Crow-street Theatre, re-engaged Arne and his wife for a revival of *Cymon*, for three nights, with the youthful Kelly in the caste.   This proved successful, and, on the fourth night of the engagement, *Lionel and Clarissa* was produced for Kelly's benefit, Pinto being leader of the band, and Bartlett Cooke as first oboe.   Subsequently, on May 1st, 1786, Kelly created the parts of Basilio and Don Curzio in Mozart's *Figaro*, at Vienna.

The era of the Volunteers, 1774-1784, was marked by band music, and almost every corps had a wind band.   One of the favourite tunes was "The Volunteers' March," by Elford, dedicated to Lord Charlemont.   Another Irish march was annexed by the Scotch and utilised for "Whistle o'er the lave o't."   A third, popular in Munster, was "The Shamrock Cockade," set to the Irish air of "Ally Croker."   After the rejection of Flood's Reform Bill in 1784, the Volunteers collapsed, and the bands dissolved.

In 1779 Giordani and Lini took the Capel-street Theatre as an opera house, but they became bankrupt

---

* Cogan published various anthems. In 1788 appeared six sonatas for pianoforte and violin (Op. 2), followed by harpsichord lessons and songs, and in 1792 he printed his concerto in E flat.—(*British Musical Biography*.)

in 1783,* and both returned to London. In January,
1782, Richard Daly produced O'Keeffe's *Son-in-Law*
at Smock-alley Theatre.   This play (first given in
London by Colman in 1779) was rendered attractive
by the number of Irish airs introduced into it, especially
a few of O'Carolan's.† O'Keeffe himself tells us that
Dr. Arnold arranged the airs of many of his songs,
and found no small difficulty with them.   Sir John
Stevenson (who was appointed a stipendary at St.
Patrick's Cathedral, July 20th, 1775, in which year he
gained the Catch Club's prize for his glee, "One night
while all the village slept,") composed some airs for
O'Keeffe's *Dead Alive* in 1780, which was performed
with success in June, 1781.   This play was followed by
The Agreeable Surprise, in which Irish airs are largely
drawn on, having been supplied by Vernon to Dr.
Arnold.   O'Keeffe's opera of the *Banditti* (November,
1781) contains " Ceann ᵒuᵇ ᵒiᴌiꞃ " and " 'Sᴀ ᵯúiꞃníꞃ
ᵒiᴌiꞃ "—the latter air being until then only known by
its Irish words.   This opera was revised and renamed
The Castle of Andalusia, with two new airs by Giordani.
The Poor Soldier (1783) was arranged by Shield, mostly
to O'Carolan's airs, chosen by O'Keeffe.

On January 3rd, 1784, Daly produced Gluck's opera,
Orpheus and Eurydice, with Tenducci and Mrs. Billington
Master Weichsel conducting.   On July 9th of the same
year the famous "Douglas" riot occurred, when the
Duke of Rutland was present on a command night at the

* On June 24th, 1782, the Irish State Lottery was first drawn at
the Opera House in Capel-street.
† On January 1st, 1779, John Lee, of Dublin, published the *fourth*
edition of *Carolan's Old Irish Tunes*, price, 3*s.* 9*d.*, at No. 70,
Eustace-street.

Theatre Royal—Home's *Douglas* being the play. At the
rising of the curtain the audience insisted on the
"Volunteers' March" being played by the orchestra,
which was accordingly done ; but no sooner did Home's
fine tragedy begin than the whole house, to mark their
disapproval of the Viceroy's recent action in refusing
to sanction the petition of the Dublin Corporation in
favour of Reform, would not allow the play to proceed,
and the Duke of Rutland had to retire, to the accompaniment of the " Volunteers' March."

Kane O'Hara, the author of *Midas* (1760), *The Golden
Pippin* (1772), *The Two Misers, Tom Thumb* (1780), etc.,
died at his house in Dublin, June 17th, 1782. He was
a fine musician, and is praised by Michael Kelly. From
the year 1778 he was totally blind, but kept up to the
last his interest in music. With him died the *Academy
of Music*.

In 1783 Mr. Robert Owenson opened Fishamble-
street as a "National Theatre," the inaugural piece
being Jephson's *The Carmelite,* followed by O'Keeffe's
Poor Soldier. Lady Morgan, Owenson's daughter, tell
us that " the overture consisted of Irish airs, ending
with the 'Volunteers' March,' which was chorussed by
the gallery to an accompaniment of drums and fifes."
This venture was short-lived.

From 1780 to 1786 concerts were held twice a
week during the summer season in the Round Room,
Rotunda, for the benefit of the Rotunda Hospital. For
these concerts the very best talent was procured, and
Irish musicians who were forced to go abroad to
become prophets, came back at handsome fees.
Andrew Ashe, who had been principal flute at the

Brussels Opera House, appeared at these concerts in 1782, and, in 1791, was engaged by Salomon for the Hanover-square concerts.

On May 3rd and 5th, 1787, a Handel Commemoration was given in St. Werburgh's Church by "amateurs of the highest distinction," including Sir Hercules Langrishe, Baron Dillon, Surgeon John Neale, Lady Portarlington, and Hon. Mrs. Stopford. In the following year, on April 12th and April 16th, a similar festival in honour of Handel was given in Christ Church Cathedral in aid of local charities, and on both occasions "the ladies laid aside their hats, feathers, and hoops."

In November, 1787, Richard Daly reopened Smock-alley and Crow-street, both of which houses had been renovated and decorated—Crow-street, in particular, being practically rebuilt. To the band of Smock-alley, on the initiative of Mr. Bartlett Cooke, as before stated, is due the establishment of the Irish Musical Fund Society for the relief of distressed musicians. In 1794 it was incorporated, and we read that "such was the feeling excited in the House of Commons upon that occasion that the Speaker and all the officers relinquished their fees."

About the year 1781, Catholic services, in consequence of Lord North's Relief Bill, began to attract attention by reason of the introduction of organs, and, in many places, small orchestras. The earliest book on the *Church Plain Chant*, was printed and published in 1782 by an Irishman, John P. Coghlan, in London. In Part II. of this rare publication are Anthems, Litanies, Proses, and Hymns "as sung in the public chapels at London." The book is in three parts, and contains two settings of the *Tantum Ergo* by Stephen Paxton; also motets by Samuel Webbe.

In April, 1789, Giordani composed a *Te Deum* for the recovery of King George III., which was sung for the first time at the conclusion of High Mass in the old chapel of Francis-street, Dublin, by Archbishop Troy. At this performance were present the leading Catholics, and also many distinguished Protestants, *e.g.*, the Duke of Leinster, the Earls and Countesses of Belvedere, Arran, and Portarlington, the Countesses of Carhampton and Ely, Lords Tyrone, Valentia, and Delvin, Messrs. Grattan, La Touche, etc.

In 1789 the Fishamble-street Music Hall was taken by the Honourable Society of King's Inns, who relinquished it, however, in less than two years, when it was again acquired as a Private Theatre, by the Earl of Westmeath and Frederick E. Jones, the opening performance, on March 6th, 1793, being the *Beggar's Opera* and the *Irish Widow*.

Dr. Langrishe Doyle (Organist of Armagh Cathedral from 1776 to 1780) who was appointed Organist of Christ Church Cathedral in 1780, was given the post of Organist of Trinity College Chapel in 1781. He was a very brilliant Irish musician, and in 1784 was elected a full Vicar of St. Patrick's Cathedral. His powers began to fail in 1804, and he was given an assistant on November 25th, 1805, in the person of William Warren, his nephew.

Music was patronised by the Earl of Camden, Lord Lieutenant of Ireland, and in 1795 he knighted William Parsons, Mus. Doc., Master of the King's Band ot Musick, who often visited Ireland. Stevenson, who

obtained Mus. Doc. of Trinity College in 1791, was
at this date coming into prominence, but he did not
receive his knighthood till 1803—being the second
musical knight.

Timothy Geary (also known as Thomas Augustine
Geary) was a very promising Irish composer. Born in
Dublin in 1773, he graduated Mus. Bac. in 1792, and
wrote some glees, duets, and songs (most of which
were sung by Dr. Spray). He was drowned in
November, 1801.

On August 12th, 1797, Frederick E. Jones purchased
Daly's patent of Crow-street Theatre—Smock-alley
having been closed three years previously.* Unfortunately, the political atmosphere from 1795 to 1800
did not make for harmony in any sense of the word,
and hence many distinguished Irish musicians obtained
their triumphs elsewhere. Tom Cooke, who was leader
of the band at Crow-street in 1798, was afterwards a
great star in London. John Field, who was a boy
pianist in 1798, and was afterwards apprenticed to
Clementi, invented the Nocturne. William Southwell
patented the Irish damper action for pianofortes in
1794, and subsequently invented the cabinet piano.
Henry Mountain was leader of the band at Covent
Garden, and was praised by Haydn. Andrew Ashe was
leader of the Bath concerts in succession to Rauzzini.
John Moorehead was a marvellous Irish violinist and
composer, and played at the Worcester Festival in
1794. Thomas Carter was musical director of the
Royalty Theatre, Goodman's Field's, and composed

---

* On the site of Smock-alley Theatre stands the Church of SS.
Michael and John, which was opened in 1815.

the comic opera *Just in Time,* in 1792, for Covent
Garden. Another Thomas Carter, of Dublin, was
musical director of the Calcutta Theatre, but returned
to London, in 1793, where he died in 1800.* John
Mahon (1755-1834) was a famous clarinet player, and performed at the Birmingham Festivals from 1802 to 1811.

Probably one of the best evidences of the cultivation
of music in Ireland in the latter half of the eighteenth
century is the number of music publishers and musical
instrument makers in Dublin at that period. In
1800 there were ten flourishing music shops, namely,
Rhames, Gough, Hill, Hime, Lee, Holden, M'Calley,
M'Donnell, Power, and Southwell, nearly all of which
were music-publishing firms. There were also eight
harpsichord and piano manufacturers, and three makers
of wind instruments—also makers of pedal harps, Irish
harps, bagpipes, and fiddles, and two organ builders.
The two Protestant Cathedrals could boast of as fine
services as in any English place of worship. As yet
the Catholics were only just emerging from the Catacombs. And, on August 1st, 1800, the royal assent
was given to the iniquitous *Act of Union,* one effect of
which was the disappearance from Dublin of the Lords
and Commons—patrons of music and the drama.

* For notices of both the Carters see the new edition of Grove's
Dictionary of Music and Musicians, by Fuller Maitland.

CHAPTER XXVII.

HARP FESTIVALS AND HARP SOCIETIES.

BEFORE describing the various harp festivals and harp societies, it may be well to glance at four distinguished harpers of the period 1750-1790, namely, Jerome Duigenan, Dominic Mongan, James Duncan, and Arthur O'Neill. Duigenan was born in County Leitrim in 1715, and, in addition to being a clever harper, was an excellent classical scholar. Many amusing anecdotes are related ot him. His patron, Colonel Jones, M.P. for Leitrim in 1740, once brought him up to Dublin for a trial of skill with a famous Welsh harper, at that time in the train of an English nobleman residing in the Irish metropolis. This Irish harper was requested to dress himself *more Hibernico*, and to wear his *cotach* and *barred*, "in which he looked uncommonly well, being a tall, handsome man." O'Neill tells us that some of the parliamentary members, hearing of the intended trial of skill, requested that it would take place on the floor of the Irish House of Commons, which accordingly was done. The competition came off previous to the commencement of the usual parliamentary business, and the decision was unanimously given in favour of Duigenan, who gained the laurel. Dominick Mongan was also a famous bard and performer on the harp. Born in County Tyrone in 1715, he was blind from infancy, and sedulousy cultivated the national instrument, but was also thoroughly conversant with the works of Corelli, Handel, Geminiani, other masters. O'Daly styles him a "gentleman bard," and quotes his "ᴀ Ꞃᴀɪᴃ ᴄᴜ ᴀᴣ ᴀɴ ᴣ-ᴄᴀꞀꞀᴀɪᴣ?" (Have you been at Carrick?) as a good specimen of his abilities. His third son, Charles, became Protestant Dean of Clonmacnoise. Among the Hardwicke Papers (1803) is the following note in reference to Dean Mongan, who had assumed the name of Warburton :—" The King has declared he will never make him a Bishop. He was a Roman Catholick originally; his name, Mongan, and his father an Irish Harper. He himself was a missionary, and acquired, by plausible manners to the amount of £2,000 a year and upwards of Church preferment." * James Duncan was also a gentleman harper, and merely pursued the avocation of minstrel in order to raise the necessary funds for carrying on a law-suit to regain his ancestral property. He won his case, "and died in 1800, in the enjoyment of a handsome competence," as the late Sir Robert Stewart writes. Arthur O'Neill deserves special notice as the last really typical Irish harper of the old school. Born at Drumnaslad, near Dungannon, in 1734, he accidently lost his sight when still a child, and was, in 1742, placed under the tuition of Owen Keenan, "the blind Romeo of Killymoon" (near Cookstown), and subsequently under Hugh O'Neill, in order to become a professional harper. Early in 1750 he began his career as a wandering minstrel, and during ten years made a circuit of the four provinces, visiting the chief families in each

* Dean Warburton (Mongan) was afterwards made Bishop of Limerick, over which see he presided till 1833, when Bishop Knox was translated from Killaloe as Bishop of the united sees of Limerick, Ardfert, and Aghadoe.

county. As an incident of his visit to the hospitable
mansion of Mr. James Irwin, of Streamstown, Co. Sligo,
in 1759, he thus writes in his Memoirs :—

"This gentleman (Mr. Irwin) had an ample fortune,
and was passionately fond of music. He had four
sons and three daughters, who were all proficients ; no
instrument was unknown to them. There was at one
time a meeting in his house of *forty-six musicians*, who
played in the following order :—The three Miss Irwins
at the piano ; myself at the harp ; six gentlemen, flutes ;
two gentlemen, violoncellos ; ten common pipers ; twenty
gentlemen, fiddlers ; four gentlemen, clarionets."

O'Neill played on the so-called "Brian Boru's Harp"
—re-strung for the occasion—through the streets of
Limerick in 1760, but he ceased his wanderings in
1778, and settled in Belfast, taking up the position of
harp tutor in the house of Dr. James M'Donnell, where
he remained till 1780.

Through the generosity of an Irish gentleman, James
Dungan, residing in Copenhagen, a harp festival was
organised at Granard in 1781. Seven harpers com-
peted, namely, Charles Fanning, Patrick Kerr, Patrick
Maguire, Hugh Higgins, Charles Byrne, Rose Mooney,
and Arthur O'Neill. Fanning got first Prize (ten
guineas) for his rendering of " An Cuilḟionn ;" Arthur
O'Neill got second (eight guineas) for the " Green
Woods of Truagh " and " Madame Crofton ;" and Rose
Mooney got third (five guineas) for " Planxty Burke."

The second Granard Festival came off on March
2nd, 1782, but only two new candidates, Edward
MacDermot Roe and Catherine Martin, presented
themselves, in addition to the seven others. Mr.
Dungan came over specially from Copenhagen to

attend the third festival in 1783, when Laurence
Keane and James Duncan brought the number of
competitors up to eleven. The fourth festival came
off on August 1st, 1784, when four premiums were
offered, but the results were not encouraging, and
the attendance of spectators showed a falling off.
However, the fifth festival was announced for Monday,
August 1st, 1785, the premiums being seven guineas
to the best performer, five guineas as second prize,
three guineas as third, and two guineas as fourth.
The stewards were Messrs. A. Burroughs, Connell,
and Edgeworth. From O'Neill we learn that this
was the last and best of the Granard Festivals, and
it was attended by a thousand persons. He adds :—
"In consequence of the harpers who obtained no
premiums having been neglected on the former occasions, I hinted a subscription, which was well received
and performed ; and, indeed, on distributing the collection, their proportions exceeded our premiums."

After a lapse of over six years, a project was launched
at Belfast, in December, 1791, for an "assembly of
harpers," the organisers being Dr. M'Donnell, Robert
Bradshaw, and Henry Joy. Accordingly, on July 11th,
12th, 13th, and 14th of the year 1792, the memorable
Belfast Harp Festival took place, when ten harpers
competed, namely, Denis Hampson, Arthur O'Neill,
Charles Fanning, Daniel Black, Charles Byrne, Hugh
Higgins, Patrick Quin, William Carr, Rose Mooney,
and James Duncan. The first prize (ten guineas) was
awarded to Charles Fanning for " An Cuilḟionn,'
whilst O'Neill got the second (eight guineas) for the
"Green Woods of Truagh" and "Madame Crofton."

In all, there were forty tunes played by the ten harpers, and Edward Bunting (assistant organist to William Ware) was deputed to take down the airs,* which formed the major part of his Collection, published in 1796.

An impetus was given to Irish music ever since the period of the Volunteers; and the publication of *Walker's Irish Bards*, in 1786, added a stimulus to the study of our old melodies. In the year following appeared Thompson's *Hibernian Muse*, from which Tom Moore drew many of his inspirations, whilst Brysson's Collection of fifty favourite Irish airs was issued in 1791, followed by Cooke's *Selection*, in 1794; O'Farrell's National Irish Music, in 1799-1802; a new edition of O'Carolan's Airs, in 1804; and Smollet Holden's Collection (two volumes), in 1804-6.

Between the years 1792 and 1802 the cultivation of the Irish harp naturally led to a development of harp-making, and John Egan, of Dublin, established a famous factory for harps. At length, on St. Patrick's Day, 1808, the Belfast Harp Society was formally inaugurated at Linn's Hotel, the White Cross, No. 1,

---

* The following is the list of the tunes played, as given in the Belfast *Northern Star*, of July 15th, 1792:—"Coulin," "Fairy Queen," "Molly Veagg, O" [Mhali bheag og], "Planksty Kingsland" "Gra go nish," "Denis Dealy," "Miss Fenning," "Collough an Tinnie," "Collendoon" [Cailin dhonn], "Carolan's Concerto," "Lady Latitia," "Planksty Reily," "Baccaugh Buia," "Scarant na Gompanaugh," "The Dawning of the Day," "Pearla an Vroley Vaun," "Cauher vac Aough," "Mable Kelly," "Lady Veaugh," "Tierna Vujoe," "Patrick's Day," "Aelion na Ruaen," "Mailin Guidey Uyain," "Nancy Cooper," "Gracy Newgent," "Carolan's Gap," "Thomas Burke," "Lady Bleany," "Mrs. Maxwell," "Pharaca na Ruarc," "Doctor Hart," "Carrie a Nuienish," "Shiely ni Conolan," "Mrs. Crofton," "Sir Festus Burke," "Cionn dhu dielish," "The Humours of Whiskey," "Denis Aily," "Cathelien Treall," "Trugh." I retain the original unique spelling of the Irish names.

Castle-street. In the list of original subscribers (one hundred and ninety-one) the total annual subscriptions amounted to £300, Lord O'Neill being appointed first president *vice* Bishop Percy, of Dromore, who declined the honour. The first teacher was Arthur O'Neill, and the classes opened with eight boy pupils and a girl, Bridget O'Reilly. Of these, two were dismissed in June, 1810, "for inaptitude to learn," thus leaving seven boarding pupils, viz., Patrick O'Neill, Patrick M'Grath, Edward M'Bride, Nathaniel Rainey, Abraham Wilkinson, James M'Molaghan, and Bridget O'Reilly, in addition to Edward O'Neill, Hugh Dornan, and John Wallace as day scholars. Harps were supplied by Messrs. White, M'Clenaghan, and M'Cabe, of Belfast, at a cost of ten guineas each. From 1809 to 1811 there were Irish classes in connection with the Belfast Harp Society, with James Cody as professor, the grammar used being that by Rev. William Neilson, D.D. In 1812 the society was in difficulties, and it collapsed in 1813, having expended during the six years of its existence about £955. To the credit of the Society, poor O'Neill was given an annuity of £30 a year, but he did not long enjoy it, as his death occurred at Maydown, County Armagh, on October 29th, 1816, aged eighty-eight.* His harp is now in the Museum of the Belfast Natural History and Philosophical Society.

Dublin, too, had its Harp Society, due to the exertions of the eccentric but well-meaning John Bernard Trotter (ex-secretary to Charles James Fox), who brought to the Irish metropolis Patrick Quinn, the

* Bunting, with his usual inaccuracy, gives a wrong date, namely, "in 1818.'

famous blind harper of Portadown, "one of the last of
the ancient race of harpers," as teacher of the Society.
It was formally inaugurated on July 13th, 1809, and
the list of subscribers embraced "noblemen, gentlemen, and professors," including Sir Walter Scott, Tom
Moore, Joseph Cooper Walker, Mrs. Liddiard, etc.
Trotter himself subsidised the Society to the extent of
£200, and took a house at Richmond, near Clontarf,
where he entertained lavishly, and kept Quinn "to
delight his guests with unheard-of strains of melody."
Further, in order to foster a love for the old Irish
airs, he conceived and successfully carried out a grand
" Carolan Commemoration " in Dublin, in 1809. Hardiman adds :—" With the impetuosity natural to Irishmen, it was held twice in the same week, but never
since repeated "—a statement which is inaccurate.

The Carolan Commemoration took place at the Private
Theatre, Fishamble-street, on Wednesday, September
20th, 1809, and was repeated on the following Wednes-
day. Sir John Stevenson, Tom Cooke, Mrs. Cooke,
Logier, Dr. Spray, Willmann, the Misses Cheese, and
Patrick Quinn assisted.

The Rules and Regulations of the Dublin Harp
Society were printed in 1810, but the movement declined at the close of that year, and became defunct
in 1812, when, owing to his profuse hospitality,
Trotter became bankrupt. After a chequered career
John Bernard Trotter died at Cork, September 29th,
1818, in the forty-third year of his age, and was buried
in the churchyard of St. Finnbar's.*

---

* In November, 1809, Trotter published, in Dublin, *Stories for
Calumniators*, in two volumes, dedicated to Lord Holland. His

After Trotter's death, the Irish Harp Society at Belfast was re-established, as the result of a meeting held to administer a fund of £1,200, forwarded by a number of public-spirited residents in India, "to revive the Harp and Ancient Music of Ireland. This meeting was held on April 16, 1819, with Thomas Verner as chairman, and classes were again started, with Edward M'Bride (1819-1822) as teacher, who was succeeded by Valentine Rennie (1823-1837). A small number of harps was ordered of the most approved construction, and the pupils were selected from "the blind and the helpless." This benevolent scheme lingered on for twenty years, regarding which Petrie writes as follows :—"The effort of the people of the North to perpetuate the existence of the harp in Ireland by trying to give a harper's skill to a number of poor blind boys was at once a benevolent and a patriotic one; but it was a delusion. The harp at the time was virtually dead, and such effort could give it for a while only a sort of galvanised vitality. The selection of blind boys, without any greater regard for their musical capacities than the possession of the organ of hearing, for a calling which doomed them to a wandering life . . . was not a well-considered benevolence, and should never have had any fair hope of success." *

Meantime, Edward Bunting (who was organist of the Second Congregation of Rosemary Street, Belfast, from 1806 to 1817) published a second volume of Irish airs in 1809, which was reprinted in 1811. He was organist of

Walks through Ireland in 1812, 1814, and 1817, was published at London in 1819, with a memoir of the author by Rev. Dr. Walshe.

* O'Curry's Manners and Customs of the Ancient Irish, vol. iii., p. 298.

St. George's, Belfast, from 1817 to 1820, and then removed to Dublin, where he published his third collection in 1840. His death occurred on December 21st, 1843, and he was buried in Mount Jerome Cemetery, where a modest slab marks the grave of a man who preserved hundreds of exquisite Irish melodies from utter oblivion.

Between the years 1803 and 1823 the harp was taken up as a "fad" by many titled dames, and hence had a passing popularity. Lady Morgan tells us that she treated herself to an Irish harp, made by John Egan in May, 1805, "as the first fruits of her literary earnings by the publication of the *Novice*." At the close of the year 1805 she published a small collection of Irish melodies, and in the year following she collaborated with Tom Cooke in an operetta entitled *The Whim of the Moment*, produced at Crow-street Theatre Royal on March 5th, 1807. In 1809 the Marchioness of Abercorn and Lady Aberdeen purchased Irish harps from Egan, and in 1811 there were further orders for the national instrument. Finally, in 1822, Charles Egan published a *Harp Primer*, "being a familiar introduction to the study of the harp," which was reprinted in 1829. He also issued *The Royal Harp Director* in 1827.

When Valentine Rennie died, in 1837, the Belfast Harp Society was moribund, but a new teacher (James Jackson) was appointed in January, 1838, and kept the school in Cromac-street for a twelvemonth. The end came in 1839, after twenty years. However, a new Harp Society was inaugurated at Drogheda on January 15th, 1842, owing to the zeal of Father Thomas V. Burke, O.P., of that town. The first year's report showed a class of fifteen pupils, and the Society had obtained twelve new harps, manufactured in Drogheda, at a cost of £3 each. Hugh Fraser was the first—and last—teacher, at a salary of £27 a year. Kohl, the German traveller, visited Drogheda in 1843, and was delighted with the harp performances he heard whilst a guest at the house of Father Burke. He praises the powers of Patrick Byrne, a famous harpist and composer, who was family minstrel to the Shirleys, and who died at Dundalk in 1863. From the printed programme of the first public concert of the Drogheda Harp Society, on Monday, February 24th, 1844, it appears that Mr. Frazer had taught sixteen pupils, including a number of blind boys. At this concert the harpers were assisted by Miss Flynn, Mr. Halpin, Mr. Dowdall, and Mr. M'Entaggart. The Society collapsed in 1845. Then came the famine, and, alas! the harp was allowed to become neglected till the Irish Ireland movement, inaugurated by the Gaelic League, and fostered by the Celtic Literary Society and kindred associations, again galvanised the national instrument into life. However, it is evident that notwithstanding those efforts, as evidenced by the harp competitions at the Feis Ceoil and Oireachtas since 1897, the national instrument is now merely heard "to show that still she lives."

CHAPTER XXVIII.

CONCLUSION.

MUCH as I should like to dwell on the musical doings of the nineteenth century, the time is hardly ripe to form an unprejudiced judgment, and therefore I shall merely touch on the more important composers, namely, Field, Cooke, O'Rourke, Wade, Balfe, Wallace, Osborne, Stewart, Holmes, and Stanford.*

John Field (O'Fihil), born in Dublin, on July 26th, 1782, showed a marvellous precocity as a boy pianist. His father and grandfather were musicians of Dublin fame, the latter an organist, and the former a violinist at Crow-street Theatre. In 1794 his father took him to London, where he appeared as a prodigy, and was then placed under the tuition of Clementi. During the Christmastide of 1799 young Field again appeared, and his playing elicited universal admiration, so much so that Clementi decided to take him on tour. From 1802 to 1804 Field astonished delighted audiences in Paris, Germany, and Russia; and Spohr writes most enthusiastically of the marvellous Irish pianist. During eighteen years he was the fashionable piano teacher in St. Petersburg, and in 1823 he removed to Moscow, where he met with even greater success. His performance in London, at a Philharmonic concert, on February 27th, 1832, showed a more robust virtuosity,

---

* Some persons may wonder at my non-inclusion of Sir Arthur Sullivan, but, though his father was Irish, he himself may be regarded as a typical English composer. Similarly, I have omitted notices of Sir Frederick Ouseley and Rev. Scotson Clarke, who were both of Irish parentage.

and was also remarkable for a concerto of his own. He died at Moscow on January 11th, 1837. Davey writes as follows :—

"Here at last we meet with a musician who *invented*, who had a style of his own—a composer and performer of European celebrity. As a player, Field is reckoned among the very greatest that ever lived. He is said to have kept the fingers almost perpendicular, and his touch was distinguished by an unprecedented richness and *sostenuto*, and by the subtlest details of expression. . . . He made an important addition to existing means of expression by his *new form*, the NOCTURNE, . . . and we owe it entirely to Field. Chopin, a man of far greater intellectual power, applied deeper science and richer poetry to the *Nocturne;* but he did not altogether eclipse Field, the original inventor." *

Amongst the numerous sonatas, concertos, divertimenti, rondos, airs varies, valses, etc., few are now heard in his native country, though well known on the continent. Of course, his Nocturnes are popular everywhere, and Liszt edited a collection with a most sympathetic foreword. However, it has often been stated that Field never drew any inspiration from the incomparable folk-melodies of his native land. This is not so. In 1818 he published an arrangement of "Go to the Devil and Shake Yourself" (The Growling Woman), a Munster tune, whilst his "Rondo Ecossaise" is also founded on an Irish air.

Tom Cooke (as invariably called) was also a Dublin man, and was born in Dublin in 1782. At Christmas, 1798, he was leader of the orchestra at Crow-street Theatre, and continued as such till 1812—composing

* Davey's *History of English Music*, pp. 436-8.

much popular music, some of which was published by himself at his music warehouse, 45, Dame-street, between the years 1810-1813. One of his earliest attempts was " The Battle of Marengo," performed at Crow-street on May 24th, 1802, followed by "Lord Hardwicke's March " in 1804.* His first benefit was on May 22nd, 1805, and he resigned the baton at Crow-street on June 21st, 1813, having proved such a success as a tenor vocalist in the *Siege of Belgrade*, the *Beggar's Opera*, the *Duenna*, etc. He became director of the music at Drury-lane in 1821, of which theatre he was principal tenor for over eighteen years. At a benefit in 1820 he proved his extraordinary versatility by performing successively on nine instruments, namely, the violin, flute, oboe, clarionet, bassoon, horn, 'cello, bass, and pianoforte. As a composer his versatility was equally great, as may be evidenced by his operas, masses, glees, catches, songs, duets, etc., besides treatises on singing.† Among his pupils were Miss Tree, Miss Povey, Miss Austin, Miss Rainsforth, the Misses Williams, and the late Sims Reeves. He died February 26th, 1848.

William Michael O'Rourke—who changed his name to Rooke—was another Dublin musician of fame. Born in South Great George's-street, September 29th, 1794, he was an excellent violinist, and was Balfe's instructor from 1815 to 1817. O'Rourke was chorus master and

---

* He collaborated with Sydney Owenson (Lady Morgan) in the music for *The Whim of the Moment*—an operetta produced on March 5th, 1807, in the Theatre Royal, Dublin, on which occasion Mr. Owenson appeared for the last time.

† One of his songs, "Gentle Zitella" (also known as "Love's Ritornella"), in *The Brigand* (1829) had a wonderful popularity.

deputy leader at Crow-street Theatre from 1817 to 1823, and, in 1818, composed his first opera, *Amilie* ; *or, The Love Test*. Removing to England in 1824, he settled in London in 1826, and his opera, after lying in manuscript for close on twenty years, was produced at Covent Garden on December 22nd, 1837, with much success. *Henrique* ; *or, The Love Pilgrim*, followed on May 2nd, 1839, but did not catch on. Two other operas, *Cagliostro* and *The Valkyrie*, were not performed. O'Rourke died on October 14th, 1847, and was buried in Brompton Cemetery.

John Augustine Wade, born in Thomas-street, Dublin, in 1796, was clerk in the Irish Record Office in 1820, and studied the violin under O'Rourke. He married Miss Kelly, of Garnavilla (Athlone), studied medicine, and removed to London in 1822.* His oratorio, *The Prophecy*, was produced at Drury-lane in 1824, and then followed an opera, *The Two Houses of Granada* (1826), in which occurs the time-honoured ballad, "Long, long ago." In the following year (1827) he published *Songs of the Flowers*, in two books, and, some years later, *Select Airs* and *Polish Melodies*. Early in 1831 he negotiated with James Power (Moore's publisher) for the publication of a *History of Music*, and in 1833 he collaborated with Hawes in *Convent Belles*. His song, "Meet me by moonlight alone," had an extraordinary popularity, and in October, 1834, the inimitable "Father Prout" published a French version of it in *Fraser's*

---

* In 1811 he composed a ballad, "I have culled every flowret that blows," which was published by Thomas Cook & Co., of 45, Dame-street, Dublin, in 1812. Sir Robert Stewart says that Wade composed "Lovely Kate of Garnavilla," but this is not so.

*Magazine.** A duet of his, "I've wandered in dreams," is still to be heard at concerts. Alas! from 1837 till his death he was the victim of intemperance, and he died in London, September 29th, 1845.

Michael William Balfe belongs to European musical history, and two excellent biographies of him have been published. Born in Dublin, at No. 10, Pitt-street, on May 11th, 1808, he studied under O'Rourke, Barton, and Horn, and his song, "Young Fanny," was published by Willis in 1823. His opera, *The Siege of Rochelle,* produced at Drury-lane on October 29th, 1835, was the first of a series of operatic triumphs. On December 26th, 1838, he was given a public dinner at Morrison's Hotel, Dublin, and in the following year he had a successful tour in Ireland. *Keolanthe* was produced on March 9th, 1841, and the *Bohemian Girl* on November 27th, 1843. From 1846 to 1852 he was conductor at Her Majesty's Theatre *vice* Costa resigned, and during that time he paid a second visit to Dublin as conductor for Lumley in 1848. In 1859 Balfe edited a collection of Moore's *Irish Melodies* for Novello, with new symphonies and accompaniments. His death occurred at Rowney Abbey, Herts, on the 20th of October, 1870. A good summary of his works will be found in Brown and Stratton's *British Musical Biography,* to which the reader is referred. A statue to his memory was unveiled in the vestibule of Drury-lane Theatre, on September 25th, 1874, and a Balfe Festival was given at

---

* His song, "Love was once a little boy," was also much in vogue during the forties and fifties. For the farewell dinner to Cramer, in May, 1835, Wade composed a song which was sung by John Parry, and accompanied by Moscheles. He travelled with Liszt, Parry, Knight, and others to Dublin at Christmas, 1840.

the Alexandra Palace on July 29th, 1876. A bust of Balfe, from the chisel of Sir Thomas Farrell, R.H.A., was placed in the Irish National Gallery on July 6th, 1878, where also may be seen a list of his operas, with dates of their production, in his own handwriting, and fragments of his manuscript diary. Finally, a tablet in his honour was placed in the north-west aisle of Westminster Abbey, which was formally unveiled on October 20th, 1882.

William Vincent Wallace also belongs to European fame. Born in the city of Waterford on March 11th, 1812, he was known as a musician of promise in his fifteenth year, having been taught by his father (band-master of the 29th Regiment) and Otho Hamilton. In 1826 the family removed to Dublin, where his father got an engagement as bassoon player in the Theatre Royal orchestra, and, in 1828, we find young Wallace as violinist in the band—his brother Wellington being second flute. At the age of seventeen William Vincent Wallace was a proficient organist, pianist, and violinist, and he could also play on the clarionet and guitar. His first public appearance was in June, 1829, at a Dublin concert, and, in the autumn of that year, (having become a Catholic), he was appointed Organist of Thurles Cathedral, and Professor of Music at the Ursuline Convent. He returned to Dublin in September, 1831, to take part in the Dublin Musical Festival, at which Paganini was the chief attraction, and this event was the turning point in the career of Wallace, who determined to get to the top of the tree in the musical profession. In this same year he married Miss Isabella Kelly, of Blackrock (County Dublin), and continued to work at the violin and composition. Winning much applause for a violin concerto of his own, which he performed at a concert in Dublin in May, 1834, he resolved to go to Australia as a larger field for his talents. His wanderings between the years 1835 and 1845 read like romance, and, at length, *Maritana* was produced at Drury-lane on November 15th, 1845, followed by *Matilda of Hungary* in 1847. From 1849 to 1853 Wallace was in Germany, France, South America, North America, etc., and his *Lurline* was given at Covent Garden on February 23rd, 1860. He died at Chateau de Bagen, Haute Garonne, France, on October 12th, 1865, but his remains were brought over to England and interred in Kensal-green. His widow* survived till July 25th, 1900, at the age of eighty-seven, and his last surviving son is now (1904) in London. It is sufficient to add that the list of his compositions fills upwards of a hundred pages of the British Museum Catalogue, of which a good summary is given in Brown and Stratton's *British Musical Biography*.

George Alexander Osborne was born in Limerick on September 24th, 1806, and was originally intended for the Church, but fixed on music as his profession. His father was organist and lay vicar of Limerick Cathedral, and so, as a youth, Osborne occasionally acted as assistant, having acquired a knowledge of the organ as well as the piano. In 1825 he went to Brussels, where he found a patron in the Prince de Chimay, and in 1830 he removed to Paris, where he completed his

---

* Wallace separated from his wife in 1835, and never saw her again. He married Helene Stoepel, a pianist, in 1850. A good water colour of Wallace, by J. Hanshew, dated 1853, is in the National Gallery of Ireland.

studies under Pixis, Fetis, and Kalkbrenner. From 1831 to 1843 Osborne was one of the principal musicians in the French capital, and enjoyed the friendship of Chopin, Berlioz, and others. In 1842 he gave his assistance to Balfe at a concert given in the Erard Salon, and in 1844 settled in London, where he became Director of the Royal Academy of Music, and was recognised as one of the most esteemed teachers in London till he retired in 1889. Commencing with three trios in A (1844), G and E (1845), for piano and strings, Osborne published an enormous quantity of music, including numerous duets with de Beriot, and piano pieces like " La Pluie des Perles," " Romance sans Paroles," etc. His ballad of " Pat Molloy," composed for Boucicault, is still sung. He died November 16th, 1893.

Sir Robert Prescott Stewart was born at No. 6 Pitt-street, Dublin, on December 16th, 1825, and was educated as a chorister of Christ Church Cathedral. In 1836 he wrote a complete service in B flat, and in 1843 an anthem, " Plead thou my cause." So conspicuous was his ability that, in 1844, he was appointed Organist of Christ Church Cathedral, and of Trinity College Chapel, and in 1852 he succeeded Mr. White as Organist of St. Patrick's Cathedral. From 1846 to his death he was conductor of the Dublin University Choral Society, the members of which subscribed the necessary expenses attending the performance of his exercise for the degrees of Mus. Bac. and Mus. Doc., in 1851, also presenting him with his graduate's robes and a jewelled baton. His " Inauguration Ode " for the Cork Exhibition, in June, 1852, and his " March " for the Dublin

Exhibition of 1853 were not ephemeral works, whilst his cantata, " The Eve of St. John," produced on April 12th, 1861, was of more than average merit. For the Birmingham Festival of 1870 he composed an " Ode to Shakespere," for solo, chorus, and orchestra. In 1871 he was appointed Professor of Music in the University of Dublin, and in 1872 he was knighted by Earl Spencer. His glees and arrangements of Irish airs are exceedingly clever, and he wrote some fine organ fantasias. As an executant on the organ Stewart was in the very first rank, and his extemporisation was phenomenal. He died in Dublin on March 24th, 1894, and a brass tablet was placed to his memory in Christ Church Cathedral. At length, on March 8th, 1898, a fine statue on Leinster Lawn, Dublin, was unveiled by the Viceroy, Earl Cadogan— truly a national monument to a distinguished Irish musician.

Augusta Mary Anne Holmes was born of Irish parents in the Rue de Berri, Paris, on December 16th, 1847, and attracted attention as a piano prodigy and singer of her own original French songs, from 1858 to 1865. Her mother died early in 1857, and she then began to study music seriously, publishing some pieces under the *nom de plume* of " Hermann Zenta." After a course of instruction from Lambert, Franck, Klose, and St. Saens, she bounded into favour with *Hero and Leander*, at the Opera Populaire, in 1874, a success which was followed up with the orchestral piece " Les Argonautes," performed at the Concerts Populaires on April 24th, 1881. However, her greatest triumph was the symphonic poem " Irlande," the pro·

duct of an inborn Irish sympathy. It was first heard on March 2nd, 1882, and was given at the first Feis Ceoil, in Dublin, on May 18th, 1897, described by Jullien as "a creation of great worth, evincing by turns a charming tenderness, ardent passion, and masculine spirit." Then came " Pologne " in 1883, and the ode " Pro Patria " in 1888, after which, in 1895, her opera *La Montagne Noire* was produced at the Grand Opera, Paris. She became a Roman Catholic in 1902, and died January 28th, 1903.*

Sir Charles Villiers Stanford was born at 2 Herbert-street, Dublin, September 30th, 1852, and studied under R. M. Levey, Miss Meeke, Miss Flynn, and Sir Robert Stewart. His first composition was a march in D flat, which was played at the pantomime of *Puss in Boots*, at the Theatre Royal, during the Christmas of 1860-1. On the first production of Mendelssohn's *Elijah,* in Dublin, on December 9th, 1847, Stanford's father sang the part of the " Prophet " with signal success, and in August, 1849, he played the cello at the Viceregal Concert given in honour of Queen Victoria's visit. The young composer went to London in 1862, and took lessons from Arthur O'Leary. Matriculating at Cambridge in 1870, he became organist of Trinity College, and took his B.A. degree in 1874, being then conductor of the University Musical Society. From 1874 to 1876 Stanford studied at Leipzig under Reincke, and in 1877 at Berlin under Kiel. In 1878 he married Miss Jennie

* On July 13th, 1904, a splendid monument was unveiled to her memory in the St. Louis' Cemetery, Versailles. A weeping muse is represented holding a lyre, and on the monument there is inscribed an appropriate quotation from her choral symphony, "Lutece."

Wetton, and proceeded M.A., settling down at Cambridge for the succeeding sixteen years. His three operas, *The Veiled Prophet* (1881), *Savanarola* (1884), and *The Canterbury Pilgrims* (1884), placed him in the forefront of "British" musicians, whilst *Shamus O'Brien* (1896) is of too recent date to need eulogy. In 1883 and 1888 he was given the honorary degree of Mus. Doc. by the Universities of Oxford and Cambridge respectively, and in 1887 he was appointed Professor of Music in the University of Cambridge in succession to Sir George Macfarren. His symphonies, masses, and suites are of European fame, and he has edited three collections of Irish airs. In January, 1901, he was appointed conductor of the Leeds Festival, vacant by the death of Sir Arthur Sullivan, and in June, 1902, he was knighted. For the Leeds Festival (October, 1904) he composed a Violin Concerto and five " Songs of the Sea."

It would be unpardonable to pass over the name of Thomas Moore (1779-1852) whose " Irish Melodies " are world-famed, and who compelled drawing-room dames to listen to the old-folk melodies of Ireland, as adapted to his own matchless lyrics.* Samuel Lover, too, ought not to be forgotten, though his best known songs were adaptations. The names of R. M. Levey (1811-1903) and J. W. Glover (1815-1899) are also associated with arrangements of Irish music. Joseph Robinson (1816-1898), as the founder of the Antient Concerts, and the youngest of four musical brothers, deserves honourable

---

* Moore's only attempt at an opera, *M.P., or the Blue Stocking*, with music by C. E. Horn, was produced at the English Opera House, London, on September 4th, 1811, but met with no success. His *Lalla Rooke* was also set to music by Horn in 1820.

mention in any work dealing with Irish musicians. His eldest brother, Francis, was given the degree of Mus. Doc., *honoris causa*, and edited a collection of Irish melodies. Short memoirs of W. H. Kearns (1794-1846), M. R. Lacy (1795-1867), H. R. Allen (1809-1876), George A. Barker (1812-1876), Wellington Guernsey (1781-1885), R. W. Beaty (1790-1883), Joseph F. Duggan (1817-1900), J. J. Gaskin (1820-1876), W. J. Cordner (1826-1870), W. Vipond Barry (1827-1872), P. S. Gilmore (1829-1892), Joseph O'Kelly (1829-1885), Rev. Edward Synge, Mus.Doc. (1829-1895), William Houghton (1844-1871), Sir W. C. F. Robinson (1839-1897), H. G. Thunder (1832-1881) Richard F. Harvey (1820-1904) and other Irish musicians will be found in Grove's *Dictionary of Music and Musicians*, and in Brown and Stratton's *British Musical Biography*. As vocalists, Catherine Hayes and Allan James Foley (Signor Foli) will long be remembered, whilst the songs of Piccolomini (Pontet), W. E. Hudson, Barker, Molloy and Harvey are occasionally heard.

It is risky to mention persons still living, but the following names are sufficient to prove that Ireland can still boast of musical sons and daughters, inheritors of the traditions of past ages—Mrs. Needham, Mrs. Milligan Fox, Mrs. Scott Ffennell, Dr. Annie Patterson, Miss Oldham, Mrs. Hobday, Mrs. Curwen, Mrs. Dutton Cook, Sister Attracta Coffey, Archbishop Walsh, Bishop Donnelly, Sir Francis Cruise, Sir Francis W. Brady, Canon Torrance, Mus. Doc.; Rev. Professor Mahaffy, Mus. Doc.; Dr. Marchant, Dr. Charles Wood, Dr. Sinclair, Rev. E. Gaynor, J. L. Molloy, J. F. Horan, Brendan Rogers, Vincent O'Brien, Rev. E. O'Keeffe,

John Power, John F. Murray, C. K. Irwin, Mackay Glover, Rev. Dr. Collisson, H. H. Harty, P. Delaney, J. Seymour, R. O'Dwyer, D. Nunan, P. Goodman, Rev. W. Butler, S.J.; Rev. G. O'Neill, S.J.; Dr. Joze, Dr. Gick, Arthur O'Leary, Dr. Malone, Dr. Power O'Donoghue, Herbert Hughes, Owen Lloyd, Arthur Darley, W. H. Pelissier, Victor Herbert, Hubert Rooney, M. Connolly, F. Manly, St. John Lacy, Wm. Ludwig, Madam Adelaide Mullen, P. J. Griffith, Norman O'Neill, Barton M'Guckin, Baron Crofton, Joseph O'Mara, Harold White, J. J. Johnson, John O'Donnell, Maud M'Carthy, W. H. Vipond Barry, Charles Manners, Plunket Greene, Denis O'Sullivan, Madeleine O'Connor, Miss Donegan, Rev. B. Donovan, G. B. Shaw, etc.

A word too might be expected on the various musical societies that flourished in Dublin during the nineteenth century, but I refer the reader to Appendix C, in which a list is given. In connection with musical societies it is only right to add that the annual music-makings at the Feis Ceoil and Oireachtas since the year 1897 have not a little influenced musical life in Ireland, whilst the various provincial and local Feiseanna have also contributed to the popularisation of Irish folk-songs in the native tongue.

Let me conclude with the hope that ere long a school of national Irish music will be founded. "If not," as Mr. A. P. Graves writes, "we shall assuredly forfeit our national birthright of song; for, Antaeus-like, our musicians have lost their power since they have been lifted from the touch of their native earth."

APPENDICES.

APPENDIX A.

LIST OF THE PRINCIPAL COLLECTIONS OF IRISH MUSIC

(FROM 1725 TO 1887.)

A.D.

1726   Neale's *Collection of Irish and Scotch Tunes* (Dublin).

1726   Neale's *Book of Irish Tunes* (Dublin).

1727-8   Wright's *Aria di Camera.*

1729   Coffey's ballad-opera, *The Beggar's Wedding.*

1738   *The Vocal Miscellany* (Dublin).*

1742   Burke Thumoth's *Scotch and Irish Airs.*

1743   Burke Thumoth's *English and Irish Airs.*

1747   Henry Brooke's ballad-opera, *Jack the Giant Queller.*

1747   O'Carolan's *Collection* (Dublin).

1748-9   Rutherford's 200 *Country Dances.*

1743-64   Oswald's *Caledonian Pocket Companion*—12 books.

1754   Lee's *Masque*—3 books. (Dublin).

1771   MacLean's *Selection of 22 Original Airs* (Dublin).

1774   Jackson's *Celebrated Irish Tunes* (Dublin).†

1775   *The Hibernian Catch Book* (Dublin).

1779   O'Carolan's *Collection* (New Edition) (Dublin.)‡

1784   MacDonald's *Collection of Highland Airs.*

---

* This is the third edition of a book of the same name of which the original was printed in London, in 1733. The *names* of the tunes are prefixed to each song.

† There have been three reprints of this collection.

‡ The date for this publication is usually given as " 1780," but it was issued on January 1st, 1779. Another edition was issued in 1783, by Hime, of College Green. I have traced four other editions between the year 1780 and 1800; and, in 1804, Broderip and Wilkinson of London, published an edition, suppressing the names of the tunes.

A.D.
1786   Walker's *Irish Bards* (Dublin).

1786   *The Musical Miscellany* (Perth).*

1787   Thompson's *Hibernian Muse.*

1782-99 Aird's *Selection.* 6 vols (Glasgow).

1791   Brysson's 50 *Favourite Irish Airs.*

1792-3 *The Edinburgh Musical Miscellany.*

1794   Cooke's *Selection of* 21 *Favourite Original Irish Airs*
        (Dublin).

1795   Gaudry's *Masonic Songs* (Dublin).

1796   Bunting's *Ancient Irish Music.*

1798   Holden's *Masonic Songs* (Dublin).

1793-9 Thomson's *Four Sets of Scottish Airs* (including
        numerous Irish Tunes).

1797-9 *Vocal Magazine.*

1787-1803 *The Scots Musical Museum.*

1801   Crotch's *Specimens.*

1800-2 O'Farrell's *Irish Music for the Union Pipes.*

1804   Mulholland's *Irish and Scots Tunes.*

1805   Miss Owenson's *Twelve Hibernian Melodies* (Dublin).

1804-6 Holden's *Collection of Irish Tunes*—two books—
        (Dublin).

1805-8 Hime's *Selection of Original Irish Airs* (Dublin).

1804-10 O'Farrell's *Pocket Companion for the Irish Pipes.*

1807   Abraham Mackintosh's *Collection.*

1808   Holden's *Periodical Irish Melodies* (Dublin).

1808   Crosby's *Irish Musical Repository.*

1809   Murphy's *Irish Airs and Jigs.*

1809   Bunting's *Second Collection.*†

1810   Mulholland's *Ancient Irish Airs* (Belfast).

1810   Power's *Musical Cabinet* (Dublin).

1812   *National Melodies of England and Ireland.*

---

* A new and enlarged edition of this work appeared in 1788,
under the title of *Calliope*, containing English, Irish, and Scots
songs, a copy of which is in my musical library.

† There were two issues of this edition, but the original was,
in 1809, by Clements, of London, containing seventy-seven airs,
price £1 6s. The second edition was published in 1811.

A.D.

1804–14 Hime's *Collection of Country Dances* (Dublin).

1808–12 Moore's *Irish Melodies*, No. 1 to No. 4 (Dublin.)*

1815 Fraser's *Highland Airs.*

1814–16 Thomson's *Irish Airs* (arranged by Beethoven). Two Vols.

1815–17 Kinloch's *One Hundred Airs.*

1813–18 Moore's *Irish Melodies.* No. 5 to No. 7 (inclusively), (Dublin).

1814–16 Fitzsimon's *Irish Minstrelsy*, by Dr. Smith (Dublin).

1818 *A Selection of Irish Melodies* (Dublin).

1818 Holden's *Favourite Irish Airs* (Dublin).

1816–18 Campbell's *Albyn's Anthology.*

1820 *Mona Melodies.*

1821 MacCullagh's *Collection of Irish Airs.* Three Vols. (Dublin).

1821–22 O'Callaghan's *Collection of Irish Airs.*

1821–24 Moore's *Irish Melodies.* Nos. 8 and 9.†

1825 Smith's *Vocal Melodies of Ireland.*

1826 Egan's *National Lyrics.*

1834 Moore's *Irish Melodies.* No. 10 and Supplement.

1840 Bunting's *Third Collection.*

1840 Clinton's 200 *Irish Melodies for the Flute.*

1840 Alexander's *Flowers of the Emerald Isle.*

1840–2 *The Citizen*, edited by W. E. Hudson.

1841 Clinton's *Gems of Ireland.*

1841 Crouch's *Songs of Ireland.*

1841–2 *National Music of Ireland.*

1843 Fitzgerald's *Old Songs of Old Ireland*, by Guernsey.

* Most authors give the year 1807 as the date of the first issue of Moore's *Irish Melodies.* The actual date was 5th April, 1808, and the publisher was William Power of No. 4 Westmoreland Street, Dublin, the printers being Messrs. Carrick, of 29 Bachelor's Walk, Dublin. This first number contained twelve airs.

† No. 8 was published by James Power, London, in 1821, with symphonies and accompaniments by Sir Henry Bishop. However, in June of the same year, a pirated edition was published by William Power, 4 Westmoreland-street, Dublin, with symphonies and accompaniments by Sir John Stevenson.

A.D.

1844 Horncastle's *Music of Ireland.*

1844–5 *The Spirit of the Nation.*

1845 Lynch's *Melodies of Ireland.* Six books.

1846 Conran's *National Music of Ireland.**

1847 Henderson's *Flowers of Irish Melody.* Two Vols.

1849 O'Daly's *Poets and Poetry of Munster.* First Series.

1850 Moore's *Irish Melodies,* by Francis Robinson. Two Vols.

1854 Surenne's *Songs of Ireland.*

1855 Petrie's *Ancient Music of Ireland.*†

1859 Moore's *Irish Melodies,* by Glover.

1859 Moore's *Irish Melodies,* by Balfe.

1860 *Gems from Ould Ireland,* by Ogden.

1860 *Songs of Ireland,* by Wellington Guernsey.

1860 O'Daly's *Poets and Poetry of Munster.* New Series.

1861 Davidson's *Irish Melodies.*

1861 Hughes's *Collection.*

1865 *Old Songs of Ireland,* by Arthur O'Brien.

1858–73 Levey's *Collection of Irish Dance Music.* Two Vols.

1873 Dr. Joyce's *Ancient Irish Music.*

1873 *Songs of Ireland,* by Molloy (Boosey's edition).‡

1877 Hoffman's edition of Petrie for Pianoforte (Dublin).

1882 *Songs of Old Ireland,* by Stanford.

1887 *Irish Music and Song,* by Joyce.

---

* Published by James Duffy, Dublin. A second edition was issued in 1850 by Johnson, of London.

† A Supplement, containing thirty four airs, was issued in 1882. However, the entire Petrie Collection, in three volumes, containing almost 2,000 airs, has been recently issued by Boosey, of London, for the Irish Literary Society, London.

‡ An enlarged edition, by Hatton and Molloy, was printed in 1882.

APPENDIX B.

MUSICAL MSS. IN TRINITY COLLEGE, DUBLIN.

(The Number is that as given in Rev. Dr. Abbot's "Catalogue," 1901.)

NO.

69   The Psalter in Latin and English. A.D. 1400.

77   Breviarium. 15th century.

82   Kilcormack Missal and fragment of Sarum Anti-phonary (written by Dermot O'Flanagan, a Carmelite Friar of Loughrea, A.D. 1458).

86   Breviariam cum Psalterio. A.D. 1489 (written by Malachy O'Loughlin of Killaloe).

95   Officia B.V.M., et Antiphonae variae. A.D. 1405.

100   Antiphonarium. 14th century.

101   Antiphonale Missarum et Horae. 15th century.

109   Antiphonarium. 15th century.

407   De Arte Musica, by John Travers. A.D. 1572.

408   A Collection of Songs and other Musical Pieces.

409   Musices Libri Tres, by James Dowson of Chester. 1600.

410   Musical Lessons set for the Lute, by Dr. Dallis of Cambridge, 1583 (with Musical Lessons by other hands).

411   Dionysius Chalcus. Hymni harmonici tres sec. modum Lydium, Graece et Latine. Dedicated to James Ussher. With notes by Edm. Chilmead. 17th century.

412   Hymns and Songs set to Music, in four or five parts (ascribed to William Ballet). 16th century.

413   Overtures, Preludes, etc., for three instruments. 17th century.

414   The Psalms in French Metre, with Music. 17th century.

432   "Quant le russinol se cesse," French song set to Music. 15th century.

1177   Traité de la Musique Moderne, par Alphonse des Vignoles. 1702.

1418   A Collection of Irish Songs. 1770.

APPENDIX C.

DUBLIN MUSICAL SOCIETIES.

(FROM 1680 TO 1880.)

A.D.

1680 The Hibernian Catch Club (still flourishing).

1716 Charitable Musical Society (of the " Bull's Head ").

1723 St. Cecilia Celebrations.

1724 Charitable Musical Society (of the " Bear ").

1729 Anacreotic Society (d. 1865).

1740 Philharmonic Society (the old Philharmonic).

1742 Charitable Musical Society (of Crow-street).

1742 Vicar-street Society.

1752 Charitable Musical Society (for " decayed musicians ").

1757 Academy of Music (d. 1765).

1765 Amicable Catch Club.

1767 Mecklenburgh Musical Society.

1810 Sons of Handel.

1813 Dublin Glee Club.

1826 Philharmonic Society (the new Philharmonic).

1834 Antient Concerts (d. 1863).

1836 Dublin Choral Society.

1837 Dublin University Choral Society (still flourishing).

1841 Sacred Harmonic Society.

1845 Amateur Harmonic Club.

1846 Dublin Madrigal Society.

1852 Royal Choral Institute.

1864 Dublin Harmonic Society (d. 1893)

1865 The Strollers (d. 1903).

1876 Dublin Musical Society (d. 1902).

INDEX.

344 HISTORY OF IRISH MUSIC.

Bicknor, Archbishop, founds a University, 133-4.
Bigger, F. J., M.R.I.A., 250.
Birkenshaw, John, 214, 219.
"Blackbird, The," an Irish air, 244.
"Blackbird's Song," in St. Gall MS., 15.
"Bonny Sweet Robin," 169, 174.
Book of Anthems (1662) for Christ Church Cathedral, 214.
"Boyne Water," 205.
Brenagh, Walter (harper), 119.
Brian Boru's Harp, 24, 25, 63-5, 113.
"Brian Boru's March," 39.
Bridge, Sir Frederick, Mus.Doc., 214.
Broadway, Richard (organist), 290.
Browne, William (organist), 153.
Bruidhean da derga, 58.
Buinne, 22, 27.
"Bull's Head Society," 266 ff.
"Bumpers Squire Jones," 231.
Bumpus, J. S., 231.
Bunting, Edward, 187, 188, 318, 321 ff.
Bunworth, Rev. Charles, 242, 246.
Burden, Irish origin of, 176.
Burney, Dr., 67.
Burns, Robert, employment of Irish airs by, 187, 193, 202, 228, 247, 251.
Byrde, Wm., 158, 185.
Byrne, Gerald, 127.
Byrne, Patrick (harper), 323.

Caerwys, Eisteddfod at, 48-9.
"Callino Casturame," 108, 165, 167, 170.
Callech (Coileach), St., *see* Gall, St.
Cambrensis Eversus, 190-1.
Cambrensis, Giraldus, 52, 58, 61 ff, 66.
Campion, B. Edmund, 66, 179.
Cantus Gregorianus, 13.
"Captain Tyrell's March," (1597), 129.

Carey, Henry (composer), 272.
Carmen Paschale, 9.
"Carman, Fair of," 25, 138, 142.
"Carolan's Concerto," 234 ; *see* O'Carolan.
Carols, Christmas, 89, 102-3.
Carolan's Old Irish Tunes, 308.
Carter, Thomas, 312-3.
Cashel, Synods of, 138, 142.
"Castle Hyde," 207.
"Castle Otway" Harp, 242.
Castrucci, Pietro, ends his days in Dublin, 294-5.
Ceana dubh dilis, 189.
Ceis, 10, 23, 59, 66.
Ceol-sidhe, 174.
Chappell, William, 38, 108.
Charitable Musical Society, 268, 274, 277, *et seq.*
Church, John (conductor), 286.
Christ Church Cathedral, 57, 85 ff, 91, 132-8, 151, 154 ff.
Cibber, Mrs., sings at first production of the *Messiah*, 279.
Cithruadh (bard), 82.
City Music (Corporation Band), 158, 265, 297.
Clagget, Charles (violinist), 303.
Clairsech, 13, 98.
Clancy, Cosney mac (piper), 182.
Clancy, Maire ni (rhymer), 121.
Clavichord, 98.
Clegg, John (violinist), 283.
Clement V., Pope, issues a Bull for founding an University in Ireland, 133.
Clinch, Patrick (organist), 146, 152.
Clive, Kitty, 292.
Cloncraff, church of, 31.
Clyn, Friar, 68-9, 73, 88.
"Coelia's my foe," *see* "Since Coelia's my foe."
Coffey, Charles, 201, 205, 207.
Colgan, Father, O.F.M., the Irish hagiologist, 5.
Cogan, Dr., organist and pianist, 306-7.
Colgan, James, bass singer, 291.

LIST OF SUBSCRIBERS.

His Majesty the King of Portugal.

His Royal Highness the Duke of Connaught, K.P.

His Eminence Cardinal Logue.

His Grace Most Rev. Dr. Healy, Archbishop of Tuam.

His Grace the Duke of Norfolk, E.M., K.G.

His Excellency The O'Neill, Lisbon.

His Excellency the Lord Lieutenant of Ireland, K.P.

Most Rev. Dr. James Browne, Bishop of Ferns.

Most Rev. Dr. O'Doherty, Bishop of Derry.

Most Rev. Dr. Brownrigg, Bishop of Ossory.

Most Rev. Dr. Henry, Bishop of Down and Connor.

Most Rev. Dr. Robert Browne, Bishop of Cloyne.

Most Rev. Dr. O'Donnell, Bishop of Raphoe.

Most Rev. Dr. Sheehan, Bishop of Waterford and Lismore.

Most Rev. Dr. Hoare, Bishop of Ardagh.

Most Rev. Dr. Foley, Bishop of Kildare and Leighlin.

Most Rev. Dr. O'Dea, Bishop of Clonfert.

Right Rev. the Lord Abbot of Mount Melleray.

Right Rev. the Lord Abbot of Mount St. Joseph.

The Lady Abbess of Stanbrook, Worcester.

Right Hon. Lord Ardilaun, D.L.

Right Hon. Lord Iveagh, K.P.

Right Hon. the Earl of Belmore, K.C.M.G.

Right Hon. Lord Monteagle, K.P.

Right Hon. Lord Castletown of Upper Ossory.

Right Hon. A. J. Balfour, M.P.

Right Hon. the Lord Chief Baron, P.C.

Right Hon. Sir Horace Plunkett, K.C.V.O.

Right Hon. George Wyndham, M.P.

Lord Walter Fitzgerald, Kilkea Castle.

Lord Power and Coraghmore.

Sir Thomas H. Grattan Esmonde M.P.

Sir Henry Bellingham, D.L.

Sir Francis W. Brady, K.C.

Sir Francis Cruise, M.D., D.L.

Sir Frederick Bridge, M.V.O., Mus. Doc.

Sir Alexander MacKenzie, Mus. Doc.

Sir A. Conan Doyle.

Rev. Professor Mahaffy, D.D., Mus. Doc., C.V.O.

Professor Dowden, LL.D.

T. M. Healy, Esq., K.C., M.P.

William O'Brien, Esq., M.P.

John P. Boland, Esq., M.P.

Edward Martyn, Esq., Tillyra Castle.

John Sweetman, Esq., Drumbaragh.

Very Rev. Canon Sheehan, D.D. (Doneraile).

Very Rev. P. Boyle, C.M. (Paris).

Rev. Professor Bewerunge.

Very Rev. J. Lennon, M.S.S.

Very Rev. A. Quigley, O.P.

Dr. M. F. Cox, M.R.I.A.

W. R. J. Molloy, Commissioner of National Education.

Dr. Douglas Hyde.

The Publication Committee of the Gaelic League.

The Society for the Preservation of the Irish Language.

The Freeman's Journal, Limited.

The Pipers' Club, Dublin.

W. H. Cummings, Esq., Mus. Doc.
J. C. Culwick, Esq., Mus. Doc.
Peter Goodman, Esq., Inspector of Music.
Vincent O'Brien, Esq.
Professor Stockley, Halifax,N.S.
J. Whiteside Dane, Esq., D.L.
Maurice Healy, Esq., Solicitor.
M. J. O'Connor, Esq., Solicitor.
Denis Slattery, Esq., Solicitor.
Francis Joseph Bigger, Esq., M.R.I.A., Ardrie, Belfast.
T. D. Sullivan, Esq.
Mrs. Milligan Fox, London.
P. J. Lynch, Esq., M.R.I.A.
Francis O'Neill, Chief of Police, Chicago.
Rev. E. O'Leary, P.P.
Rev. T. Meehan, P.P.
Rev. John M'Cann, P.P.
Rev. John Dunne, P.P.
Rev. R. J. FitzHenry, C.C.
Rev. D. A. Kavanagh, C.C.
Rev. John Butler, C.C.
Rev. W. Harper, C.C.
Rev. Denis O'Connor, C.C.
Rev. M. B. Kennedy, C.C.
Rev. J. Kelly, PH.D., M.S.S., St. Peter's College, Wexford.
Rev. J. Quigley, M.S.S.
Rev. P. Murphy, M.S.S.
Rev. E. L. Curran, C.C., New· foundland.
Rev. James Mockler, D.I.
Rev. Denis Pettit, P.P.
Rev. T. Byrne, C.C.
Rev. R. FitzHenry, M.S.S.
Rev. E. A. D'Alton, C.C.
Rev. H. C. Lyster, B.D.
Dr. W. Cookman, J.P.
M. A. Ennis, Esq., J.P.
James Donohoe, Esq., J.P.
Henry J. Roche, Esq., J.P., Enniscorthy Castle.
Samuel B. Bamford, Esq., J.P., Uttoxeter.
Patrick Byrne, Esq., J.P.
Thaddeus Bolger, Esq., J.P.
John Anderson, Esq., J.P.
C. P. Kingston, Esq., Tulla more.

Royal Academy of Music, London.
Guildhall School of Music, London.
Trinity College, London.
Loreto Convent, Gorey.
Do.   Wexford.
Convent of Mercy, Callan.
Do.   Enniscorthy
Do.   Wexford.
Do.   Athy.
Convent of the Faithful Companions, Newtownbarry.
Presentation Convent, Enniscorthy.
Do.   Wexford.
Do.   Waterford.
National Library, Dublin.
Library, Maynooth College.
Do.   ClongowesWoodCollege
Do.   University College.
Do.   St. John's College, Waterford.
Do.   St. Peter's College, Wexford.
Do.   Clerkenwell, London.
Do.   Hammersmith,London
Do.   Dublin Corporation.
Do.   St. Patrick's College, Thurles.
Do.   Christian Brothers, Wexford.
Do.   Christian Brothers, Enniscorthy.
Do.   Linen Hall, Belfast.
James Buckley, Esq., London.
Bernard H. Roice, Esq., Tagoat.
Patrick O'Daly, Esq., Gen. Sec. Gaelic League.
John A. O'Connell, Esq., Sculptor, Cork.
John Bennett, Esq., Enniscorthy.
William Fortune, Esq., Enniscorthy.
Thomas Keane, Esq., Enniscorthy.
Patrick Kehoe, Esq., Enniscorthy
David Keating, Esq., Wexford.
P. Cousins, Esq., Wexford.
John M. Walsh, Esq., Wexford.

J. Ennis Meyler, Esq., F.R.S.A.
Clement Goff, Esq., Ballyorrell, Ferns.
Walter Marston, Esq., Barnes, London.
James Coleman, Esq., Queenstown.
Andrew Gibson, Esq., Belfast.
Herbert Hughes, Esq., Belfast.
Patrick O'Leary, Esq., Graiguenamanagh.
Richard Gahan, Esq., Montreal.
M. J. Whelan, Esq., Enniscorthy
William Hume, Esq., Lugar, Scotland.
Thomas C. Malone, Market-st., Mountmellick.

C. O'Leary, Esq., Tralee.
John Ribton Garstin, Esq., D.L., Bragganstown.
Rev. Michael J. Masterson, St. Mel's, Longford.
Maurice Healy, Esq., Lismore.
Rev. T. Quin, Clonmore, Enniscorthy.
Very Rev. Canon Ryan, P.P., V.G., Tipperary.
Very Rev. A. M. Skelly, O.P. (Prior), Waterford.
John F. Boyle, Esq., Dungarvan.
Messrs. Hodges, Figgis & Co., Dublin.
J. L. Wayland, Esq., Cork.
W. Birrell, Esq., Cork.

Printed by BROWNE AND NOLAN, LTD., *Dublin.*

DATE DUE
